overshot SIMPLY

UNDERSTANDING THE WEAVE STRUCTURE

38 Projects to Practice Your Skills

SUSAN KESLER-SIMPSON

STACKPOLE
BOOKS
Guilford, Connecticut

Thank you to Tom Knisely for his encouragement to write the book, to my husband Dave for his support and patience, and to Francie Appleman (my crazy friend) who spent a lot of time giving this book a thorough technical review.

Stackpole Books
An imprint of The Rowman & Littlefield Publishing Group, Inc.,
4501 Forbes Blvd., Ste. 200, Lanham, MD 20706
Distributed by
NATIONAL BOOK NETWORK
800-462-6420

Photography by Kathleen Eckhaus and Susan Kesler-Simpson

British Library Cataloguing in Publication Information Available

Library of Congress Cataloging-in-Publication Data
ISBN 978-0-8117-1678-9 (paperback)
ISBN 978-0-8117-6799-6 (e-book)

™ The paper used in this publication meets the minimum requirements of American National Standard for Information Sciences–Permanence of Paper for Printed Library Materials, ANSI/NISO Z39.48-1992.

CONTENTS

Projects

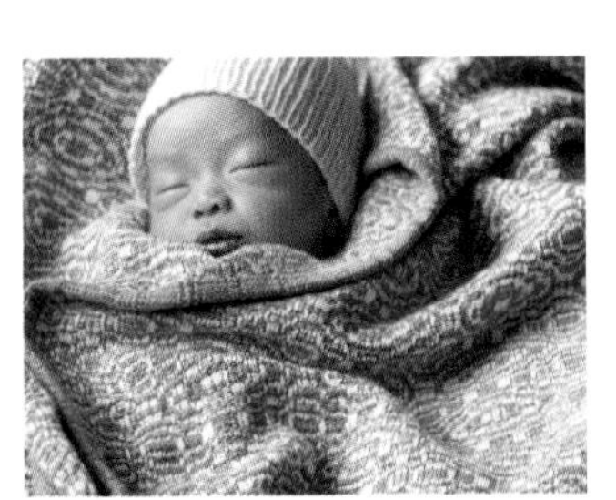

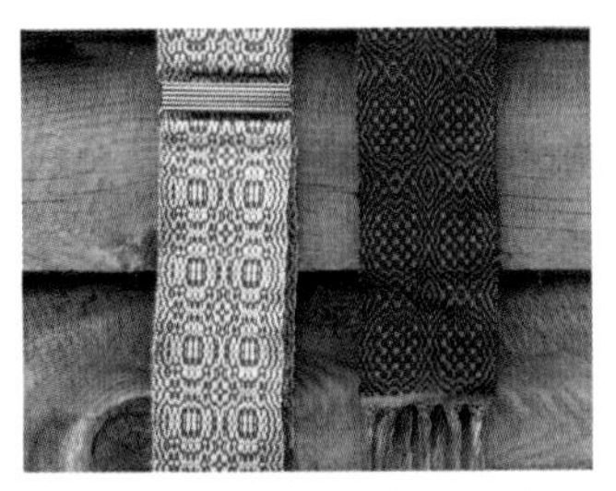

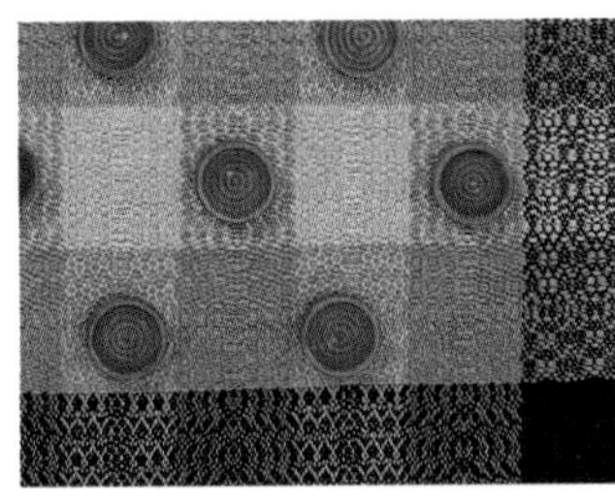

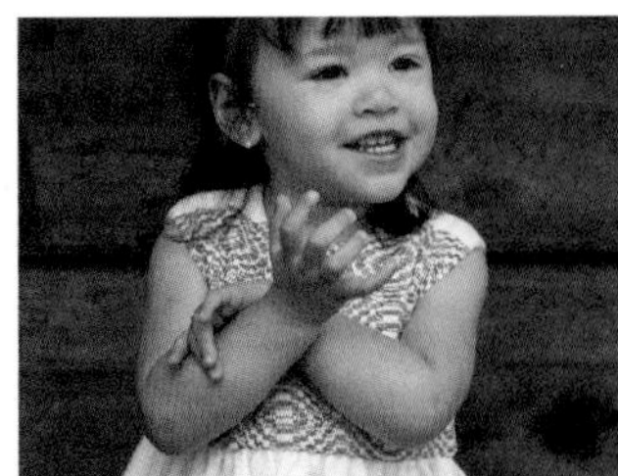

FOREWORD

On a cold January morning last year, I was taking the train to New York to do a lecture on rug weaving. I figured this would be the perfect time to sit back and read Susan's manuscript. She had given it to me a few days before and asked me to go through it and give her my opinion. As I sat back in my seat and started to read, I couldn't get over how clear and straightforward her explanations were. Like any good author, Susan has given you the background of overshot and how it has evolved out of simple twills to become the king of weave structures. Susan's explanations are to the point and easy to understand. When you read through the chapters, it's as if Susan is sitting there with you, telling you in a friendly voice how to weave overshot step by step. I was glad to see Susan covers thread sizes and choices for the projects that you want to weave. There are suggestions on how to tie up your loom's treadles to make the weaving go more smoothly. Susan covers the little things, as any good teacher should, to make readers more confident, especially if they may be weaving overshot for the first time. Even if you are a veteran to weaving overshot, you will gain a lot of good information from this book.

I was so glad to see that Susan's vision for overshot has taken her beyond the coverlet. As you go through the pages of projects, it helps you to see that this is a marvelous way to weave patterned fabric and that these fabrics have many more applications than you might have thought. Susan has used her background in fashion design and tailoring to bring us project ideas that are fresh and new. Bravo! I have to tell you that I was touched when Susan offered to weave a liturgical stole for my daughter Hannah. She recently became ordained, and Susan wove an original overshot pattern for the stole of her own design.

As one of her teachers, I am thrilled to see how Susan has taken her passion for overshot to such levels. I only planted the seed. It takes nurturing and the love of the subject to create a book of this caliber.

Congratulations, Susan, for all your hard work. I am so proud of you for taking on this project, and the weaving world will come to thank you also.

Tom Knisely

INTRODUCTION

When I began to weave, I was immediately drawn to the overshot weave structure. The complexity of the designs fascinated me. And as someone who was drawn to antiques, I had seen many old coverlets in a variety of colors and patterns and was always intrigued by the beautiful patterns. However, the overshot weave structure seemed to be way above anything I could accomplish, ever! But soon I had done enough tabbies and twills and needed a challenge. I began by taking the overshot shawl class taught by Tom Knisely at The Mannings. It was a wonderful way to be introduced to a weave structure without so much angst. During the class, I realized that overshot was not such a complicated weave structure. If I was careful and precise in the threading and treadling, this weave structure was not very hard at all!

Not all of us are fortunate enough to be near someone who can share their knowledge in the classroom. We have to resort to books! The purpose of this book is to help the weaver gain a better understanding of the overshot weave structure in a style that is unintimidating and straightforward. The patterns are simple and easy to follow. You will learn about the weave structure and how the fabric is constructed. We will cover how to add borders to your work, giving it a more finished and professional appearance. A section on thread and color choices and how they affect your finished piece is included. And, of course, after you have worked with this weave structure, you may find that you want to create your own designs, so you will be presented with some very simple techniques to use as a starting point. All of this is written so that the weaver can understand the basics of overshot. Use this book as a starting point for all of the other wonderful books written on overshot.

This book is full of original patterns for you to enjoy. You may find that you like a certain pattern but want to use it in a different end product, for instance, a scarf instead of a table runner. Absolutely! Change the colors, change how the pattern is used, change the type of thread, but, most important, enjoy what you are making! Make it your own personal work of art!

CHAPTER 1

Overshot Weave Structure

This weave structure is called overshot because the pattern thread "shoots over" the underlying weave structure, creating a float. These floats are what create the beautiful design on your piece. Overshot can easily be woven on a four-harness loom. Additional harnesses will allow you to create more complex patterns. Four-harness patterns are more frequently seen in books, and there is a great variety of patterns available to the weaver. Eight-harness patterns have more half-tones and often are considered busier patterns. Half-tones are areas in which the pattern weft is woven into the structure instead of floating over or under the fabric.

Overshot is a derivative of the twill weave structure. If you look at the threading for overshot you will see that it follows familiar twill sequences. You will also find that, just as in a twill pattern, your threading will always follow the odd-even rule. For example, 2 or 4 will follow 1, 1 or 3 will follow 2, and so on. This is important to remember when creating your own designs.

When you look closely at the overshot weave structure, you can see that it is made up of two components: the pattern thread, which creates the design, and an underlying tabby weave structure, which gives the piece integrity. Without the tabby, the fabric would be loose and sloppy. So the tabby is an essential and important part of overshot. If you have ever looked at antique coverlets, often you will see areas where the pattern threads have worn away, leaving a plain tabby fabric construction.

Overshot is a tied weave structure, sharing harnesses during the weaving process. It is the sharing of the harnesses that allows the soft curves that are created in the motif. The term "shared harness" means that one harness will be used with another harness during the weaving process. For example, harness one will be shared with harness two and harness four. Harness two will be shared with harness one and harness three and so on. If you have more than four harnesses, each harness may be shared multiple times to create the pattern.

				T	T
		4	4		4
	3	3		3	
2	2				2
1			1	1	

Example of a shared harness tie-up.

Tie-Up

The tie-up for the overshot weave structure is the same as a 2/2 twill. They may be in a different sequence, but it is still the same tie-up.

Because you will always be throwing a tabby thread, you will want to include this in your tie-up. The treadles can be set up so that both treadles are on the

		4	4
	3	3	
2	2		
1			1

	4	4	
3	3		
2			2
		1	1

4	4		
3			3
		2	2
	1	1	

4			4
		3	3
	2	2	
1	1		

Examples of the same 2/2 twill tie-up but different sequences.

T					T
			4	4	4
3		3	3		
	2	2			2
1	1			1	

T	T				
	4			4	4
3			3	3	
	2	2	2		
1		1			1

				T	T
		4	4		4
	3	3		3	
2	2				2
1			1	1	

Examples of placement of the tabby treadles.

left side, both are on the right side, or they are split with one on the left and one on the right. My preference is to split the tabby treadles, knowing that if my shuttle is on my right, I should depress the tabby treadle on the right, and if the shuttle is on the left, I depress the tabby treadle to my left. You need to find your own personal preference and do what is comfortable for you.

My loom has 10 treadles and, while I can use all of them at one time, many times I am using fewer. In order to be more efficient and to help me identify the treadles more quickly, I came up with an idea that has been a huge help to me and that you may find useful, too. I purchased two packages of Velcro, one with sticky back and the other without. I cut 10 one-inch (2.5 cm) *soft* sticky-back pieces. These I put onto the treadles in a place where they did not interfere with my feet but were visible to me. Then I cut 12 one-inch pieces of the *non-sticky hook* Velcro. I numbered these from 1 to 10, plus two with a T, for tabby. I can put these on whichever treadles I choose, depending on my tie-up and what is comfortable for me. The Velcro tags are easy to use and easy to move! Just be sure to put the soft side on the treadle so you don't catch your socks! Now I can quickly look at the treadles and see the numbers, making me less prone to mistakes.

Thread Choices

When weaving overshot, you will be working with two threads and two shuttles. Traditionally the thread that you use for your warp will be the same thread you use for your tabby thread, although you will find I break that rule for many of my projects. Your pattern thread

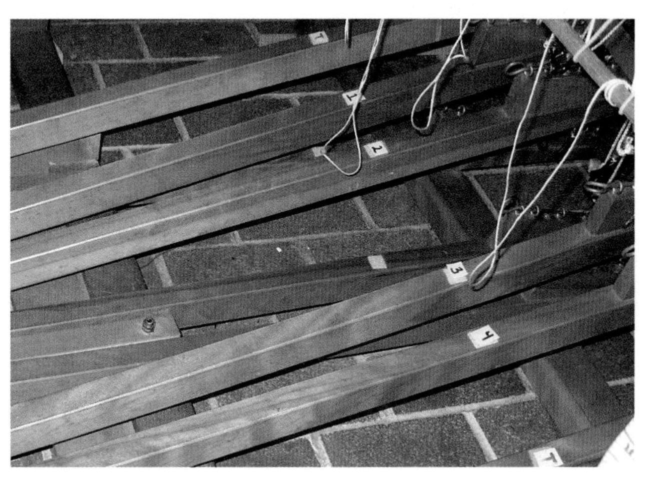

To help you identify your treadles quickly, put numbers on them.

I use Velcro to attach the treadle numbers.

should be at least twice the size of the tabby thread. If you are using 10/2 perle cotton for your warp, your pattern thread would be 5/2 perle cotton or a thread of similar size. Another choice for the pattern thread to go with the 10/2 perle cotton would be Jagger Spun Maine Line 2/8 wool or Harrisville Shetland wool.

Yarn choices will affect the dimension of the pattern and its appearance. Fluffy yarns, such as the wools, will hide the tabby threads and give a softer appearance. They may also increase the size of the motif. The tighter woven cottons will allow the tabby to be more visible but not so much that it will impact the pattern. And sometimes the tabby becomes a part of the overall design, such as when you are working with color.

Because this book is meant for the beginner, I have tried to work with less expensive and easily accessible threads. These will include mill ends, garage sale finds, yarns/threads that have been given to me by fellow weavers, and the like. The more experienced weavers can easily substitute their preferences. I used UKI brand perle cotton unless otherwise specified. For yarns that you have been given or picked up at a sale, be sure to check the integrity of the thread to make sure it is reliable and strong. Also, do a burn test to find the content of the thread: cut a piece of the yarn, hold it in tweezers over a sink, and, using a match, light the end of the thread and then blow it out.

- Wool will smell like burnt hair, with little smoke. The fire will burn slowly and often extinguish on its own. The ash is gritty or has an easily crushable bead.
- Cellulose (cotton) ignites and burns quickly. Often a small ember will remain after the fire is blown out. Cellulose will smell like burnt paper and leave a white or light gray soft ash.
- Synthetic will ignite quickly and burn fast, often continuing to burn after the flame is removed. The fiber will shrink from the flame, melt, and can drip so *use caution.* It will also leave a hard plastic-like bead. Fumes from burning synthetic fibers can be hazardous, so use caution when doing burn tests!

When you are weaving overshot, you will first create your hem/edge by weaving a plain tabby. Then you will weave the main portion of your piece to the desired length after allowing for your fringes. Generally the hem/edge is ½ inch (1.3 cm). If you are doing a rolled hem, you will want this to be three times the width of the desired hem. This is generally 1½ inches (3.8 cm).

Now let's begin with the pattern! You will throw your shuttle with the pattern thread first, beat, and then throw the shuttle with the tabby thread and beat again. Because you are putting two threads in a place where your graph shows one, you will want to use a firm beat. You will continue in this manner: first the pattern thread, then the tabby thread.

The first time you weave overshot, it would be best to put on some extra warp so that you can practice your beat and adjust your motif or your beat if necessary. When you are weaving with two threads, you may find that your motif appears somewhat distorted. It may no longer be square but more of a tall rectangle. This is simple to adjust. Simply reduce the number of pattern threads symmetrically throughout your pattern. This is important so that you can maintain the balance of the design. However, if you are happy with the motif as it is, then don't mess with it. Always remember, each piece you make is *your* design!

Example 1 shows the original draft of circles and squares, highlighting in green the threads that can be

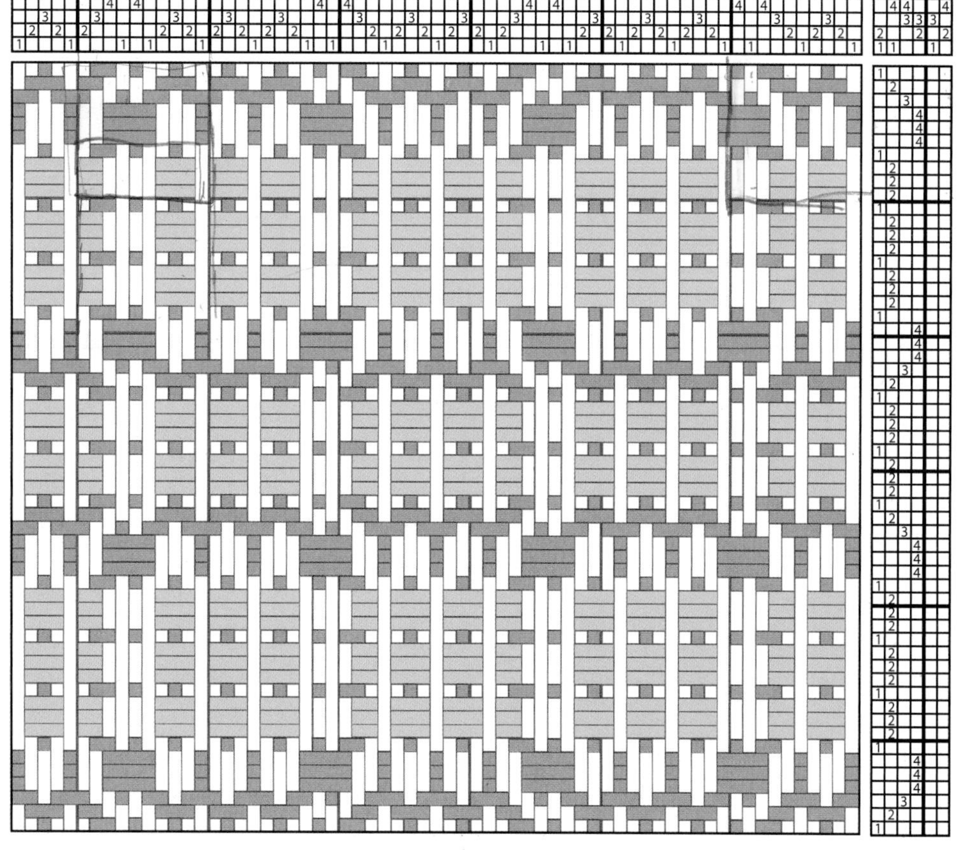

Example 1

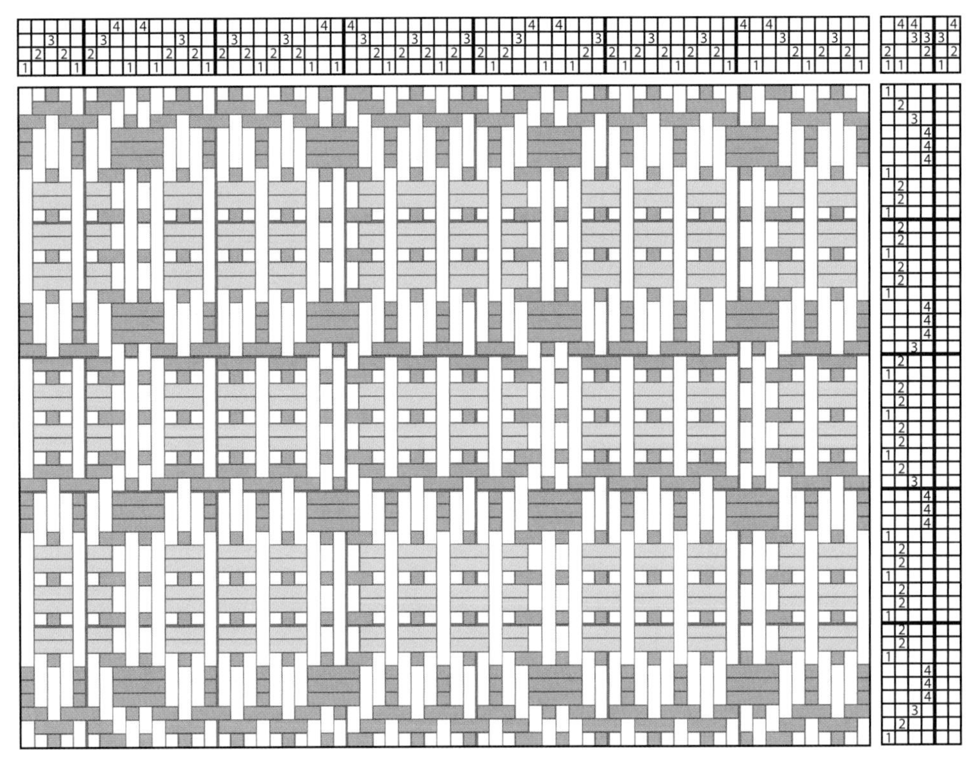

Example 2

adjusted. Example 2 shows an adjusted draft with weft threads removed in a balanced manner. In the original draft, the threads were groupings of three, and in the adjusted draft, the threads are in groupings of two. This will affect the height of the pattern and would keep your motif squarer.

Warp

When planning your warp, be sure that you do not crowd the threads. If the range is 22–26 epi, use 24. Remember that you are putting a lot of thread into the weft, and if your warp threads are too tight it will be more difficult to keep the shape of the motif. In addition, it will affect the drape of your project. Warp threads that are too tight will result in a firmer product.

When calculating the thread yardages required, you have to remember to calculate your tabby thread. Let's say that you need 600 yards (550 m) of 10/2 perle cotton for a scarf set at 24 epi, 10 inches (25.4 cm) wide and 60 inches (152.4 cm) long. You are going to use 5/2 perle cotton for the pattern thread. It is approximately 16 epi, so you would need approximately 300 yards (275 m) to finish the scarf. But remember, you also have the tabby thread to consider. A good rule of thumb is to use the same yardage requirement for the pattern thread for the tabby thread. So, your overall thread requirement would be:

Pattern thread: 5/2 cotton, 300 yards (275 m)
Warp thread: 10/2 cotton, 600 yards (550 m)
Tabby thread: 10/2 cotton, 300 yards (275 m)

If the tabby and the warp threads are the same, you can just add them together for the total required.

Floating Selvedge

When weaving overshot, you will want to use a floating selvedge. A floating selvedge will catch the edge threads with every pick thrown. To create a floating selvedge, you simply thread one matching warp thread at either side of the warp, through its own dent in the reed, but not through a heddle. When the warp is closed on a jack loom, you will see the two floating selvedge threads will float above the warp. When a shed is opened, they will float in the center of the shed. On a countermarch loom, the threads will rest in the same place as the warp, but when the shed is opened, the floating selvedges will once again be in the center of the shed opening. I always go over the floating selvedge when entering the shed, and exit going under it–that way, no matter which side of the weft you are working on, your selvedge threads will catch evenly. If you find the reverse works better for you, that is fine, too. You will find that the edges of your projects will always look better if you use a floating selvedge.

Color

Traditionally the tabby color is the same as the warp color and is not meant to be a part of the design. But as you look through my designs and projects, you will quickly discover that I don't always stick to tradition. Many times the use of a different color enhances the overall look of the project.

In many pieces, you will find that I use more than one color for the warp. Sometimes I alternate the colors, but most of the time I choose randomly–whichever color I grab is the one I thread. The Rose Path Shawl (page 121) is one of those projects that includes two colors in the warp. The placement of the colors was random. There was one of each color in a dent, and the first one I picked up was the one that I threaded at that time. Using two colors in this manner often softens the appearance, as your eye will blend the two colors.

Even though the tabby is not a part of the design, this doesn't mean that you can't make it so. Look at the Springtime Place Mats (page 133). In each place mat, a different color tabby was chosen although the pattern thread and the warp never changed. You can see how much it affects the overall color of each piece. Just be sure that your color choices work together well. If you are unsure, do a small sample piece to see if it is the look you want.

One tip to make things easier: sometimes I will choose the same color for the pattern and the tabby, just a different size thread. I put a sticker on one of my shuttles to designate that one as carrying the pattern thread. It is an inexpensive and quick way to be certain that I am always working with the proper size thread at the proper time.

The most important thing about color is that *you* are pleased with the results! Break a few rules, try something new . . . it's fun!

Notes on Patterns

Any time you are working from a new book, make sure you know what type of loom the patterns have been designed for. All the patterns in this book are created for a jack loom. Converting a tie-up for a jack loom to a countermarch loom or vice versa is a simple process.

Colored stickers can help you mark your shuttles if you use the same color thread in two different sizes.

In the jack loom tie-up, you will see that treadles 1 and 2 are tied up, then 2 and 3, and so on.

When converting to the countermarch, the treadles will be the opposite. Instead of 1 and 2, you will tie up 3 and 4. Instead of 2 and 3, you will tie up 1 and 4, and so on. Use the same process for an eight-harness loom.

If you forgot to do this and tied up your countermarch loom with the jack tie-up, don't worry. Just note that when weaving, you will be seeing the wrong side of the fabric. The right side will be on the underside of what you see on your work.

		4	4
	3	3	
2	2		
1			1

2/2 twill tie-up
Jack loom

4	4		
3			3
		2	2
	1	1	

2/2 twill tie-up
converted for
countermarch loom

The patterns in this book have been designed to read from the bottom up. This is important to remember. This is so that you are reading the pattern just as you would see your finished fabric being woven on the loom.

When working overshot, be assured that you will *always* weave a tabby thread after the pattern thread. Overshot patterns may or may not say "use tabby" along the side, but you must always use it regardless.

All of the patterns in this book use a floating selvedge, with the exception of the Shawlette.

Computer Weaving Programs

I studied Marguerite Davison's book, *A Handweaver's Pattern Book*, but found that looking at the pictures and then moving to the drafts was sometimes complicated. At times it took a great deal of study and concentration to find her starting and end points comparing the drafts to the pictures. Later, of course, after finishing a coverlet, my husband got me a wonderful Christmas present . . . Fiberworks Bronze . . . a computer drafting program that I would highly recommend to anyone who loves to design her own patterns. This tool has proved invaluable in deciphering drafts. By putting in the tie-up, threading, and treadling, you can immediately see the structure of the cloth and the beginning and end points! Words of caution, however . . . don't use this as a substitute for knowing how to do a manual drawdown. Being able to do a manual drawdown gives you a better understanding of the weave structure and how the threads interact. And do remember that Davison's book is written for a countermarch loom, not a jack loom!

CHAPTER 2

Creating an Overshot Pattern from a Twill Pattern

One of the best ways to totally understand how twill and overshot are related is to create an overshot pattern from a twill pattern. Follow through on this exercise, and you will gain a better understanding of this relationship.

We are going to start with the basic birdseye twill pattern. One of the most outstanding characteristics of overshot is the repetition of the *same treadle* in the treadling pattern. So let's begin here. The treadling pattern for birdseye twill begins with 1, 2, 3, 4, 3, 2, 1, and so on. In Example 1, we simply increased each time the treadle was used from 1 to 2 times. We now see 1, 1, 2, 2, 3, 3, 4, 4, 3, 3, 2, 2, 1, 1, and so on, elongating the pattern.

Now let's change the threading and see what happens. In Example 2, you will see that at the top and bottom of the peaks a 1, 4, 1 or 4, 1, 4 has been added in the threading pattern. Now the pattern is getting more width and looks more balanced. But this could also pose a problem. If you look closely at your weft threads, you will see areas where the thread floats over 5 warp threads. If you are working with fine threads, such as 10/2 cotton, this may not present a problem. At 24 epi, 5 threads will be a float that is only ¼ inch (6.3 mm) long. However, larger threads will result in a much longer float, which would be a great toe-catcher. Wool set at 10 epi would result in a float ½ inch (1.3 cm) long. So, how do we correct this?

Birdseye twill

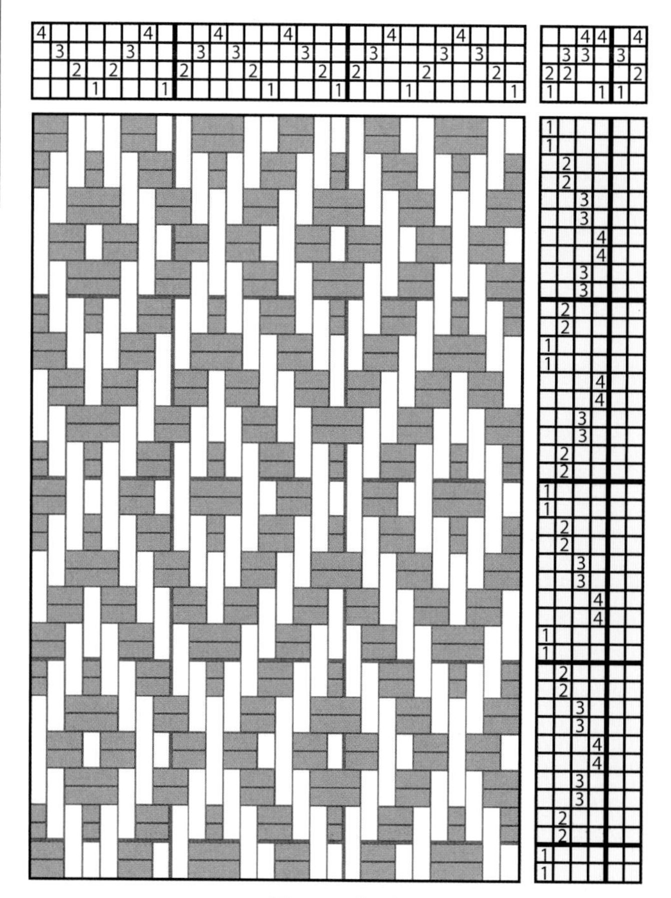

Example 1

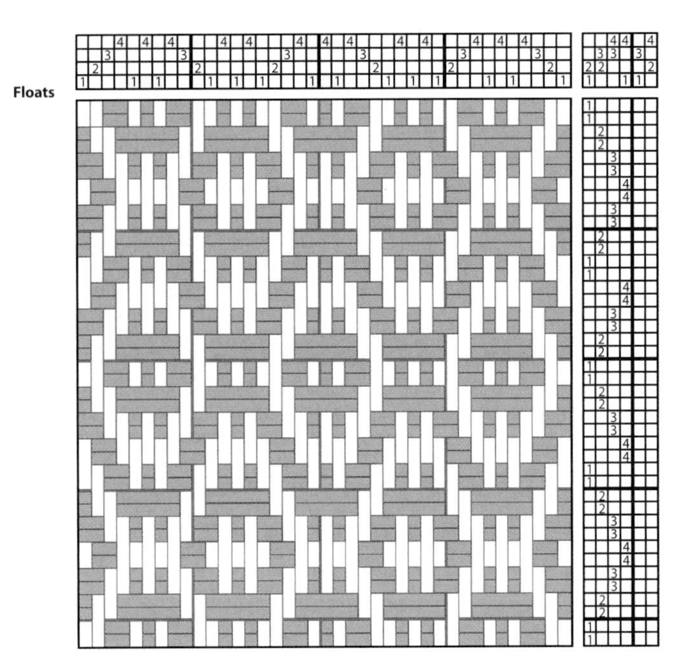

Example 2

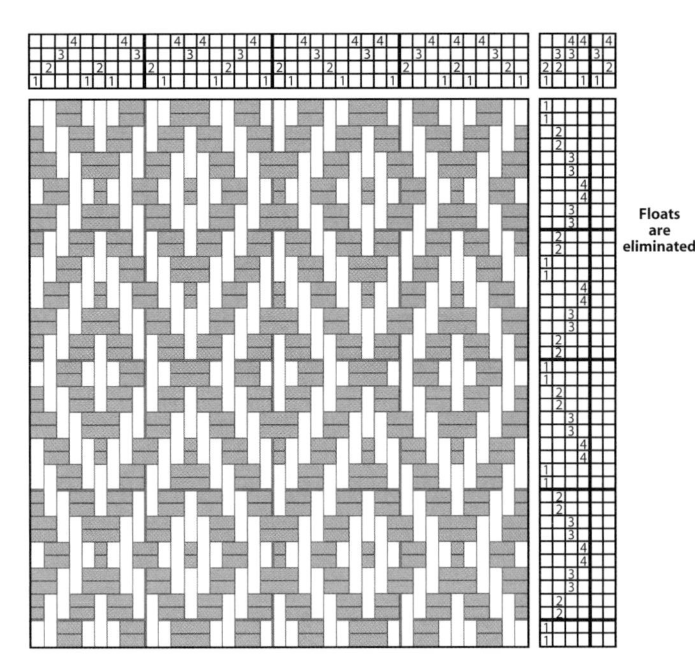

Example 3

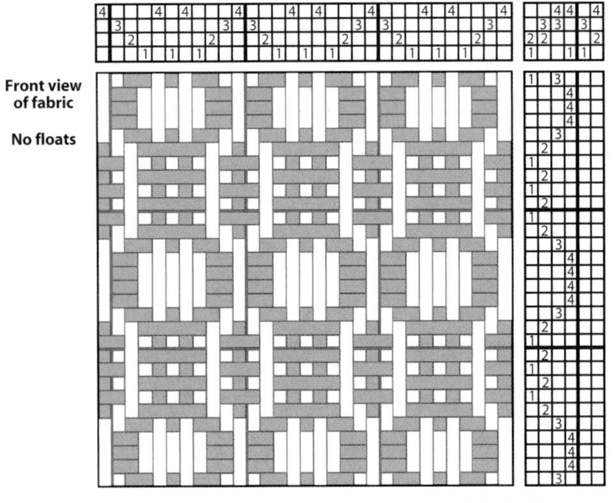

Example 4: Front view of fabric

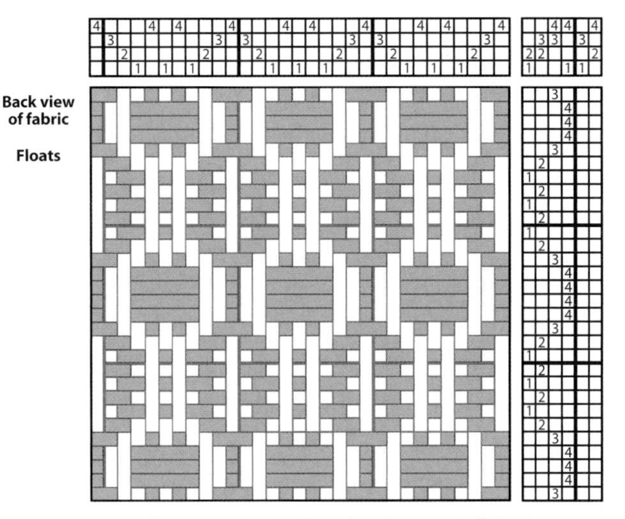

Example 5: Back view of fabric

In Example 3, the 1, 4, 1 was changed to 1, 2, 1 (remember odd to even) and the 4, 1, 4 was changed to 4, 3, 4. If you look closely at the drawdown, you will see that the long float has now been interrupted and your weave structure is more stable. When you are creating an overshot pattern, what may appear to be a long *warp* float is not a problem. After you throw the shuttle with the pattern weft, you will *always* follow with a tabby shot. This tabby automatically secures the warp threads and creates a stable fabric.

Sometimes it is not easy to see those floats! If you look at Example 4, all appears to be fine, no long weft floats. But if you look at the reverse side of the fabric in Example 5, those pesky floats jump out at you.

Again, the solution is simple, in this case substituting 3 for 1 in the threading. This allows the weft thread to be tied down and secure. Many times these changes will result in a more interesting pattern. Examples 6 and 7 (page 9) show the new threading that eliminates the long float. Again, remember the size of the thread you are working with and the end result of your piece.

Example 6 is a great jumping-off point to creating your own overshot pattern. Using that as a beginning point, I added more components to the threading and the treadling, expanding the design as you can see in Example 8 (page 9). You should be able to pick those out if you look closely. This would be a great design

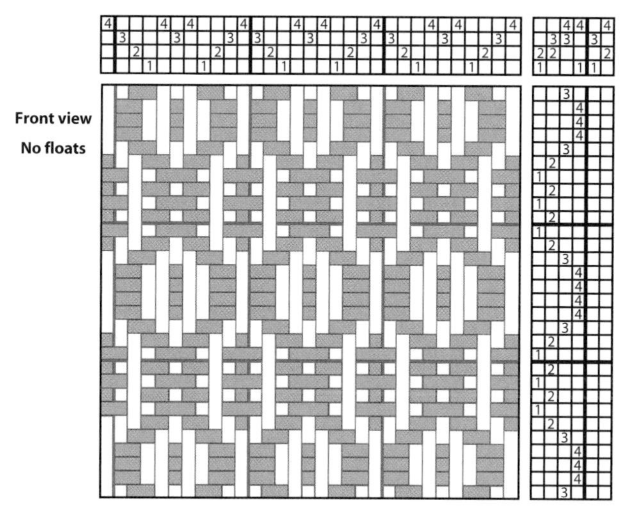

Example 6: Front view of fabric (no floats)

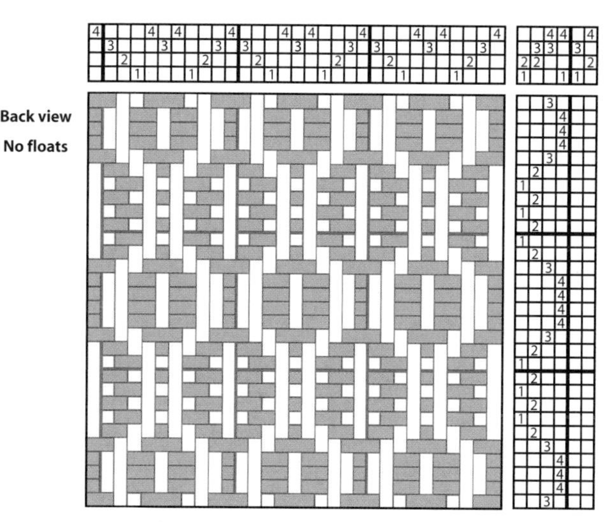

Example 7: Back view of fabric (no floats)

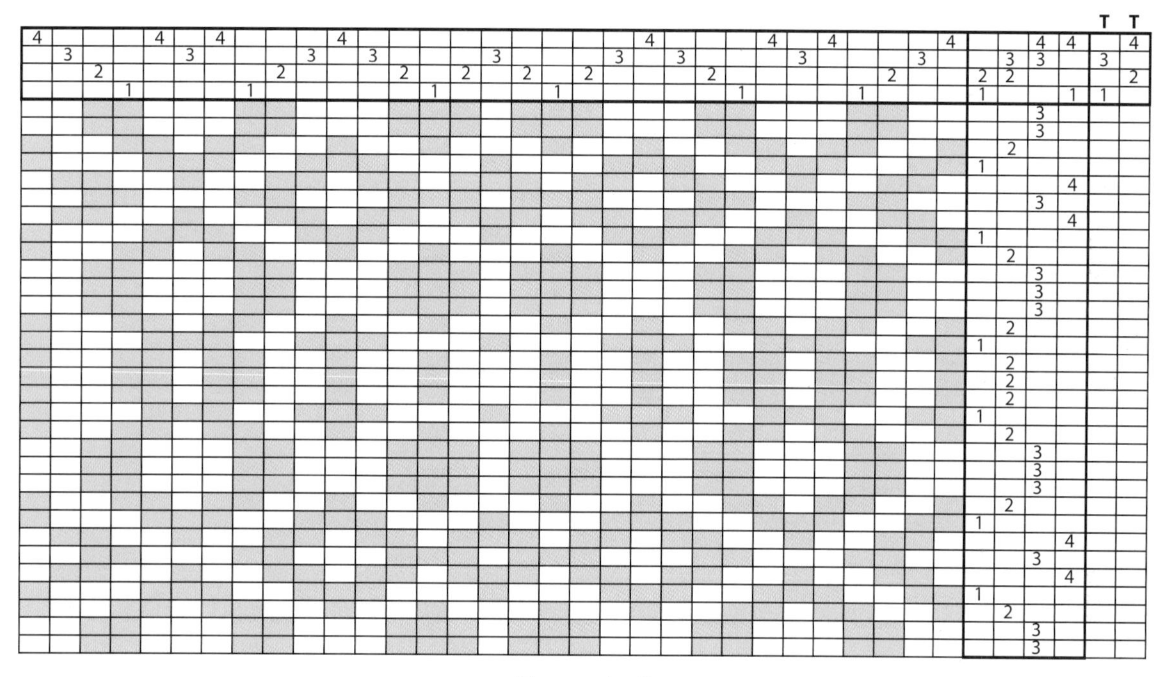
Example 8

for a scarf, as a border for a valance, or for many other projects. Just a thought! When creating your pattern, did you like the back view better than the front view? Not a problem! Make that your right side! The important thing is to be creative and start designing your own patterns.

Partial/Balancing Motifs

Because of the size and complexity of overshot threading and treadling patterns, you will find that many of them consist of Block/Motif A, Block/Motif B, and so on. In order to have balance in the pattern, it may be necessary to repeat Block A at the end. In other cases, it may only be necessary to have a portion of the motif to balance your pattern.

Let's look first at the threading pattern for Indiana (page 10). You can see that this threading has borders on each side. These are highlighted in yellow. The threading then begins with Motif A (green), then Motif B (blue), repeating until the end of the threading. But notice that it ends with Block A, just before the last border begins. This balances the overall threading.

Now let's look at the threading for Colorado (page 10). Again, we see borders on each side. In this threading there is only one motif, or block. But notice that after the last repeat of the motif, there is a balancing thread. If you were to isolate just the motif, start from the center and look at each half, you would see that it is a mirror image from the center. When the motif is repeated, the 1 thread is automatically in place because it is at the beginning of the motif, but at the end of the last repeat, you must include the 1 to balance the motif, shown in pink. Sometimes this balancing motif/block will be one thread as in this case. Other times it will be more. It depends on the pattern you are working with. Study each threading to determine what is necessary to balance your patterns.

Let's revisit creating a treadling pattern. When you create your own overshot, you need to decide where you want these repeats to be. Look first at a draft that is "tromp as writ," or treadled as written, below.

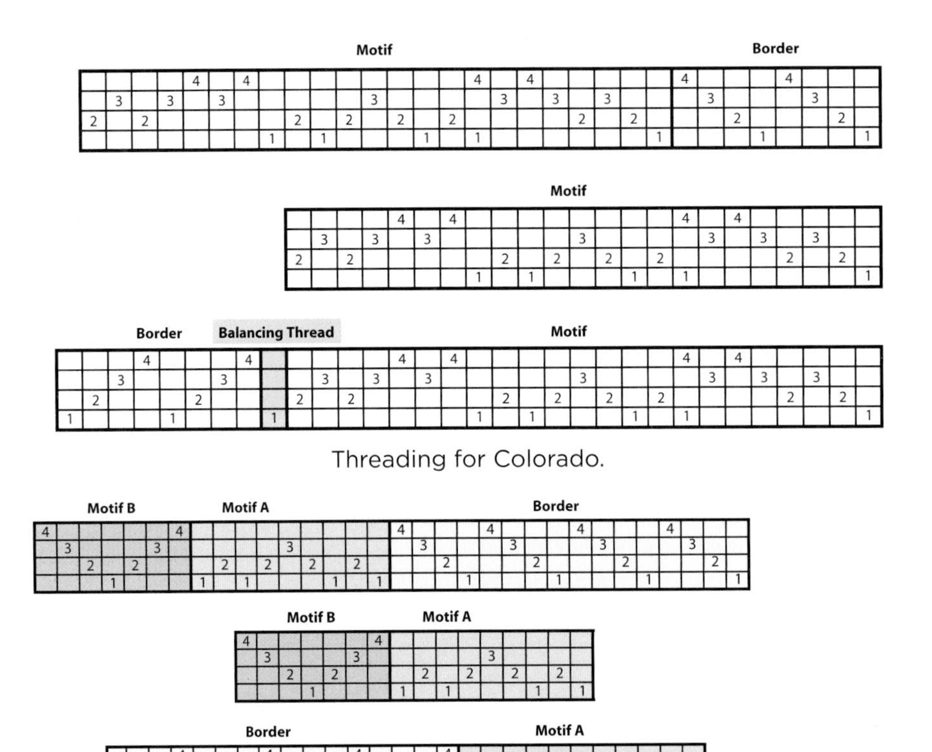

Threading for Colorado.

Threading for Indiana.

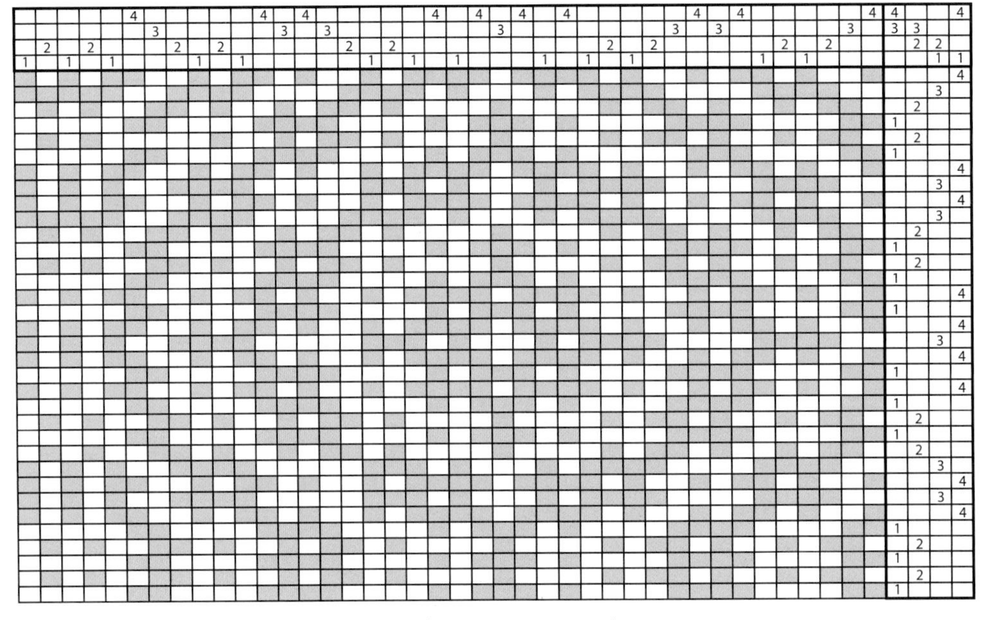

Overshot tromp as writ.

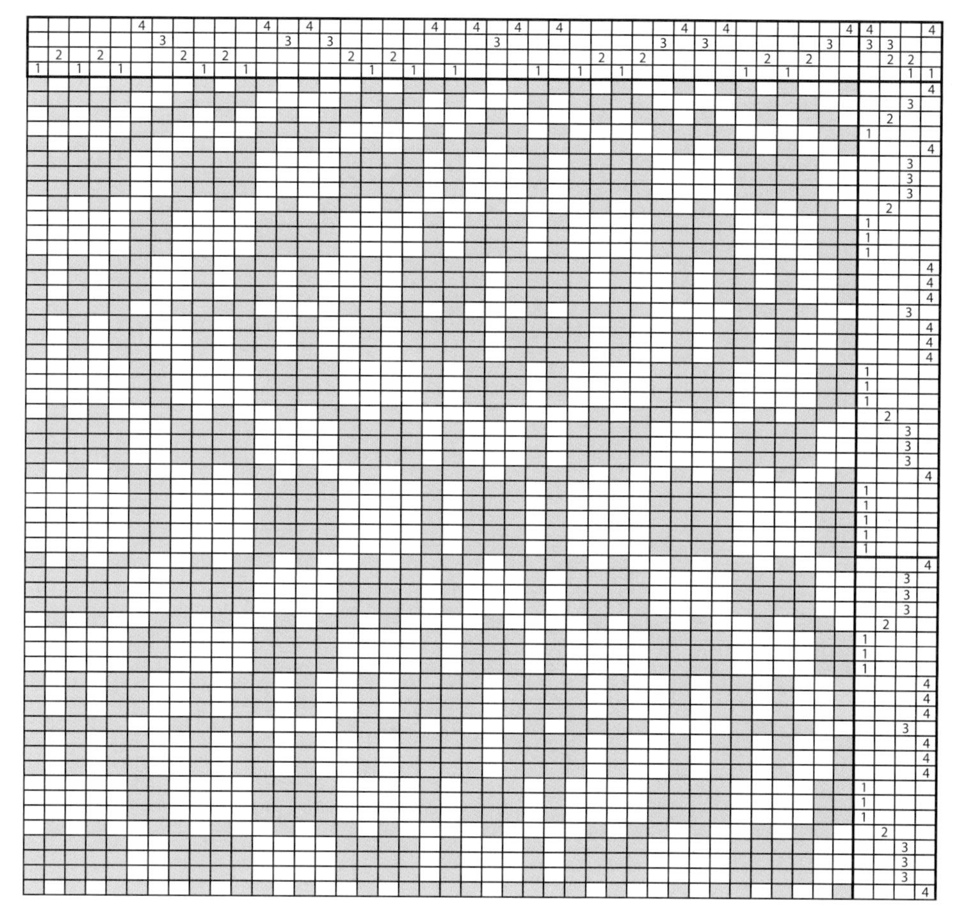
Overshot with transition.

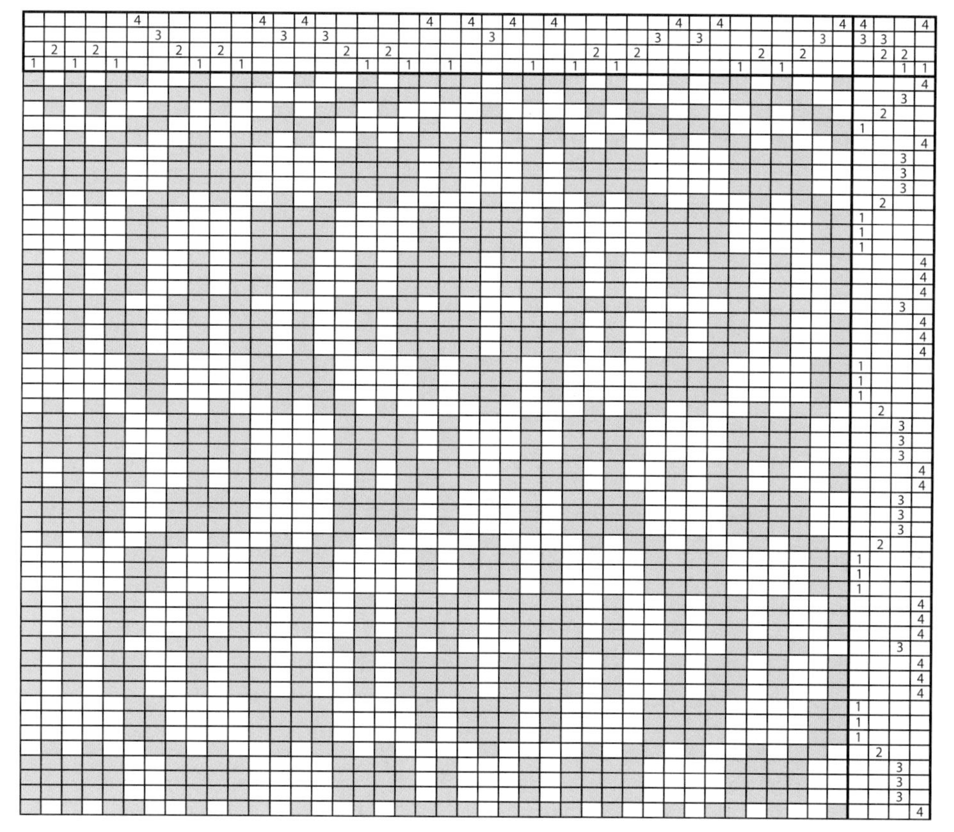
Overshot *without* transition.

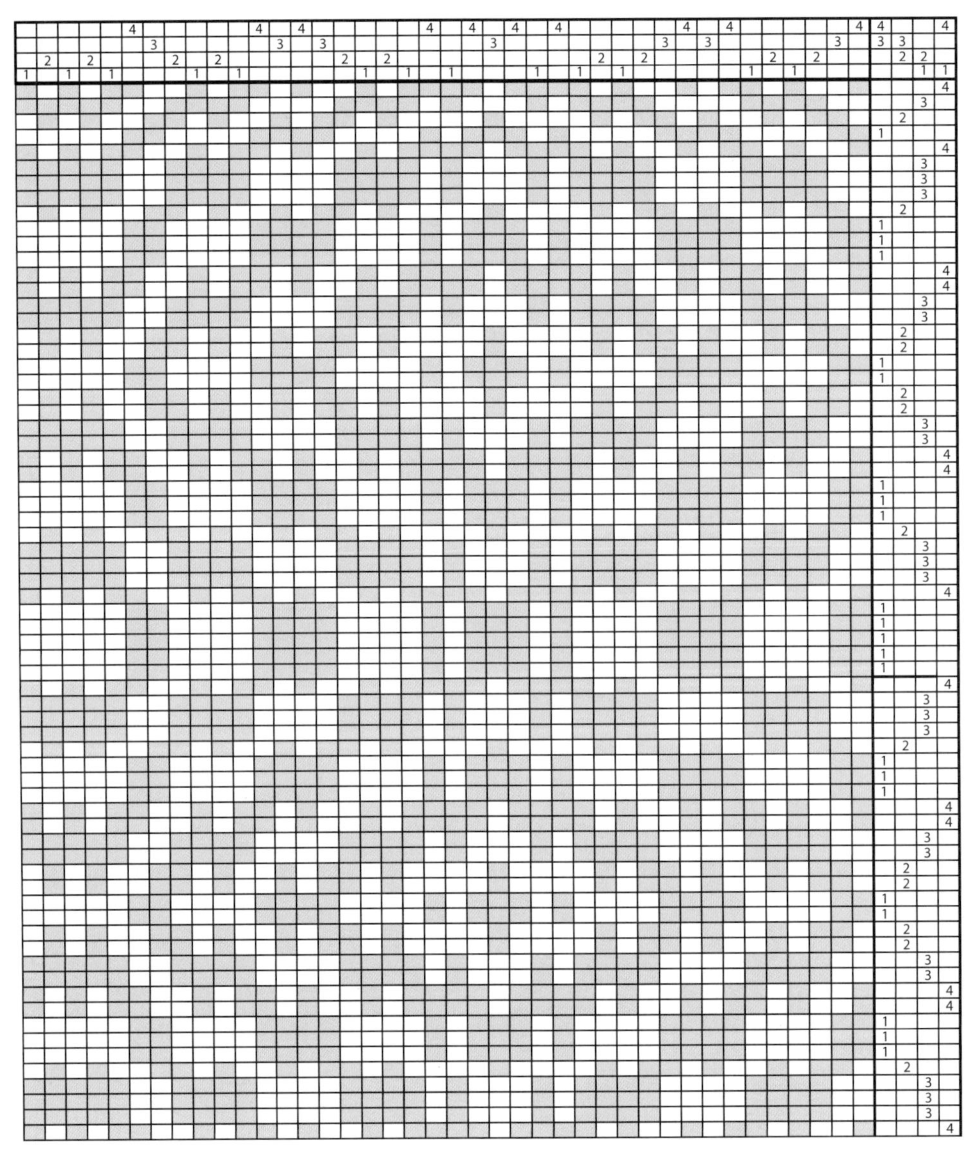

Overshot with transition and additional threads.

Looking at the treadling, you can see that the treadles are depressed one time and then you move to another treadle. The motif is circular and well balanced.

Now let's look at the same draft but as an overshot draft (see top of page 11). The motif has been repeated twice in this draft. And if you look closely, you can see some additional treadling—a transition—between the two motifs. In this draft, this transition is five number 1 treadles. This is optional and can be done with any pattern and with any treadles. It does not have to be a series like in this draft, but could follow a point twill.

Look at the draft at the bottom of page 11. In this draft, those transition threads have been removed. You can see that the motifs are now closer together.

And finally, let's look at the draft above. In this draft, the transition threads have been left in. But look closely and compare this with the first Overshot with Transition draft. You will see that there are changes made. Additional threads have been added and the treadling changed.

What does all this mean? It means that when you are setting up your treadling, the sky is the limit as far as designing. You can do the basic and just add a few additional threads, and you will have a beautiful design. Or you can really be creative and change the treadling to create a whole new image. This is where the computer software for weaving is wonderful. It will allow you to make these changes with ease and quickly see the motif you are creating.

Have fun in this process!

CHAPTER 3

Borders

Adding borders to your weaving is not a difficult process and will give your piece a finished look by framing the design portion of your piece. Always keep in mind the size of your finished piece. A small piece will usually look good with narrower borders, and a larger piece can have wider or mutiple borders. Of course, there can always be exceptions. If the border becomes an essential part of the design, then a larger border is to be expected. An example of this would be Norse Kitchen in the Davison book. In this design, the border is an integral part of the overall design. Also notice that more than one border has been used.

Borders are also a wonderful way to increase the size of your project. Maybe you want to increase the size of your piece but not as much as a full repeat. Some of the overshot repeats are quite lengthy. Adding a border not only frames your piece but can give you that little bit of additional width you want.

The size of your threads will also be a factor in creating a border, so you will need to consider the epi when creating borders for your pieces. If you have designed a project that is 24 epi and the border design is only 36 threads wide, your border will be 1½ inches (3.8 cm). However, if the project is 10 epi, that same border will

Norse Kitchen

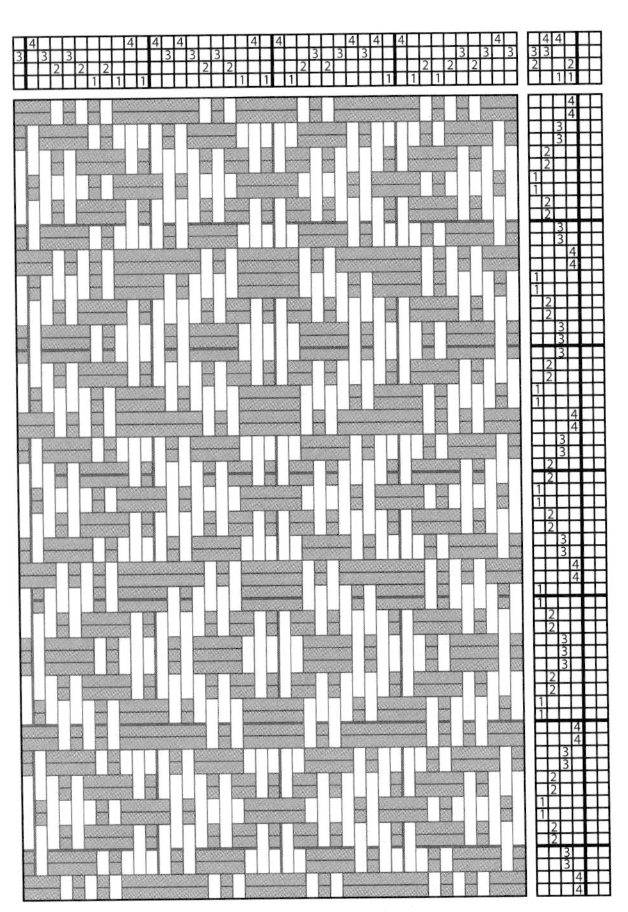

Example 1

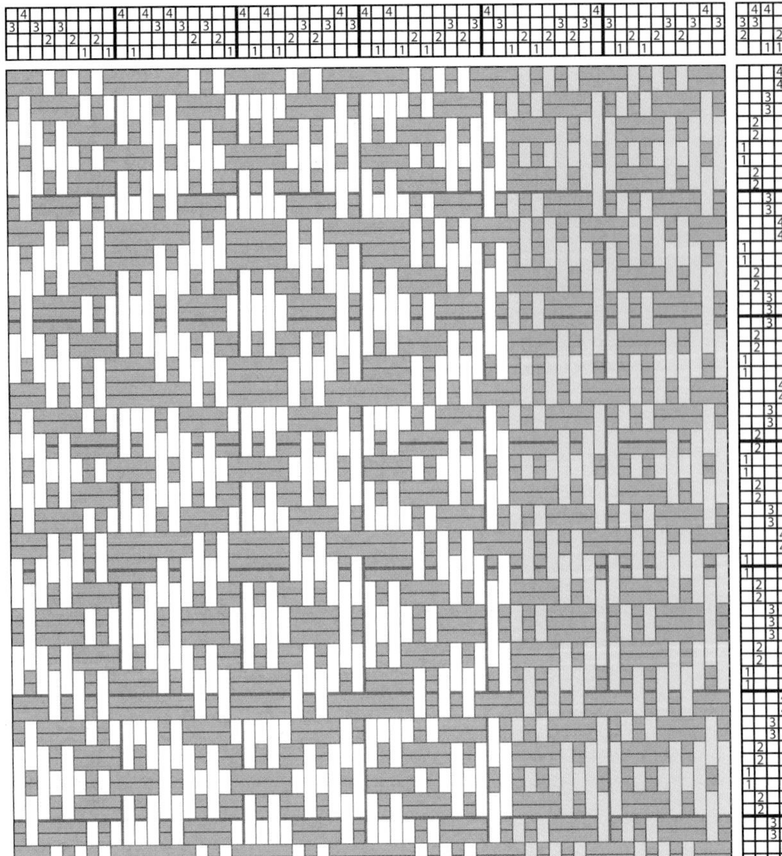

Example 2

be 3.6 inches (9.1 cm). Make sure you are getting the finished look that you want.

Let's start with the side borders. We will be working with the weaving draft Example 1. This is a basic twill/overshot pattern. You will see that the first 9 threads of the threading pattern are 3, 4, 3, 2, 3, 2, 1, 2, 1. Looking at the pattern it creates when woven, you will see an attractive sideways V design. Simply take that portion of the threading and add it to the beginning of the draft and then repeat the desired number of times. In Example 2 it has been repeated two times for a total of three sets of this threading design.

Now let's look at the opposite, or left side, of Example 1. The last set of threads is the reverse of the right side: 1, 2, 1, 2, 3, 2, 3, 4, 3. To create the second border we will again repeat this set two times for a total of three times as seen in Example 3. We have now created borders for both of the sides.

Next we will look at borders for the bottom of the piece. Look closely at the end of the treadling, and you will see a very simple and logical grouping of threads to use for a border: 1, 1, 2, 2, 3, 3, 4, 4. You can see these have been added in Example 4.

Next look at the top of your treadling and again you will see that the treadling is the reverse of that at the bottom of the treadling. You can add two repeats to the top and now you have added borders on all four sides of your piece as seen in Example 5 on page 16.

These borders can be increased, decreased, or changed. If these borders are not the look you want, keep experimenting. If you just want a simple border, these should work fine. Many times you will find that a simple 1, 2, 3, 4 or 4, 3, 2, 1 will make a very nice border. If you want something more complex, try looking at different components of your draft and see what might work. Larger motif drafts will give you more options. But you could put in something completely new and see what the result is. The more you work with adding borders, the easier it gets. And it is so much fun!

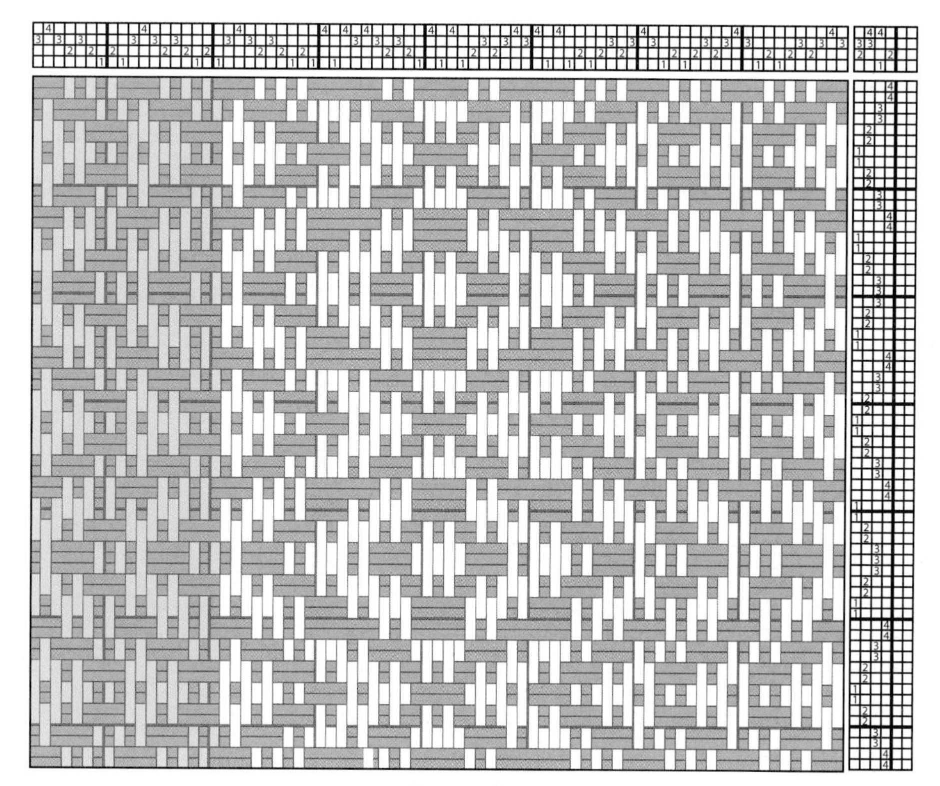
Example 3

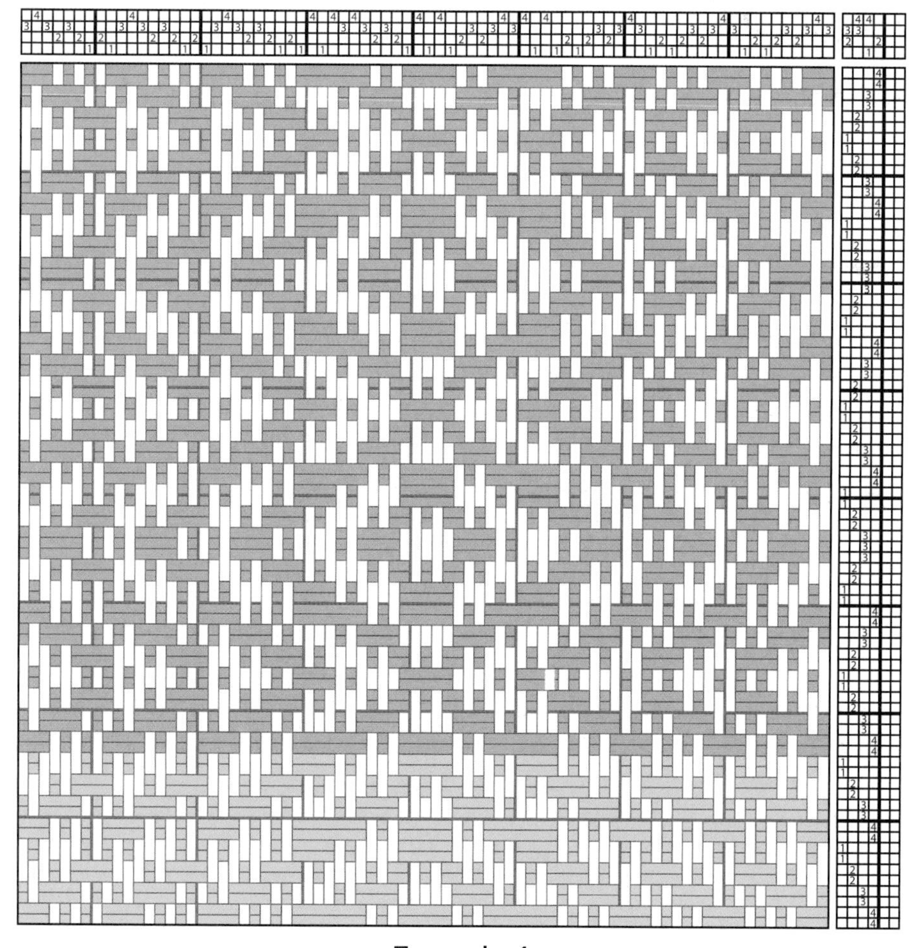
Example 4

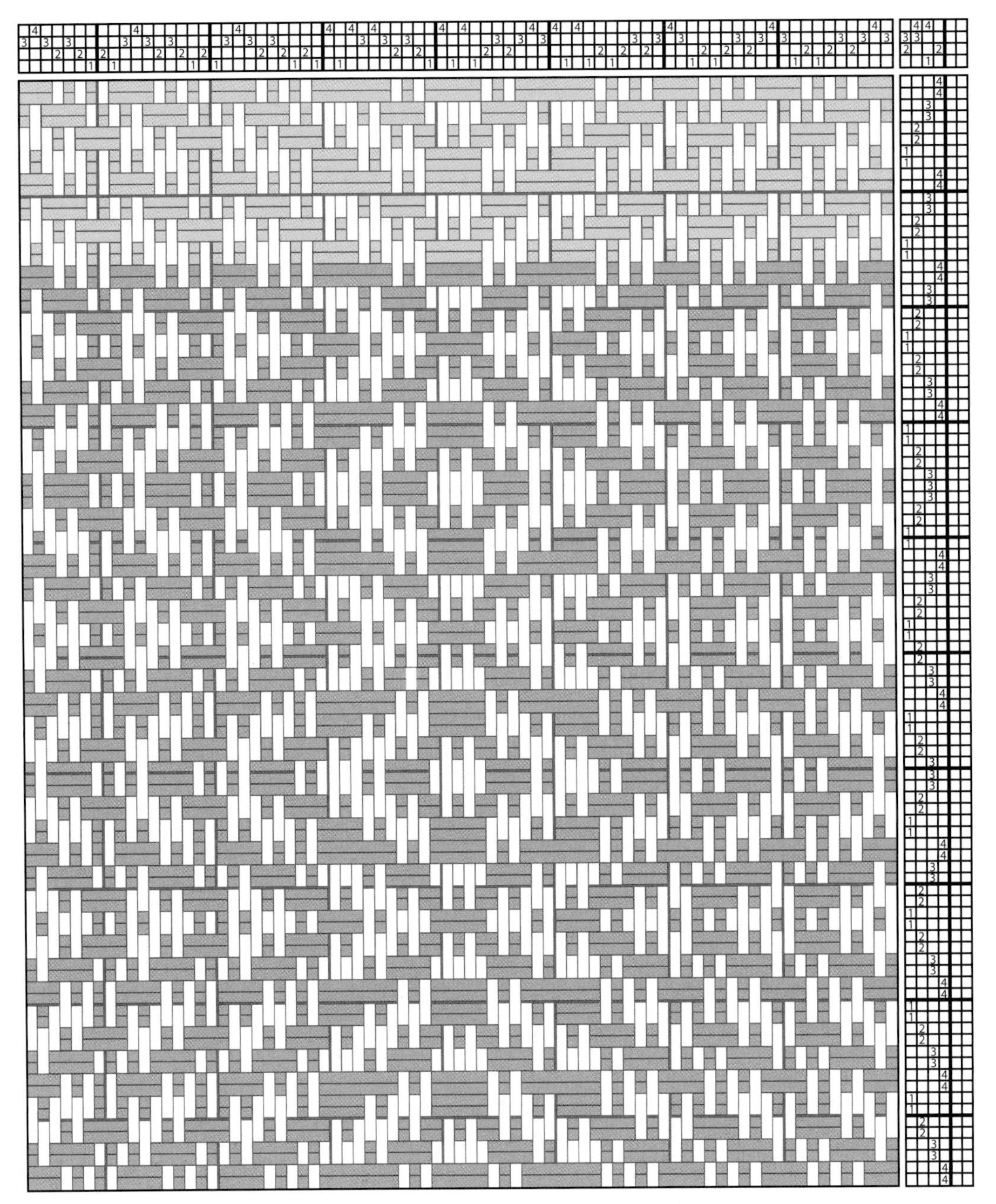

Example 5

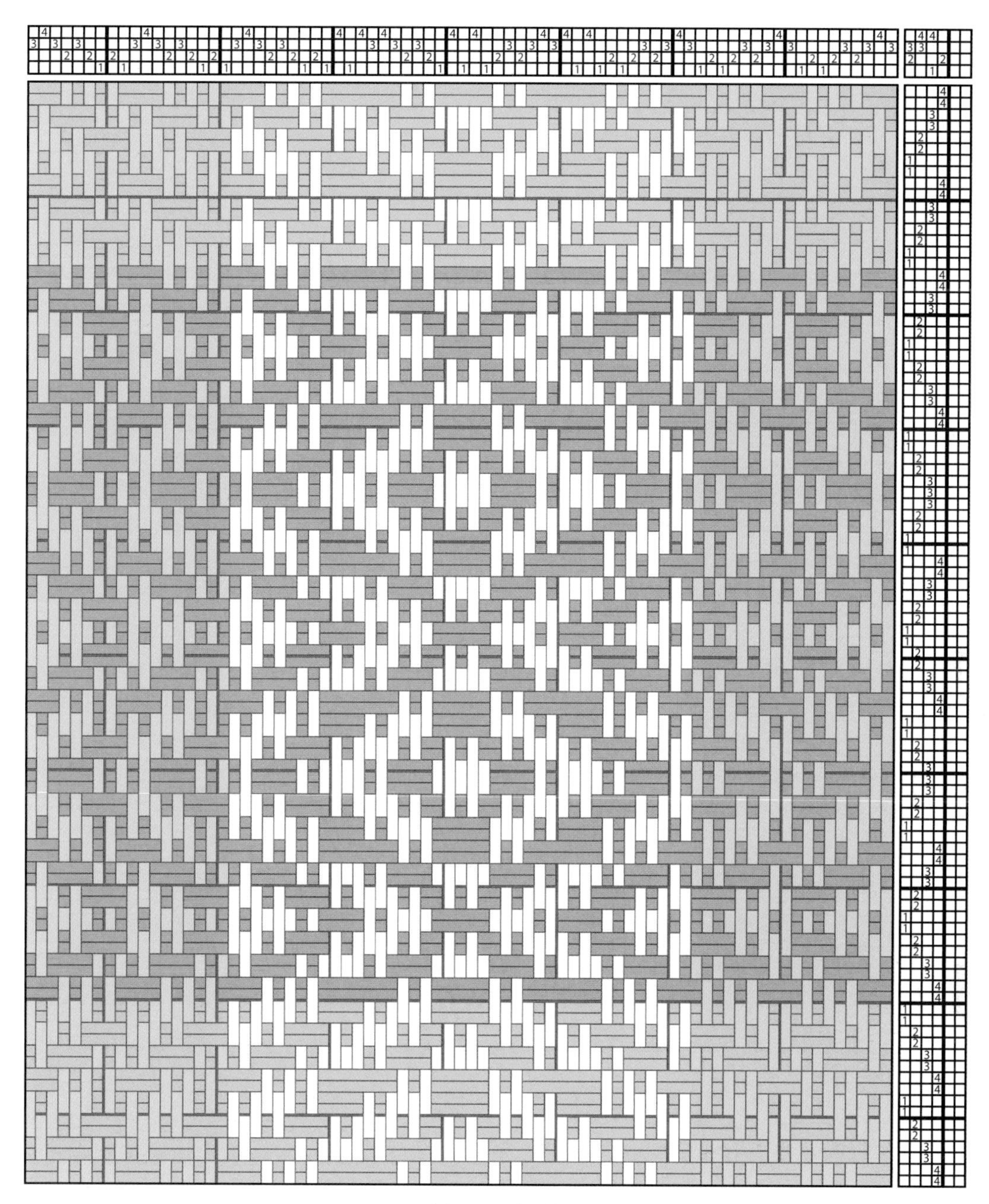

Example 6

Borders shown on all four sides.

CHAPTER 4

Changing Treadling to Change Pattern

This is one of the easiest and, in my opinion, the most fun ways to create a new pattern, especially if you have a computer program! The ability to immediately see results is wonderful.

Often when I dress the loom I like to put on enough warp to weave more than one piece. If the warp is a neutral color, I can change the treadling pattern and the weft color and create a totally new look. The overshot weave structure is especially suited for this as the tie-up is generally a more complex pattern than a tabby or twill.

Let's look at Example 1, which is the weaving draft for the large blooming leaf, a very popular pattern. As you can see, the threading for the pattern repeat is quite long, 70 threads. This will give you many options to create a new pattern. Example 1 is the traditional blooming leaf threading and treadling pattern.

Now look at Example 2. The threading and tie-up have not changed, just the treadling. But there is a dramatic change in the pattern. It's hard to believe that you started with the same threading!

Now move on to Example 3. Again, the threading and tie-up have not changed, just the treadling. And, again, you have a new pattern.

This is an especially fun exercise if you are making Christmas presents. Put on enough warp for two or more table runners or scarves and then weave each with a different treadling. Your recipients will be most impressed.

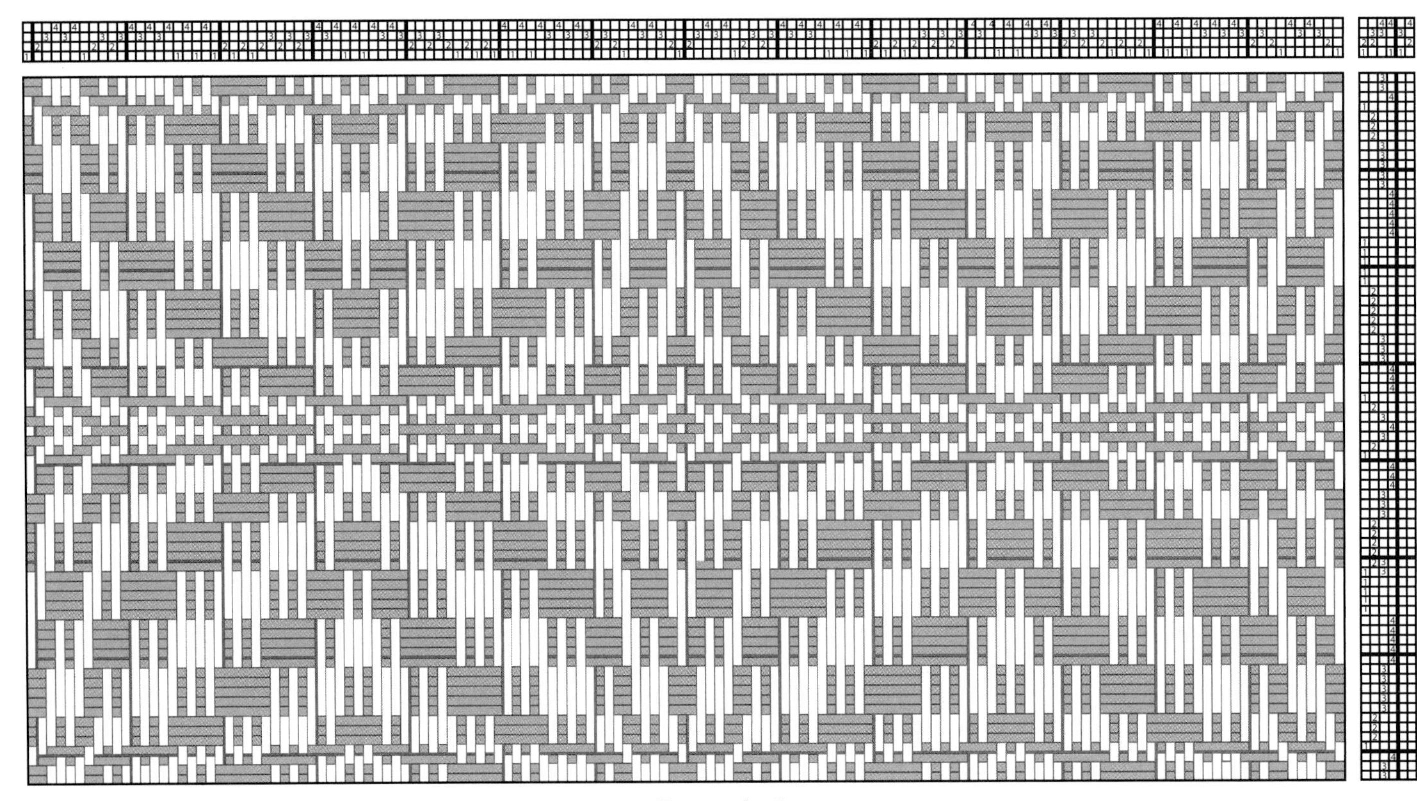

Example 1

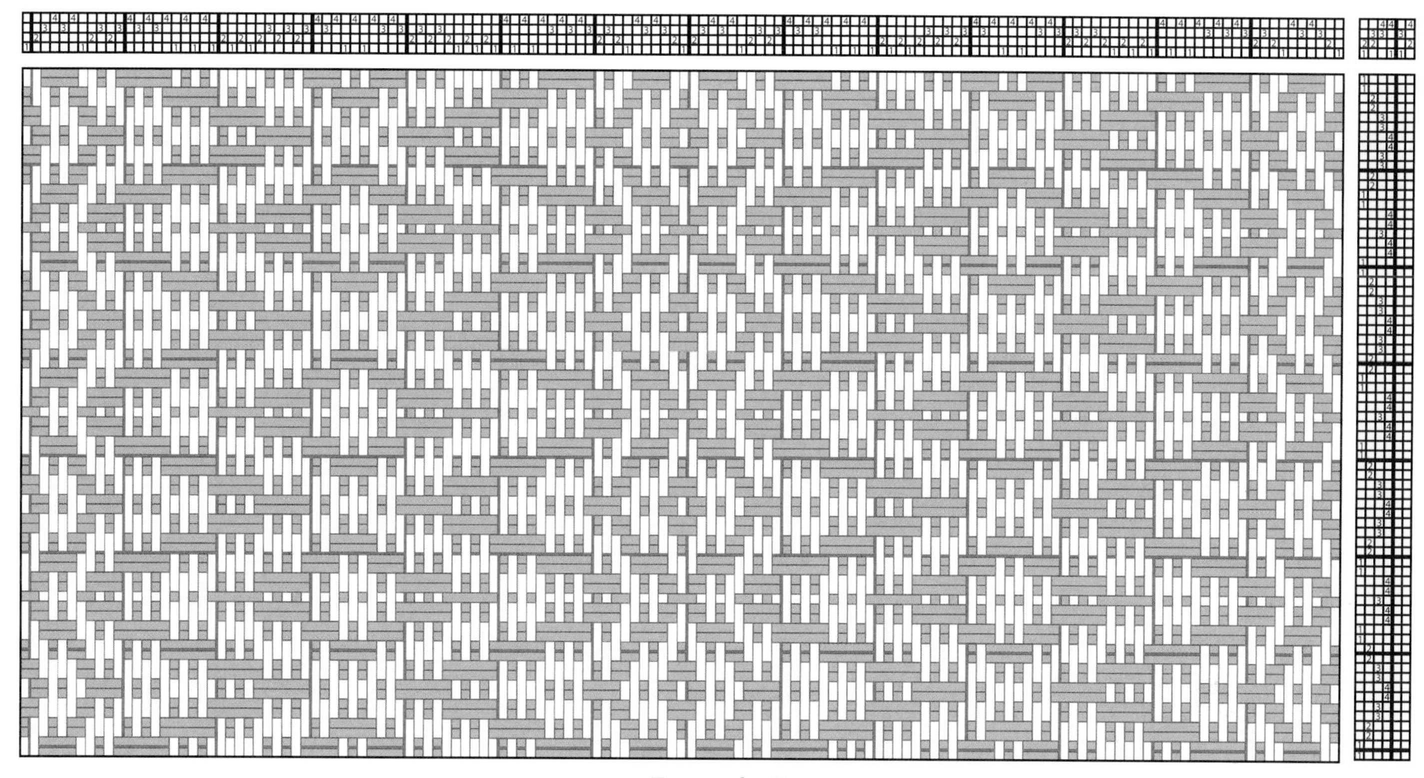
Example 2

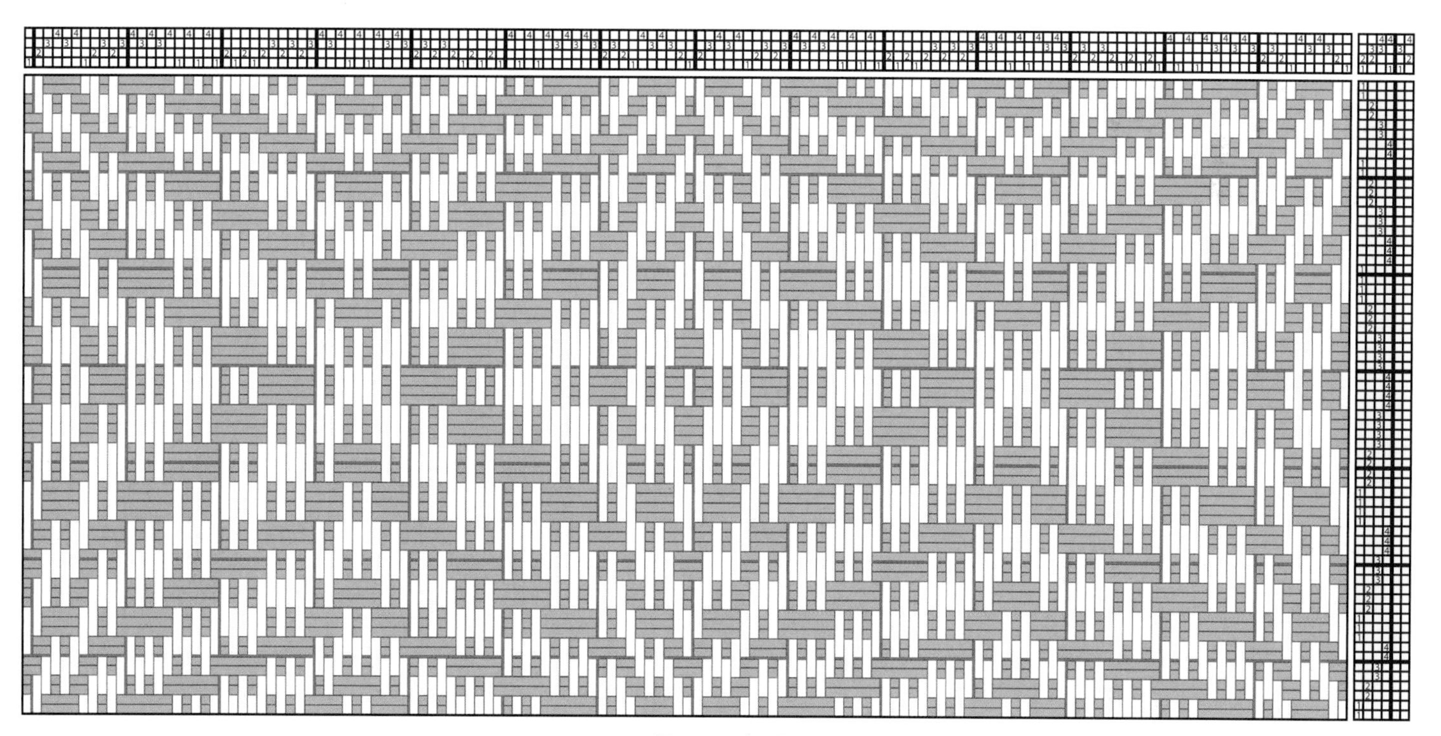
Example 3

CHAPTER 5

Making an Overshot Gamp

An overshot gamp is a wonderful way of seeing how changing the treadling creates a new pattern. When you use different colors for the warp and vary the tabby color throughout the project, you also see how the interaction of the threads affects the color. In an area where you have a blue warp and use a yellow tabby thread, that section will take on a green hue. If your warp is red and you use a blue tabby, that section will take on a purple hue. So a gamp can be a great learning tool as well as resulting in a beautiful finished project.

The Summertime Table Runner on page 143 is a gamp project. These are the threading patterns we used:

Wheel of fortune
Cat tracks and snail trail
Small honeysuckle
Leaves

A gamp can be created using patterns of any size, although it is best to keep the patterns proportional within one project. Patterns with a significant size difference may make your piece appear unbalanced, especially if you use many colors. If you want to use a particular pattern that is too small in comparison to the other patterns, consider doubling it to balance your piece.

Combining overshot patterns does require attention to detail. Remember that you must always follow the odd-even rule! A 3 must be followed by a 2 or 4; a 2 must be followed by a 1 or 3, and so on. If the chosen threading pattern ends with a 3 and the next threading pattern starts with a 1, you must add an *incidental,* or additional, thread. In this case, it would be a 2 or 4. This incidental thread would then keep the odd-even

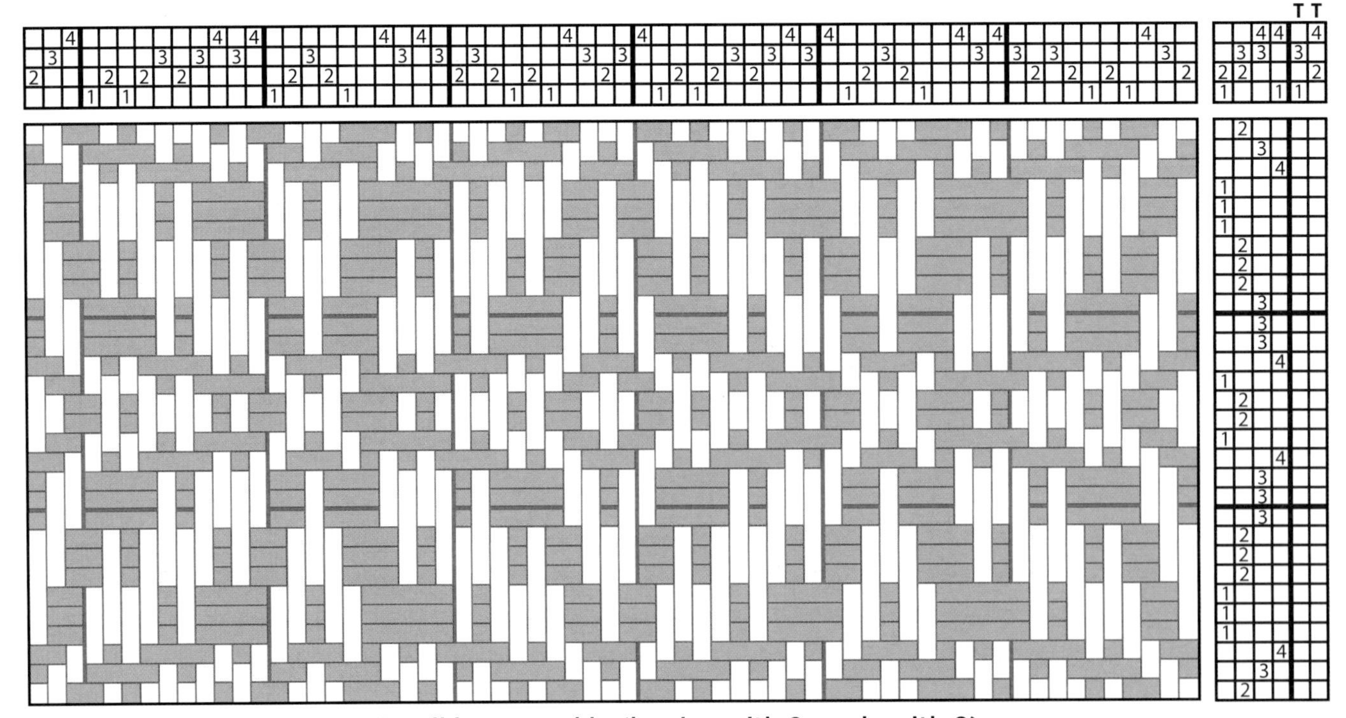

Small honeysuckle (begins with 2, ends with 2)

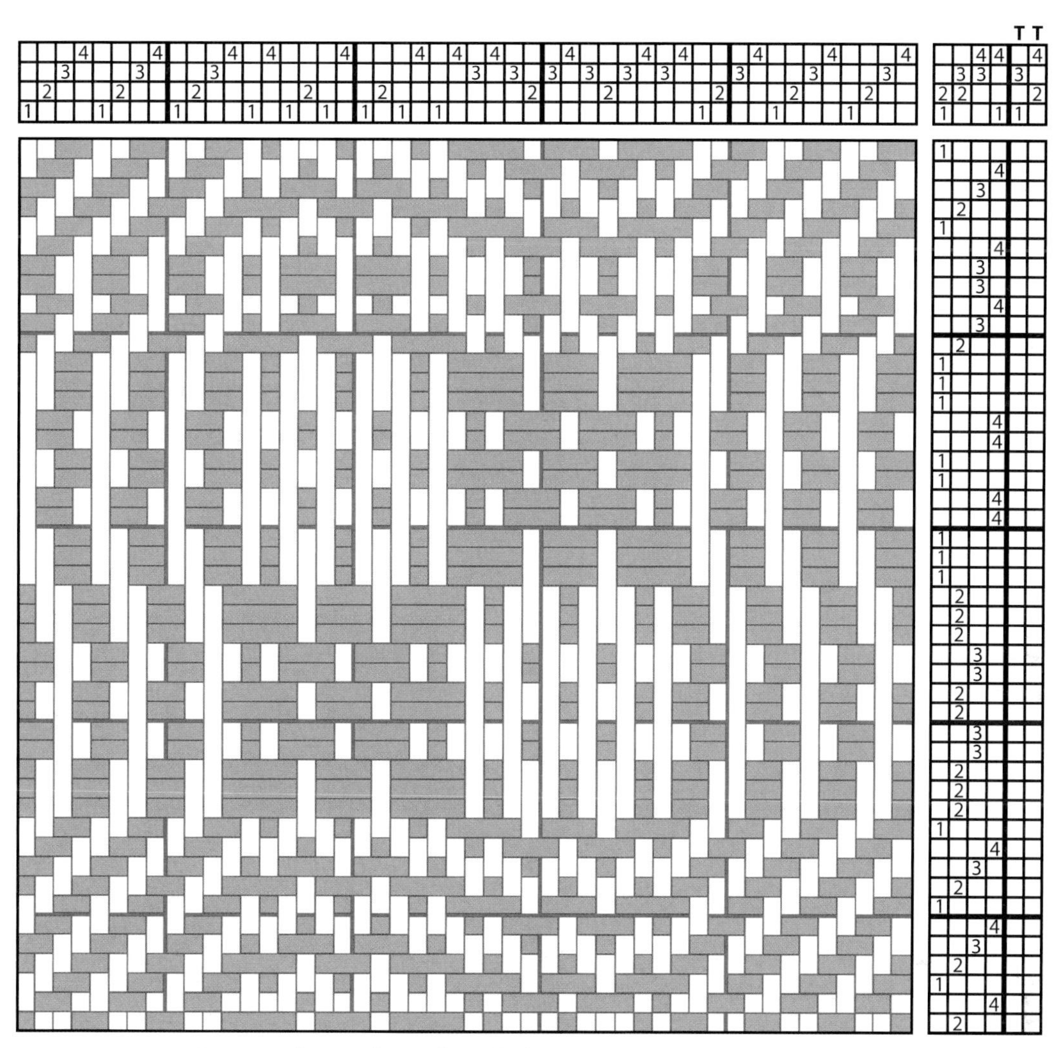

Cat tracks and snail trail (begins with 4, ends with 1)

4		4								4				4								4		4						4		4								4		
	3		3		3						3		3						3		3		3				3				3		3		3						3	
				2		2		2				2				2		2		2						2		2						2		2		2				2
							1		1						1		1								1				1								1		1			

			4		4				4				4				4			4								4		4					
3		3		3				3				3				3			3						3		3		3				3		
	2						2				2				2			2				2		2		2						2		2	
						1				1				1							1		1								1				1

			4				4				4		4				4				4		4		4				4
		3				3				3														3		3		3	
	2				2				2						2				2								2		
1				1				1				1		1		1		1		1		1							

Example 1. 4 and 2 are together, breaking the odd-even rule.

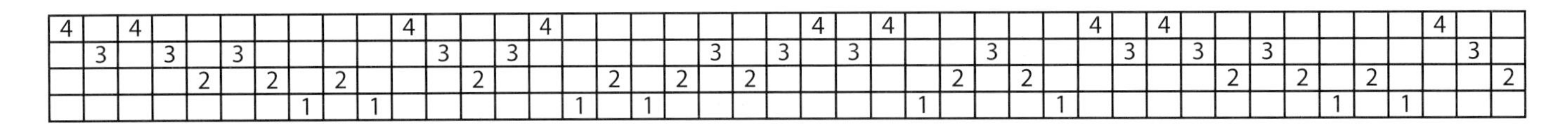

4		4								4				4								4		4						4		4								4		
	3		3		3						3		3						3		3		3				3				3		3		3						3	
				2		2		2				2				2		2		2						2		2						2		2		2				2
							1		1						1		1								1				1								1		1			

			4		4				4				4				4				4								4		4					
3		3		3				3				3				3		3		3						3		3		3				3		
	2						2				2				2				2				2		2		2						2		2	
						1				1				1								1		1								1				1

			4				4				4		4				4				4		4		4				4
		3				3				3														3		3		3	
	2				2				2						2				2								2		
1				1				1				1		1		1		1		1		1							

Example 2. A 3 has been added! Now we have odd-even again. The 3 is called an "incidental."

patterning. The incidental thread does not have to be just one thread, either. If you choose, you can create a small grouping of threads for the transition from one pattern to another—1, 4, 1–2, 3, 2–1, 4, 3, 2, 1—as large or as complex as you desire.

Let's isolate two of the weaving patterns from the Summertime Table Runner: cat tracks and snail trail and small honeysuckle. We want to start our piece with the small honeysuckle. It begins with a 2 and ends with a 2. The next pattern, cat tracks and snail trail, begins with a 4 and ends with a 1. Look at Example 1 (page 21) where the patterns are side by side. Remember the odd-even rule! There has to be an incidental thread added before these two patterns can be used together. At the minimum, we will need to add either a 1 or a 3 between these patterns. Let's choose the 3. Now the first pattern ends with a 2, we added a 3, and the second pattern begins with a 4. We now have 2, 3, 4 and we are back to the odd-even patterning we need. You can see the correct threading in Example 2 above.

Have fun creating overshot gamps. They are a wonderful learning tool and create some of the most beautiful projects. You could make a full-size shawl using a complementary colorway that would be striking. A shawl could utilize the large overshot patterns that are so beautiful. Using some of the smaller overshot patterns would create a lovely scarf. There is no end to the creative projects using this technique. Each time you change the treadling throughout the piece, you have created a new pattern. Keep track during your work of threading and treadling, as you may want to use one of the patterns again.

CHAPTER

6 Setting Up the Loom

One of the most daunting tasks with the overshot weave structure is threading the loom. All of a sudden you have gone from short, very repetitive tabby or twill threading to a very long pattern repeat that looks impossible. Overshot drafts can have over 100 threads just for one motif. Let's look at the full threading pattern for Indiana 3 in Example 1.

The first thing we will do is to isolate the different components of the threading pattern. It includes a border on each side—two repeats of Block A and three repeats of Block B. I use a pencil and draw lines to separate the components and then label and number these sections. If the motif is repeated many times I know I will need only one copy of the motif threading, but I would still mark all of them. It is a great way to make sure your threading is correct. In Example 2 you will see these sections broken down.

Next I cut these sections apart as seen in Example 3 and take them to the loom. It makes no difference whether you thread from front to back or back to front, except that if you thread from front to back, you will want to turn your threading sections upside down, putting the 1 harness on top and the 4 harness on the bottom.

I have found that I am less prone to making threading errors if I isolate the heddles needed to complete each section before I begin threading it. So for the border, pull over 4 heddles on harness 1, 4 on harness

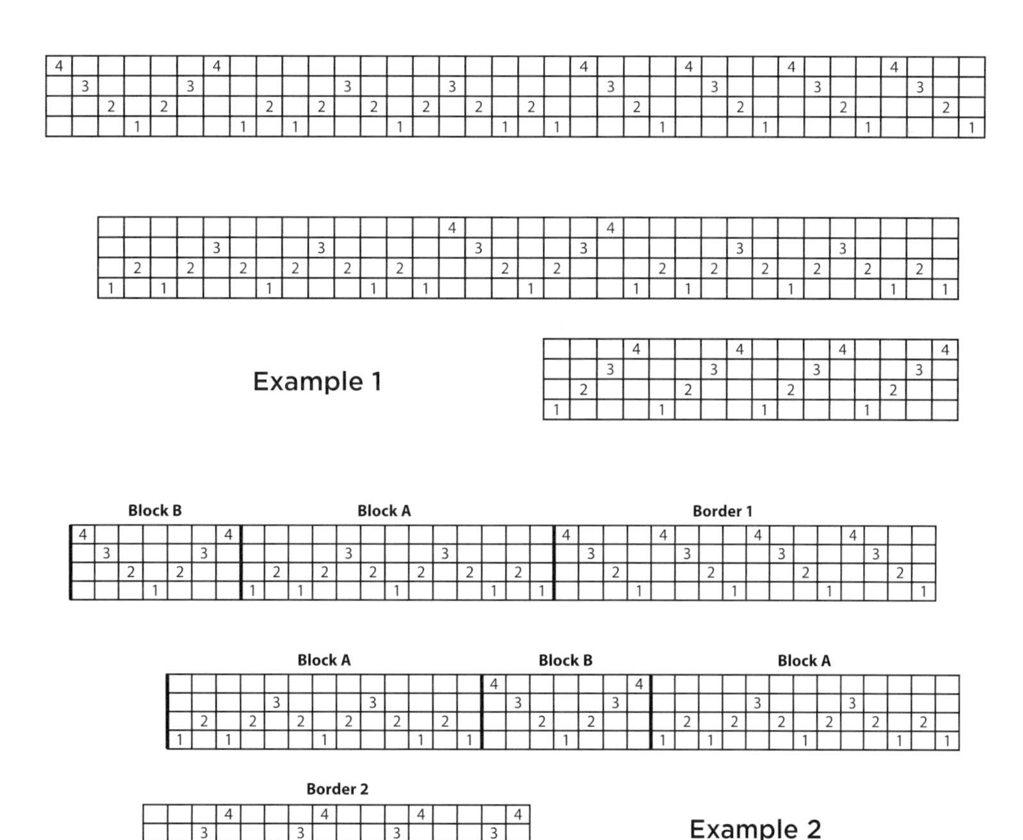

			4				4				4				4
		3				3				3				3	
	2				2				2				2		
1				1				1				1			

Border 2

4						4
	3				3	
		2		2		
			1			

Block B

				3				3				
	2		2		2		2		2		2	
1		1				1				1		1

Block A

4				4				4				4			
	3				3				3				3		
		2				2				2				2	
			1				1				1				1

Border 1

Example 3

If you thread from front to back, turn your draft upside down as you work.

2, and so on. Lay your thread between these heddles and the rest of the heddles to keep them separated. Then, and only then, will you begin to thread the heddles from the left of the design. If you end up with additional heddles on one harness and not enough on another, you have probably made a mistake and need to check the threading before continuing.

After threading the border, loosely knot this group and then move on to threading Block A. A loose knot is easier to remove if you find you have made a mistake. Sometimes a motif will have numerous threads. If this is the case, break down the motif into smaller sections working in 1-inch (2.3-cm) increments. Depending on the size of thread you are working with, you might break it down into two or more sections. Again, pull over only the required heddles to complete your section. Once you have finished threading you can tie on to the back beam with your chosen method.

Hair clips can help you keep track of the portion you are threading.

Isolate the heddles needed for a section before you begin threading.

When working with your threading draft, and especially a large threading draft, it is easy to get lost or confused as to where you are. To avoid this, use this trick: hair clips. I use hair clips to "outline" the section that I'm working with, one at the beginning and one at the end. These hair clips move easily from section to section and are a life-saver when you are interrupted. Using these will allow you to return quickly to where you left off.

Random Pickup versus Alternating Colors

In many of the projects I have used two colors in the warp. There are a few reasons I may choose to do this. I might like the blending of the two colors and the way it softens the overall design. It may simply be because I want to get started on a project and by using two similar colors I have enough thread for my warp, whereas if I used one color I wouldn't have enough. Using two colors is a good way to use up some of the smaller cones that I have left over. And, when using two colors, I can wind my warp using the two colors at the same time, making the process much faster.

When using two colors I do not worry about which color thread I'm picking up—a process known as a random pickup. Whatever thread I take hold of is the one I use. Another option would be to selectively alternate the threads, light then dark. I have provided two samples with the same pattern and colors to show you the results of the two different methods. There is really very little difference. One word of warning, however: if you choose to alternate your threads, any mistake will be glaringly obvious and will need to be fixed.

Random

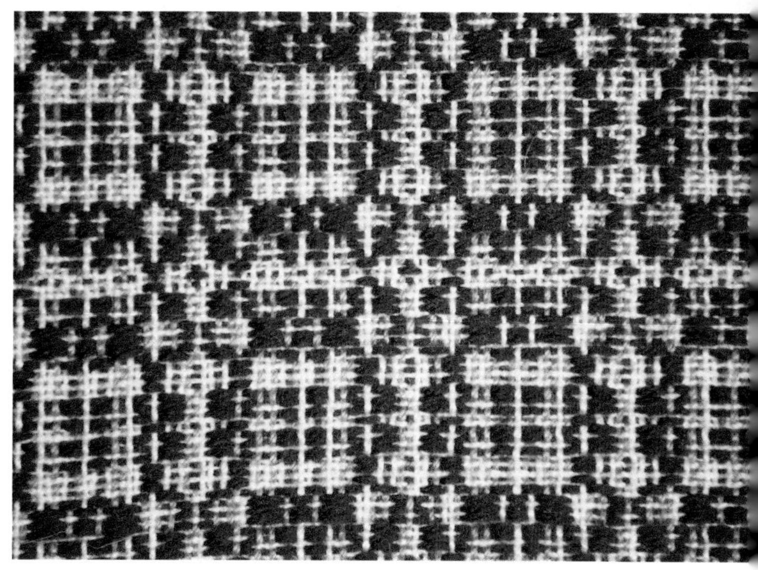

Alternating

CHAPTER

7 Treadling

In my projects, I always start weaving from the bottom of the treadling draft. Why? Because I generally add borders, it is important to read the draft in the same manner that the piece is being woven on the loom. So, you would read the draft from the bottom up.

Would it make much difference if you were to read the treadling from the top down? It could make a huge difference as the borders might be reversed and, if there is a finishing/partial motif, it might be moving in the wrong direction. While all of this may seem strange, think of it this way: You will be treadling in the direction that the fabric is being woven or in the same way the fabric is coming off the loom.

Now you are ready to start weaving. When you look at the treadling of an overshot pattern, you see a more complex treadling than for a tabby or twill. Let's go back to the Indiana 3 draft (see Example 1 at right). Again, you will see that I have begun with the borders, just as in the threading pattern. Starting from the bottom of the treadling, you will see 4, 3, 2, 1. This is fully treadled three times. The fourth time would be 4, 3, 2, as the next 1 is part of the pattern block. I have broken down the treadling into the Beginning border, Block A, Block B, Block A (to balance), and finally the balancing/partial treadling block and then the Ending border. Be sure to fully read any treadling patterns before starting to weave a project to make sure you understand all the components.

Remember, my patterns are to be treadled from the bottom up. Set up your notes in a way that is easy for you to understand (see Example 2 at right). I also use a hair clip when weaving to keep track of where I am in my sequence. For me, it is best to place the clip under the next treadle that I am to depress. If I am called away from the loom, I will place the hair clip on top of the treadle that I am to start with. Do what works for you and take your time.

Another tip for you. When weaving, after you have woven 3 or 4 threads in your pattern, place a T pin under the first thread. As you weave, move this T pin along with the fabric, keeping it at the first thread in each sequence. If you lose your place, you will only have to look within that sequence since you have the T pin marking the beginning.

Use these ideas for yourself as a starting point in your journey. One of the advantages of being with other weavers and taking classes is all the little bits of information and techniques that are shared that make weaving more successful and fun.

1				Ending Border
	2			
		3		
			4	
1				
	2			
		3		
			4	
1				
	2			
		3		
			4	
1				
	2			
		3		
			4	
		3		Partial Balancing
	2			
1				
1				
1				
	2			Block A
		3		
			4	
		3		
			4	
		3		
			4	
		3		
	2			
1				
1				
1				

	2			Block B
		3		
			4	
			4	
		3		
	2			
1				
1				
1				
	2			Block A
		3		
			4	
		3		
			4	
		3		
			4	
		3		
	2			
1				
1				
1				
	2			Block B
		3		
			4	
			4	
		3		
	2			
1				
1				
1				

	2			Block A
		3		
			4	
		3		
			4	
		3		
			4	
		3		
	2			
1				
1				
1				
	2			Beginning Border
		3		
			4	
1				
	2			
		3		
			4	
1				
	2			
		3		
			4	
1				
	2			
		3		
			4	

Example 1

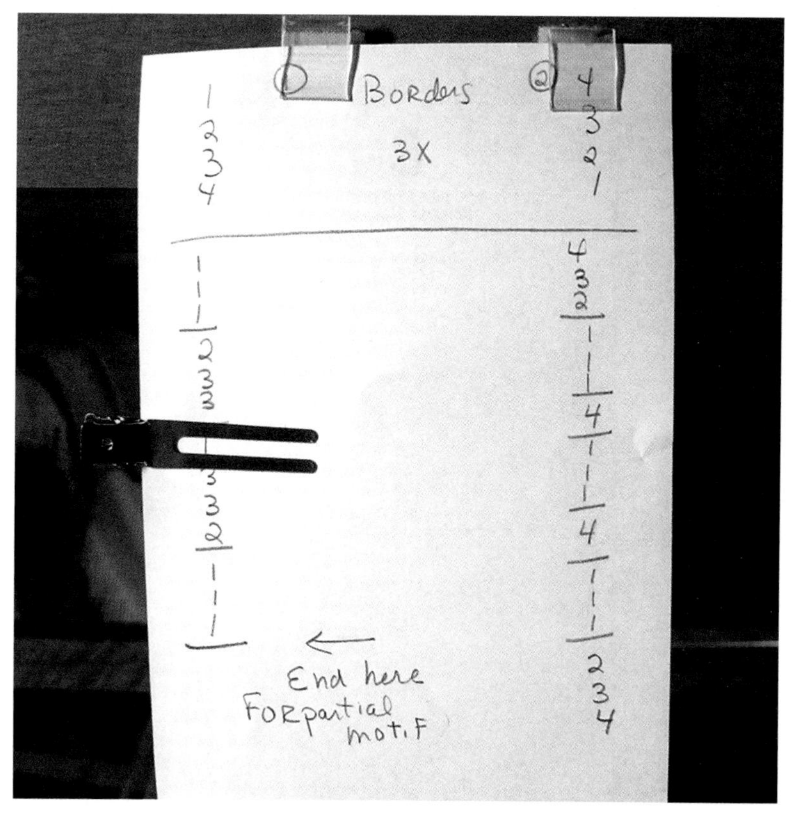

Example 2

CHAPTER

8 Bits and Pieces

There are many projects that can be made with small pieces of weaving, either samples or just pieces left from finishing that extra warp left over from a project. In this chapter, I want to share a few ideas. If you are sampling some overshot but want to make what you've woven into something useful, give these pieces a try.

Book covers are easy but can be very special when given as gifts. If you don't have enough woven fabric for an entire cover just use a motif and applique it to purchased fabric. I cover inexpensive notebooks so the recipient can reuse the cover many times once they have used up the original notebook.

Brooches and pins are wonderful for using up those very small scraps. Use cardboard or a large covered button for the backing. You could embellish with beads or trim, or leave some fringe for decoration. There is no limit to the creativity for this project.

It is very easy to create your own necklaces from small snippets of weaving. Back the piece with an iron-on interfacing to give it stability before cutting. Jewelry findings are readily available at craft stores in all sorts of materials and designs. Each stunning piece you make will be one of a kind!

Leave the fringe long and make a keychain! I used a small piece of leather with a hole punched in it for the basic structure of the keychain shown on page 29. This gives it great stability for longer use.

For some of the larger pieces, how about covered buttons? One set of the buttons on page 29 emphasizes the motif from an overshot piece. The other set is a plain weave from the faux ikat warp created for a scarf. These buttons could be used on another woven garment or replace the buttons on a purchased piece. They would definitely be the finishing touch.

Book covers

Necklace

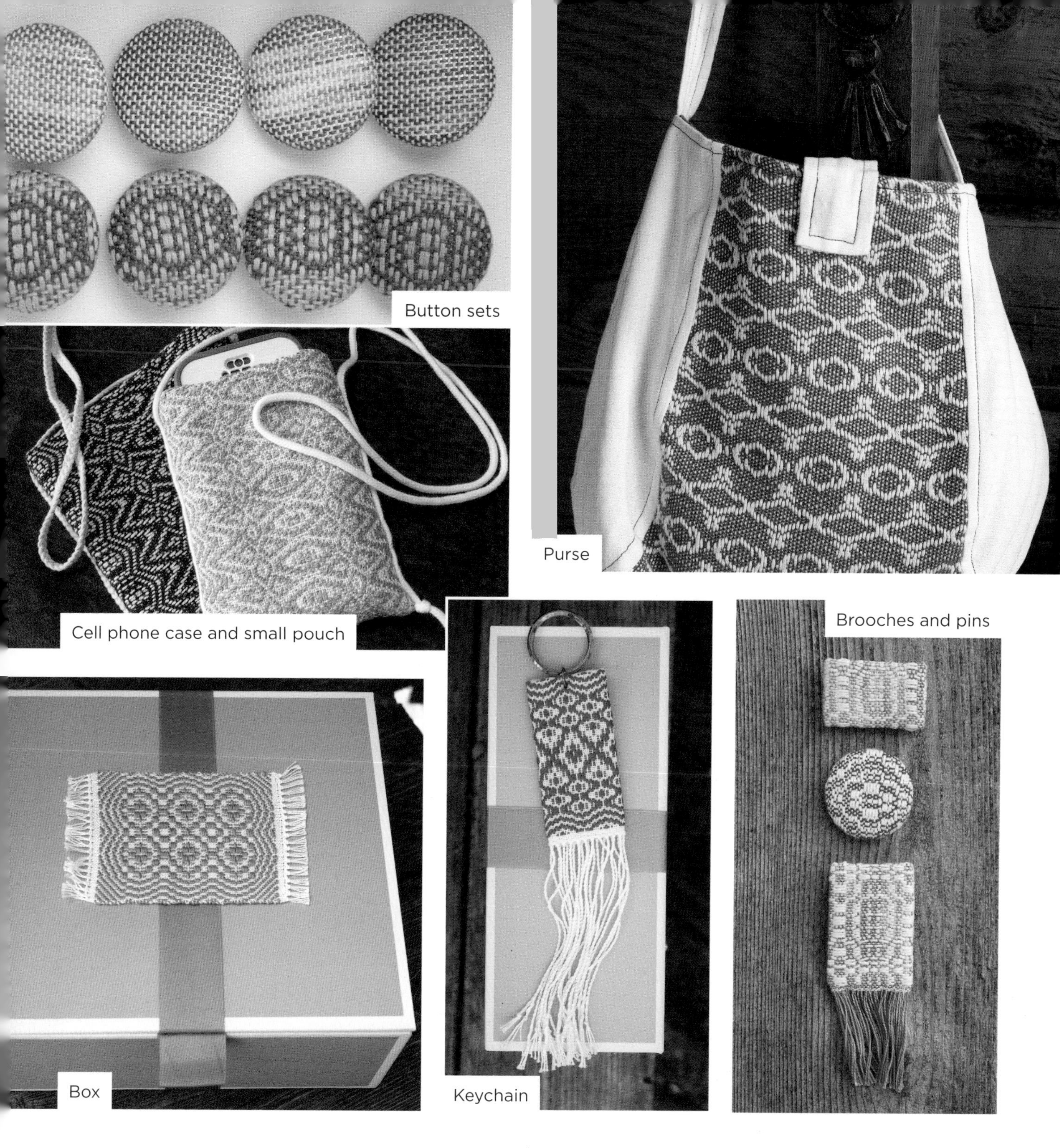

Button sets

Purse

Cell phone case and small pouch

Brooches and pins

Box

Keychain

Another use for a larger scrap would be a small cell phone pouch. Add a trim, too, so you can hang this around your neck and you will never misplace your phone again. Or use it as a purse and you will have your hands free to shop for more yarn for your next project.

How about making a purse? Find a pattern that has pieces that will fit your scraps, add purchased fabric, and you have a unique piece. If you can't sew an entire purse, you could embellish a tote with an interesting woven pocket!

And the box! This box once contained tea but was such a nice container that I wanted to save it. So I covered the writing with a piece of my handwoven fabric. I also covered all of the writing inside with nice cardstock, and the result is a wonderful place to keep my special memorabilia.

These are just a few ideas for those pieces that we all have lying around. Have fun creating your own unique and wonderful pieces!

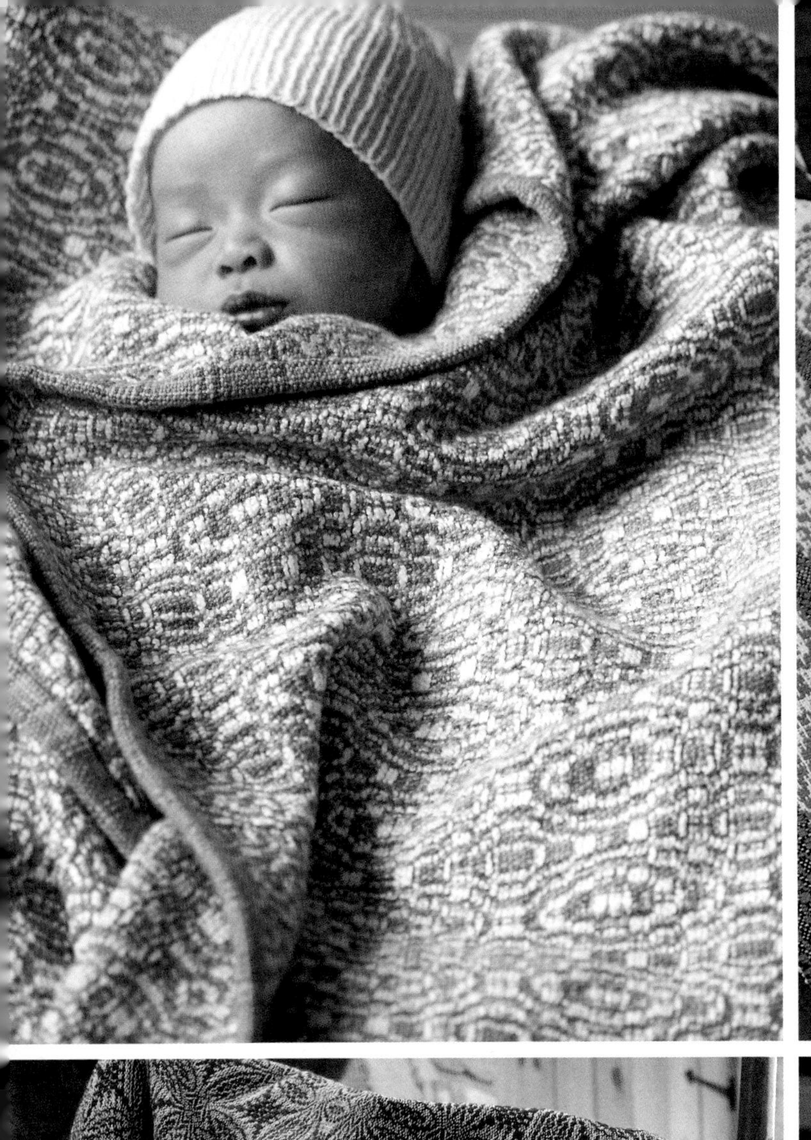

Projects

All Trimmed Out!

Who says you have to weave a whole piece of fabric? Why not weave just the trim to embellish that special garment? I adapted an old poncho pattern so that the trim became the focal point. The outside of the poncho is off-white 100 percent wool, and the lining is 100 percent wool in a lovely rich copper color. This makes for a sturdy and warm cape. I wove approximately 9½ yards (8.7 m) of trim to outline the entire piece. Yes, that was quite a bit but the results were worth the work.

You can also add trim to a purchased garment. And it doesn't have to be this extensive, maybe just trim in the front or even a pocket. But it would definitely enhance a purchased piece and make it one of a kind!

In doing the finishing work for this cape, I was unable to find closures that would work with this piece. This is often a problem when you are creating something so unique. So I created my own by using purchased buttons, some leather strips, and triangular pieces of the lining fabric. Think outside the box, look at the purchased closures, and consider how you can create your own. Try using slices of deer horns or wood, cover buttons, or make beaded buttons. Use your imagination but make the closures as beautiful as the garment!

There are no borders included in the *treadling* draft but you can easily create your own borders. This draft could be increased by adding two additional motifs in the threading and you would have a lovely scarf.

Dimensions: 4½ inches (11.4 cm) wide. Length as desired for project.

Pattern origin: Original

Warp

Sett: 24 epi; 12-dent reed, 2 threads per dent

Length: Length as desired for project

Threads: 10/2 perle cotton

- Light Rust, 32 ends plus 2 floating selvedges = 34 ends
- Oak, 32 ends
- Natural, 45 ends

Floating selvedge: 10/2 perle cotton, Light Rust

Weft

Tabby thread: 10/2 perle cotton, Natural

Pattern thread: Jaggerspun Maine Line, 2/8 Copper; calculate amount according to project

Begin

			4				4				4				4				4				4				4
		3				3				3				3				3				3				3	
	2				2				2				2				2				2				2		
1				1				1				1				1				1				1			

Tie-Up

				T	T
	4	4			4
		3	3	3	
2			2		2
1	1			1	

			4						4		4		4				4											
		3				3		3				3										3				3		
	2				2		2								2				2		2		2		2		2	
1				1						1				1		1		1		1				1				1

						4				4		4		4						4				4			
	3										3				3		3				3				3		
2		2		2				2								2		2				2				2	
			1		1		1		1				1						1				1				1

End

4				4				4				4				4				4			
	3				3				3				3				3				3		
		2				2				2				2				2				2	
			1				1				1				1				2				1

Threading and Color Placement

109 ends

Repeat entire threading 1 time for trim.

Light rust

Oak

Natural

End

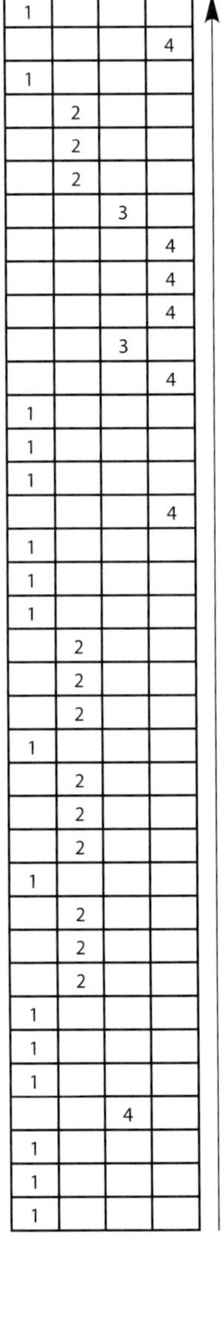

1			
			4
1			
	2		
	2		
	2		
		3	
			4
			4
			4
		3	
			4
1			
1			
1			
			4
1			
1			
1			
	2		
	2		
	2		
1			
	2		
	2		
	2		
1			
	2		
	2		
	2		
1			
1			
1			
		4	
1			
1			
1			

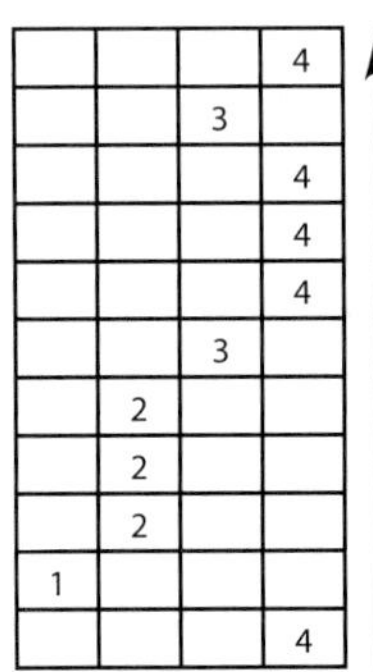

			4
		3	
			4
			4
			4
		3	
	2		
	2		
	2		
1			
			4

Use tabby

Begin

Treadling

Add tabby.

Repeat treadling to desired length.

Read and weave treadling from the bottom up.

Artemis Dog Coat

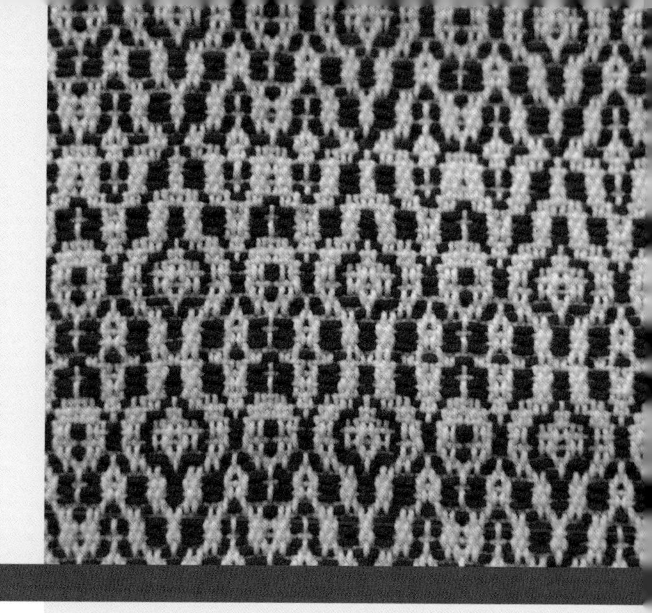

Let's make one for our furry friends! There is no reason why we can't weave a wonderful coat for our dog to keep him or her warm during these bitter cold winters. I used unmercerized cotton yarn rather than a more upscale yarn since the wearer would likely use this coat in a somewhat aggressive manner. Also, I designed the weave structure with relatively short floats so they are not as likely to get caught on branches and rocks.

When calculating the yardage required for a garment that will have to go through many washings, I always add 20 percent. It's always better to have extra than not enough. And you can always use the pieces for smaller projects.

KwikSew Pattern K3260 was used for this dog coat. I lined this piece with a quilted cotton/poly blend, although in a warmer climate this would be unnecessary.

This pattern could be used for a multitude of projects. Add a border and adjust the number of motifs, and you would have a lovely scarf or shawl. Unleash your creativity!

ANNA SIMPSON

Dimensions: Determined by project

Pattern origin: Original

Sewing Pattern: KwikSew pattern K3260

Warp

Sett: 24 epi; 12-dent reed, 2 threads per dent

Length: Length as desired for project

Thread: 8/2 unmercerized cotton, Natural

Floating selvedge: 8/2 unmercerized cotton, Natural

Weft

Tabby thread: 8/2 unmercerized cotton, Natural

Pattern thread: 4/8 cotton rug warp, Red

ANNA SIMPSON

4						4		4			
	3						3		3		
		2		2						2	
			1		1						1

Begin

Threading

38 ends
Repeat motif to desired width

				T	T
4	4			4	4
3			3	3	
		2	2		2
	1	1		1	

Tie-Up

End

		4		4						4		4						4						4	
	3		3						3				3										3		
2						2		2						2		2				2		2			
					1		1				1				1		1		1		1				1

End

	2		
		3	
		3	
		3	
			4
1			
1			
1			
	2		
		3	
			4
			4
			4
		3	
	2		
1			
1			
1			
			4
1			
1			
1			
	2		
		3	
			4
			4
			4
		3	
	2		
1			
1			
1			
			4
		3	
		3	
		3	
	2		
1			

Begin

Threading

38 ends

Repeat motif to desired width.

Treadling

Add tabby.

Repeat treadling to desired length.

Read and weave treadling from the bottom up.

Autumn Leaves Table Runner

I will admit it, fall is my favorite season. The hot summer days are past and the beautiful colors are now emerging. Numerous shades of red, brown, gold, and green create a breathtaking landscape in Pennsylvania. I love sitting under our tree while the leaves are falling and, yes, I even like to rake the leaves.

Autumn also brings us some wonderful holidays, especially Thanksgiving, and of course the need for a distinctive table runner for the season. Combining the different colors of fall along with the rich green of the evergreen trees, I created this table runner to celebrate the end of summer. The use of the Blooming Leaf weaving motif is the perfect choice. Do remember, these colors are suggestions. Do you have a different green you want to use? Then use it! Or maybe you would like to use fewer colors . . . by all means, make the change. Remember, this is your table runner and you can personalize it in any way you choose.

I began and ended with 1½ inches (3.8 cm) of plain tabby and then made a rolled hem. You could make a fringe if you prefer. Weave ½ inch (1.3 cm) of plain tabby and finish with the hem stitch.

Dimensions: 16½ x 45 inches (41.9 x 114.3 cm)
Pattern origin: Large Blooming Leaf

Warp

Sett: 24 epi; 12-dent reed, 2 threads per dent
Length: 2½-yard (2.3-m) warp
Threads: 10/2 perle cotton

- Loden Green, 49 ends plus 2 floating selvedges = 51 ends, 125 yards (115 m)
- Tangerine, 70 ends, 200 yards (183 m)
- California Gold, 70 ends, 200 yards (183 m)
- Burnt Orange, 70 ends, 200 yards (183 m)
- Scarab, 70 ends, 200 yards (183 m)
- Mead, 70 ends, 200 yards (183 m)

Floating selvedge: 10/2 perle cotton, Loden Green

Weft

Tabby thread: 10/2 perle cotton, Loden Green, 450 yards (412 m)
Pattern thread: 5/2 perle cotton, Loden Green, 450 yards (412 m)

Threading and Tie-Up

Border 1: 6 times, Loden Green
Motif: 5 times each color repeated one time
Border 2: 1 time, Loden Green

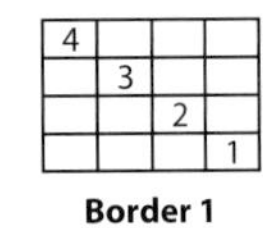

Border 1
Repeat 6X

Border 2—25 ends
1X

Tie-Up

Begin

End

Motif—70 ends
Repeat 5X

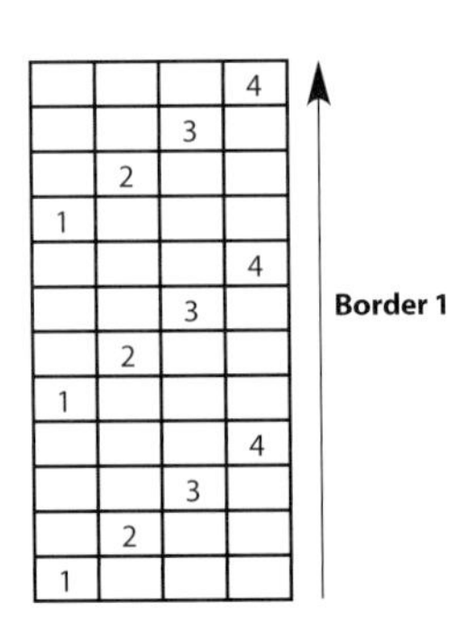

Border 1

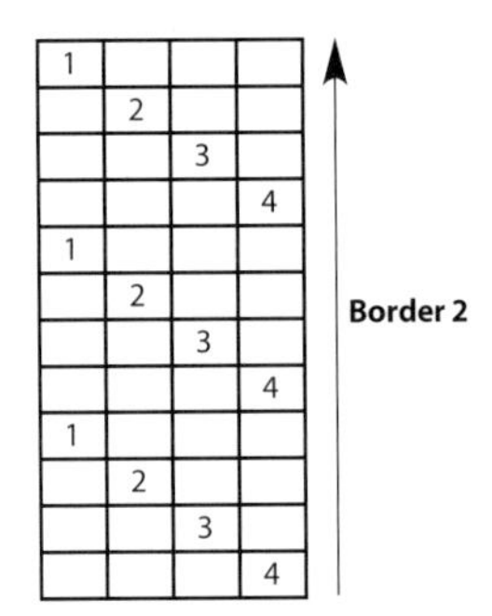

Border 2

End of
Partial motif

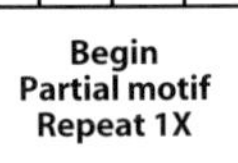

Begin
Partial motif
Repeat 1X

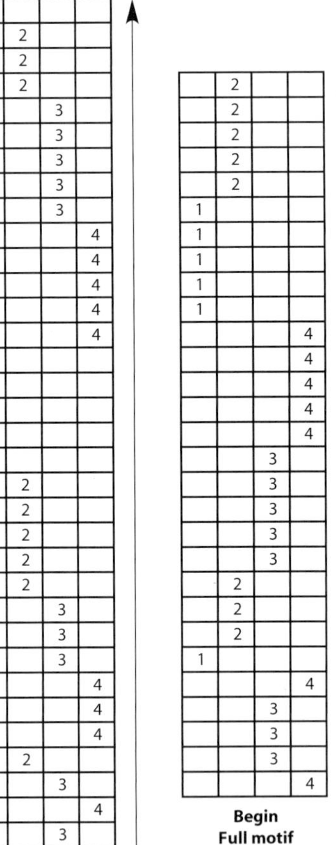

Begin
Full motif

Treadling

Begin with Border 1.
Repeat full motif to the desired length of your project.
Then repeat partial motif 1 time.
Finish with Border 2.
Add tabby.
Read and weave treadling from the bottom up.

Baby Blues Blanket

This blanket is a perfect gift for an expectant couple! This is an original pattern based on the phrase "our little angel." Using the rayon Natural color Ric-Rac for the pattern weft added a bit of texture to this piece. Plus the rayon makes the blanket very soft with a lovely drape. This would also be a wonderful gift for an older person who is housebound or in a nursing home. The fabric is very easy to care for. It would be easy to substitute 5/2 perle cotton for the pattern weft if the Ric-Rac isn't available. A 1½-inch (3.8-cm) plain tabby was woven at each end for a rolled hem. If you prefer, you could make fringe instead.

Dimensions: 34 x 50 inches (86.4 x 127 cm)

Pattern origin: Original

Warp

Sett: 20 epi; 10-dent reed, 2 threads per dent

Length: 2½-yard (2.3-m) warp

Thread: 8/2 unmercerized variegated cotton, blue tones, 697 ends plus 2 floating selvedges = 699 ends, 1,750 yards (1,601 m)

Floating selvedge: 8/2 unmercerized variegated cotton, blue tones

Weft

Tabby thread: 8/2 unmercerized variegated cotton, blue tones, 900 yards (823 m)

Pattern thread: Ric Rac (mill end) Natural, 98% rayon/2% nylon, 900 yards (823 m). Alternate comparable thread would be 5/2 perle cotton

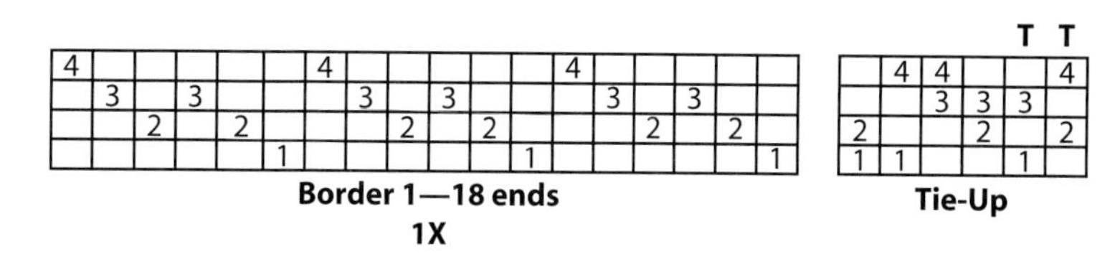

Border 1—18 ends
1X

Tie-Up

Full motif—42 ends
Repeat 15X

Threading and Tie-Up

Border 1: 1 time
Full motif: 15 times
Partial motif: 1 time
Border 2: 1 time

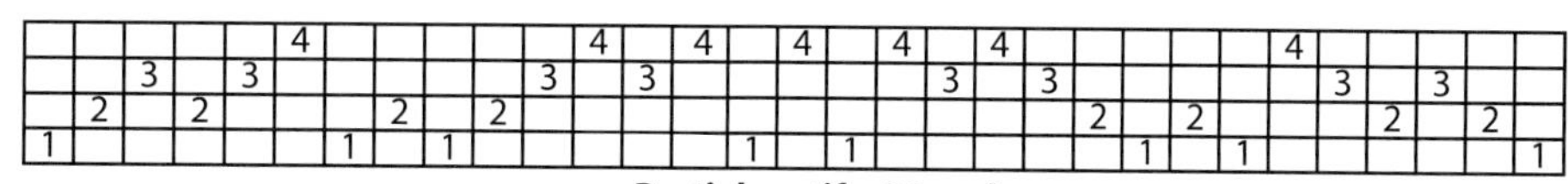

Partial motif—31 ends
1X

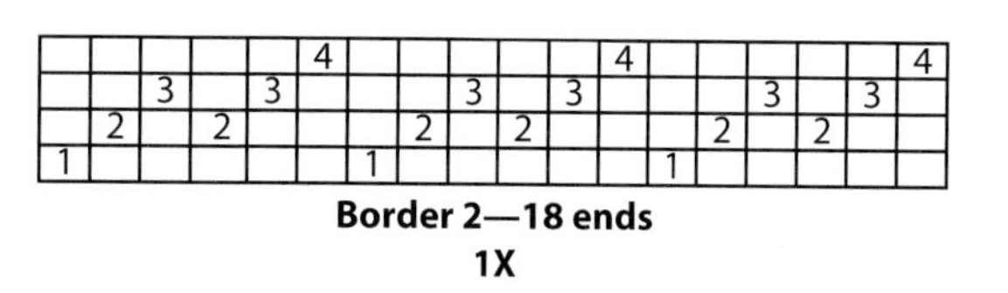

Border 2—18 ends
1X

Treadling

Add tabby.
Treadling sequence:
Border 1: 1 time
Full motif: to desired length
Partial motif: 1 time
Border 2: 1 time
Read and weave treadling from the bottom up.

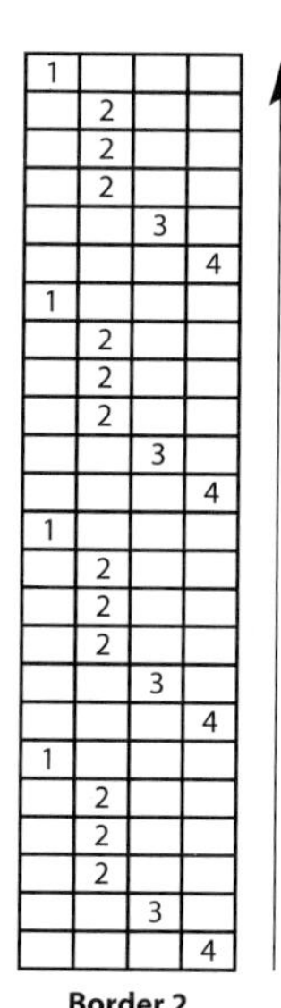

Border 2

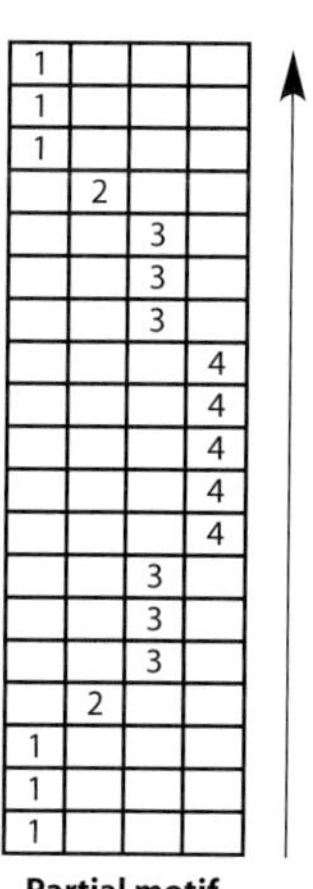

Partial motif

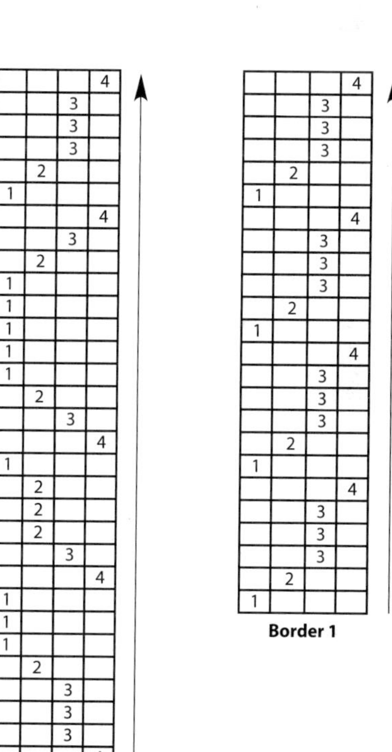

Full motif
Repeat to desired length

Border 1

Belts: Denim Blue and Sassy Brown

What could be more fun than to create and wear a belt in the overshot weave structure! These patterns are simple and weave up very quickly.

Denim Blue is the perfect accessory for that special pair of blue jeans. You can easily weave the belt as long as needed for the intended wearer. This belt was finished with a repurposed closure from an old belt. I left the fringe for accent. If you haven't got a closure, you can just increase the length and tie the belt in a loose knot.

Begin weaving with Border 1 and then repeat Motifs A and B to within 4 inches (10.2 cm) of the desired length. You will want to end with Motif A before you finish with Border 2. This will balance the repeats on your piece.

Sassy Brown has a unique and beautiful pattern. This pattern could easily be made into a scarf by increasing the repeats in the warp. In the threading you will have motif A and motif B, ending with motif A. Be sure you include the threading border on each side. I used two different colors in the warp with a random pickup. You can easily use the same color if you prefer. Make the belt as long as desired for the wearer. I planned to just tie this belt in the front, but you could add a closure.

DENIM BLUE

Dimensions: 3½ inches (8.9 cm) wide by desired length

Pattern origin: Original

Warp

Sett: 24 epi; 12-dent reed, 2 threads per dent

Length: Calculate yardage requirements according to desired length of project

Thread: 10/2 perle cotton, Cobalt, 85 ends plus 2 floating selvedges = 87 ends

Floating selvedge: 10/2 perle cotton, Cobalt

Weft

Tabby thread: 10/2 perle cotton, Cobalt

Pattern thread: 5/2 perle cotton or 5/2 Dragon Tale rayon, White or Natural

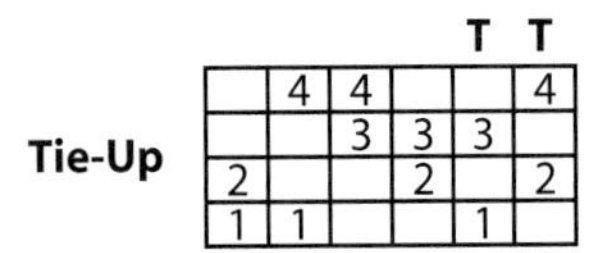

Tie-Up

				T	T
	4	4			4
		3	3	3	
2			2		2
1	1			1	

Begin

			4		4								4		4				4				4		4										4				4			
		3		3				3				3														3				3				3		3				3		
	2						2		2		2						2				2						2		2		2		2				2				2	
1						1				1				1		1		1		1		1		1				1				1						1				1

			4				4										4		4				4				4		4								4		4		
		3				3		3				3				3														3				3				3		3	
	2				2				2		2		2		2						2				2						2		2		2						2
1				1						1				1				1		1		1		1		1		1				1				1					

End **Full motif**

Threading and Tie-Up (Denim Blue)

85 ends

Repeat motif 1 time

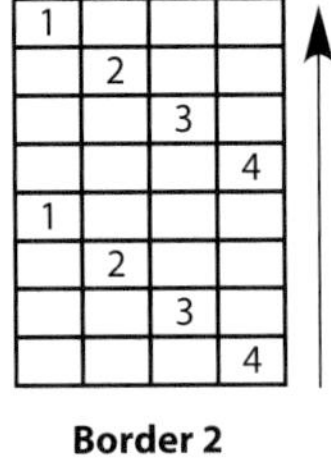

1			
	2		
		3	
			4
1			
	2		
		3	
			4

Border 2

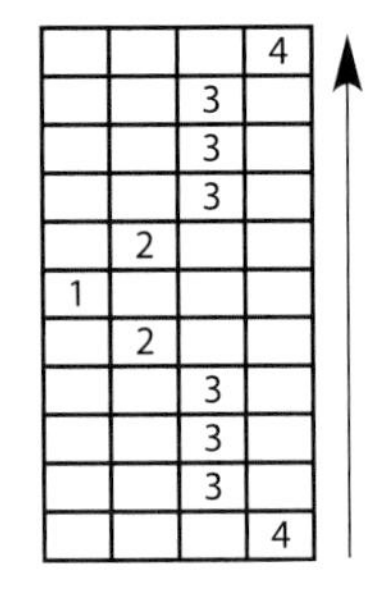

			4
		3	
		3	
		3	
	2		
1			
	2		
		3	
		3	
		3	
			4

Motif B

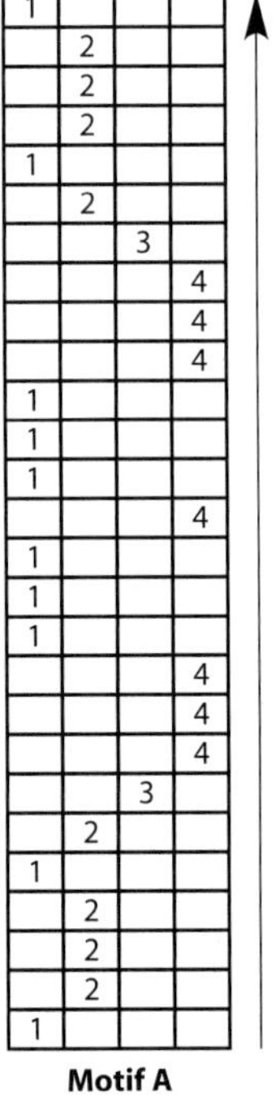

1			
	2		
	2		
	2		
1			
	2		
		3	
			4
			4
			4
1			
1			
1			
			4
1			
1			
1			
			4
			4
			4
		3	
	2		
1			
	2		
	2		
	2		
1			

Motif A

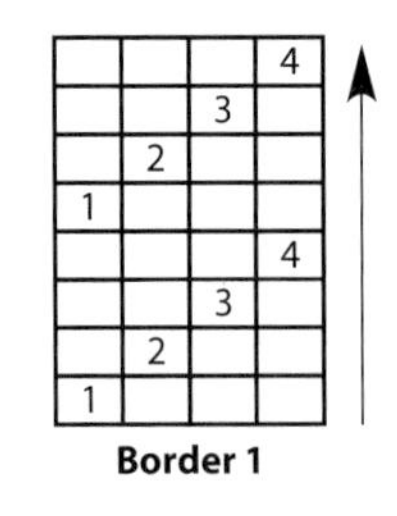

			4
		3	
	2		
1			
			4
		3	
	2		
1			

Border 1

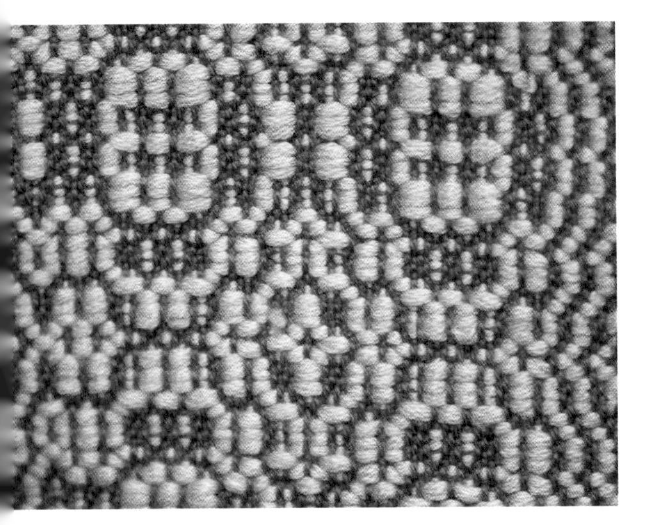

Treadling (Denim Blue)

Use tabby.

Treadling sequence:

Border 1: 1 time

Motif A then Motif B: repeat to desired length, end with Motif A.

Border 2: 1 time

Read and weave treadling from the bottom up.

Motif A—27 ends
1X

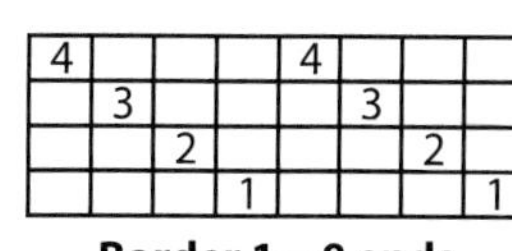
Border 1—8 ends
1X

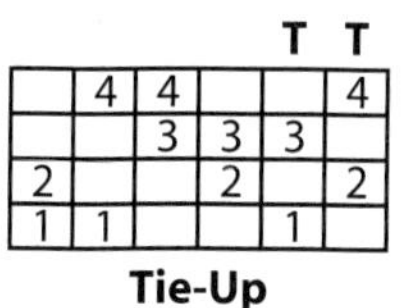
Tie-Up

Threading (Sassy Brown)

Border 1: 1 time
Motif A: 1 time
Motif B: 1 time
Motif A: 1 time
Border 2: 1 time

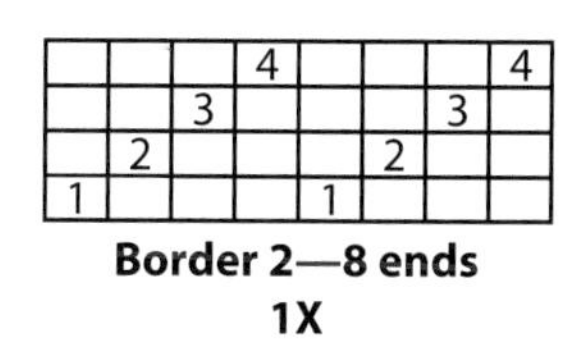
Border 2—8 ends
1X

Motif B—15 ends
1X

Border 2

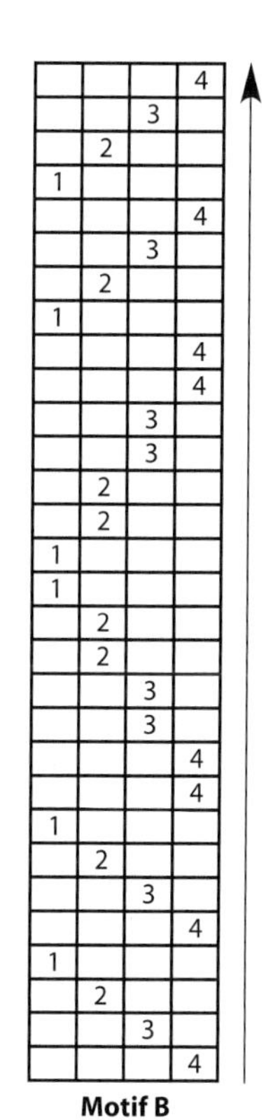
Motif B

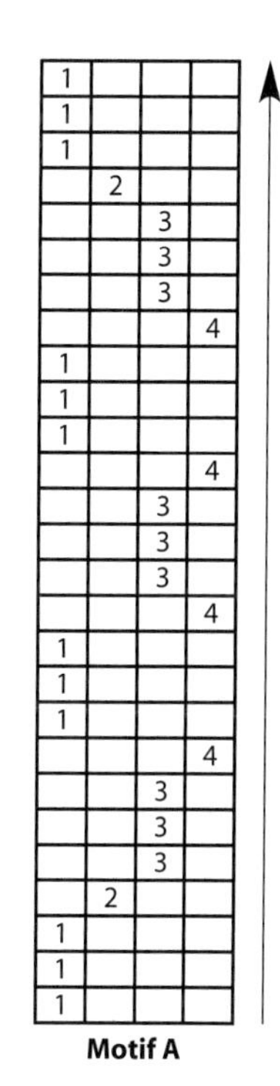
Motif A

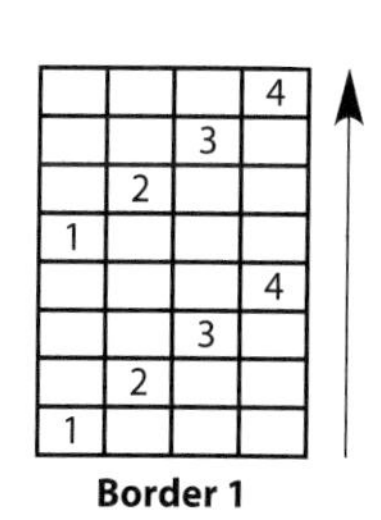
Border 1

Treadling (Sassy Brown)

Add tabby.
Treadling sequence:
Border 1: 1 time
Motif A then Motif B to desired length, end with Motif A.
Border 2: 1 time

SASSY BROWN

Dimensions: 3½ inches (8.9 cm) wide by desired length
Pattern origin: Original

Warp

Sett: 24 epi; 12-dent reed, 2 threads per dent
Length: Calculate yardage requirements according to desired length of project

Threads: 10/2 perle cotton
- Flaxon, 42 ends plus 2 floating selvedges = 44 ends
- Oak, 43 ends

Floating selvedge: 10/2 perle cotton, Oak
Note: I did a random pickup when warping the loom.

Weft

Tabby thread: 10/2 perle cotton, Flaxon
Pattern thread: 6-ply rayon (mill end), Dark Brown. Comparable threads to use are 5/2 perle cotton or 5/2 Dragon Tale Rayon.

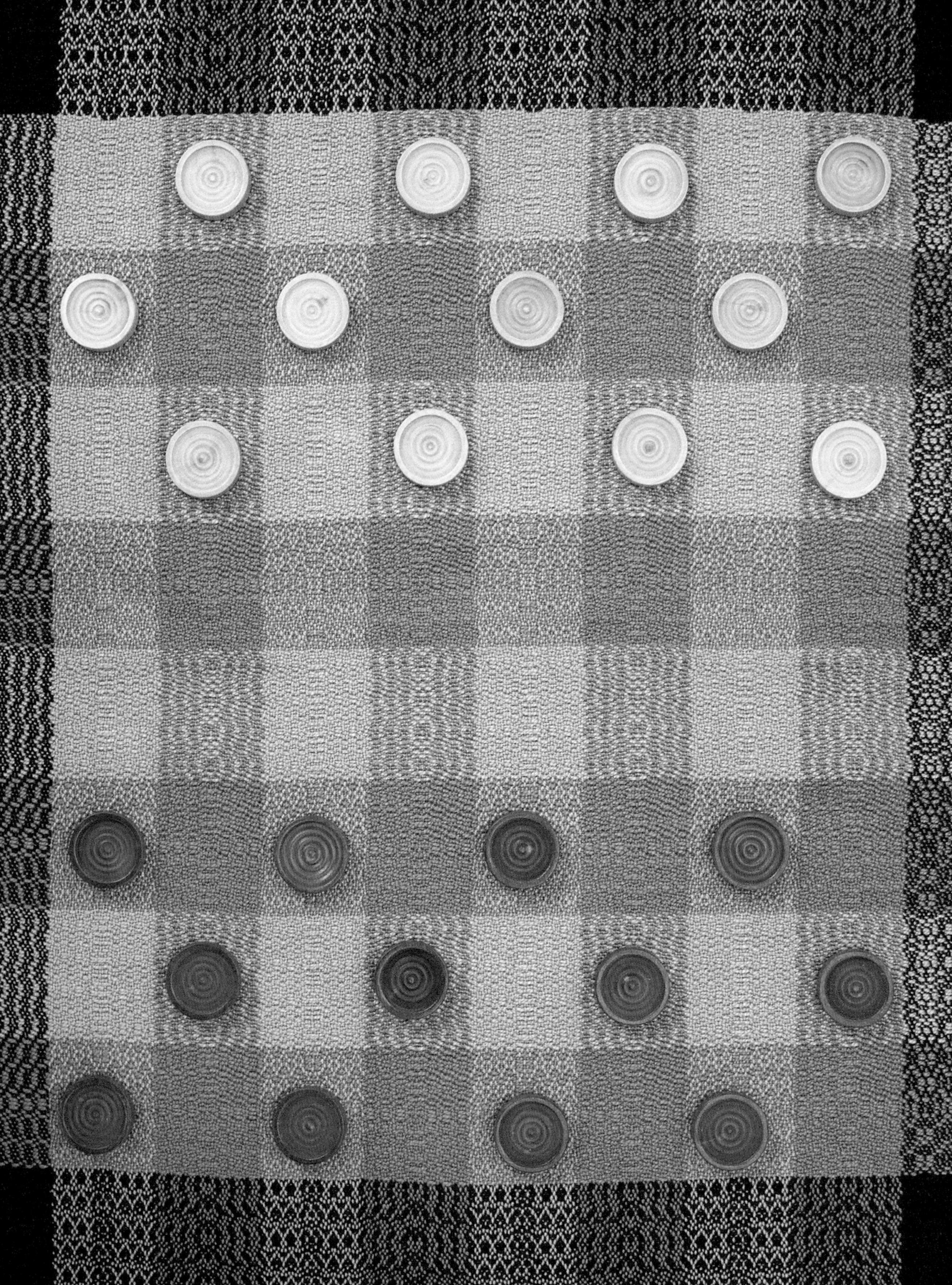

Checkerboard Table Runner

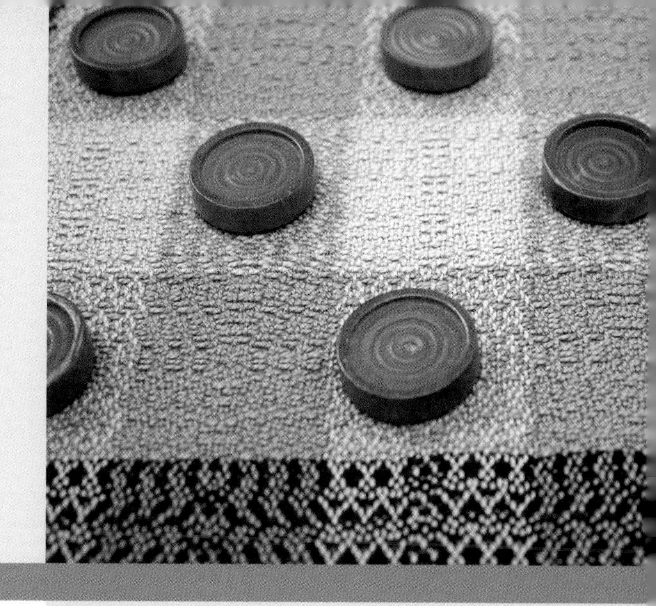

How about a game of checkers? This small table runner is patterned after a true checkerboard, eight by eight squares. You could play a game on this piece by using solid-color squares versus two-color squares. Find your own set of game pieces and choose the colors accordingly.

If you like the idea but are troubled by what appears to be a lack of balance, you could easily add another dark stripe in the warp and weft to make the piece more symmetrical. Either way, you will have a beautiful accessory for your table.

Thread your loom according to the color scheme given. You will have four blocks each of Spice and Beige. As you weave this piece, you will begin by weaving 1½ inches (3.8 cm) of plain tabby using 10/2 perle cotton Black. Then weave Border 1, continuing to use Black for the tabby. When you begin the body of the piece, weave Block A with Spice for the tabby, then Block B with Beige for the tabby. Alternate until you have woven four blocks of each color. Then weave Border 2 with Black tabby, finishing with a 1½-inch (3.8-cm) plain tabby using 10/2 perle cotton Black. Finish the piece with a rolled hem at each end.

Dimensions: 24 x 20 inches (61 x 50.1 cm)
Pattern origin: Original

Warp

Sett: 24 epi; 12-dent reed, 2 threads per dent
Length: 2¼-yard (2.1-m) warp
Threads: 10/2 perle cotton

- Spice, 172 ends, 400 yards (366 m)
- Beige, 172 ends, 400 yards (366 m)
- Black, 146 ends plus 2 floating selvedges = 148 ends, 350 yards (320 m)

Floating selvedge: 10/2 perle cotton, Black

Weft

Tabby threads: 10/2 perle cotton

- Spice, 100 yards (92 m)
- Beige, 100 yards (92 m)
- Black, 100 yards (92 m)

Pattern threads: 5/2 perle cotton

- Spice, 100 yards (92 m)
- Beige, 100 yards (92 m)
- Black, 75 yards (70 m)

Threading and Tie-Up

Border 1

Motif A and Motif B, repeating this sequence 4 times (you will have 4 blocks of each color)

Border 2

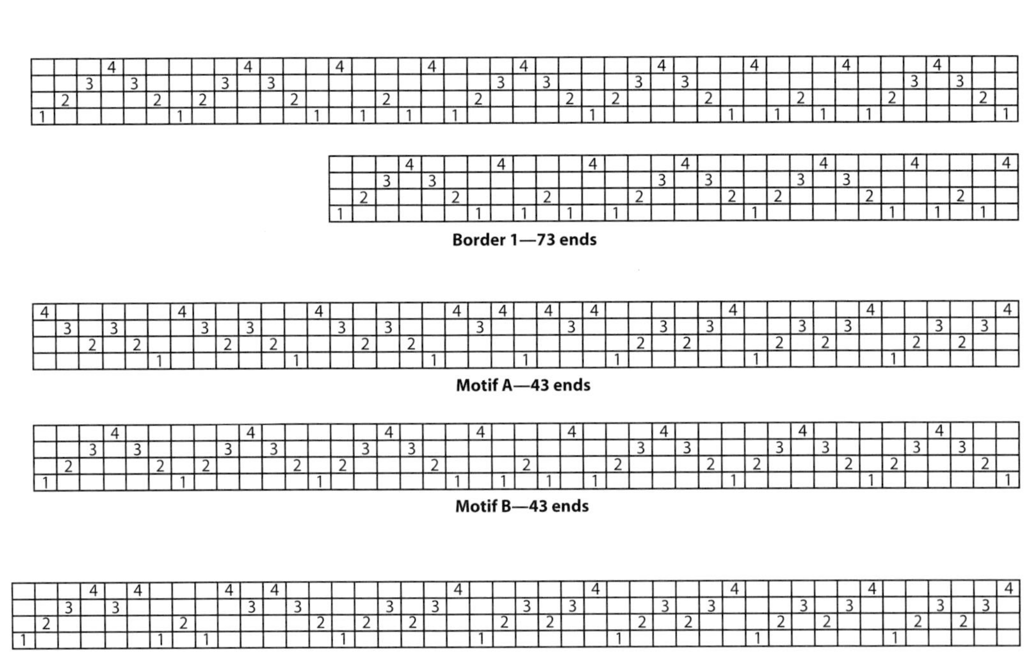

Border 1—73 ends

Motif A—43 ends

Motif B—43 ends

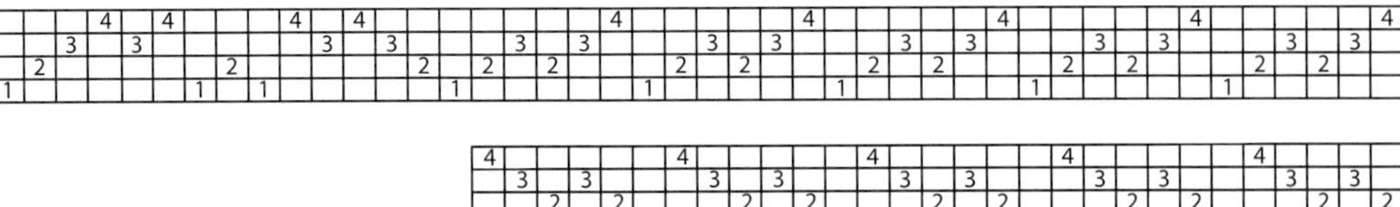

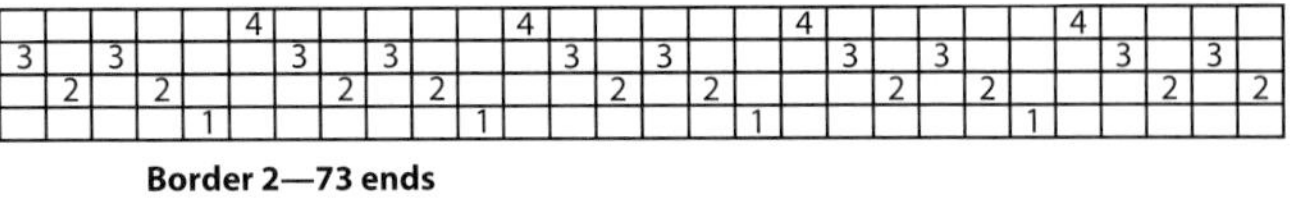

Border 2—73 ends

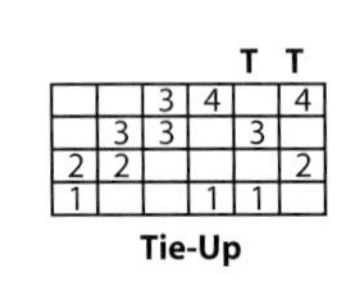

Tie-Up

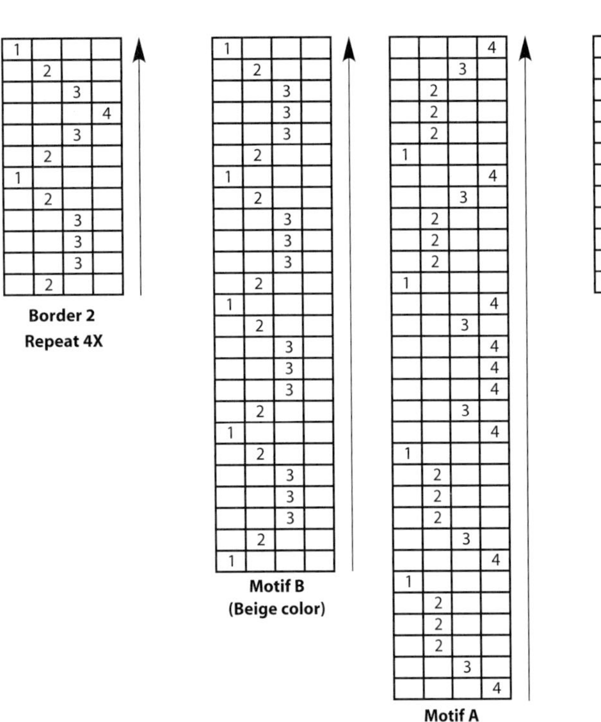

Border 2 Repeat 4X

Motif B (Beige color)

Motif A (Spice color)

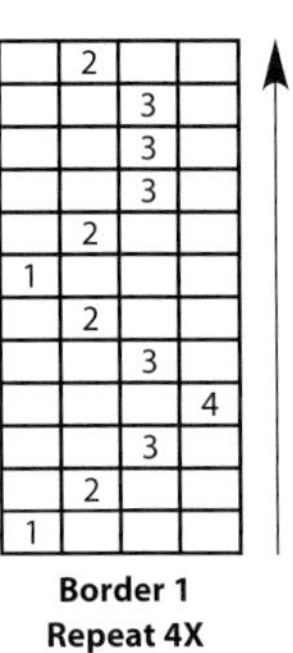

Border 1 Repeat 4X

Treadling

Begin with Border 1 in Black thread.

Repeat Motif A and Motif B 4 times, alternating colors Beige and Spice.

End with Border 2 in Black thread.

Read and weave treadling from the bottom up.

Add tabby. Match tabby thread color to pattern thread color.

Christmas Ornaments or Coasters

Christmas is such a wonderful and festive time of year! We bring out all those special ornaments that we have made and collected over the years to decorate our homes. These simple and lovely woven pieces are beautiful ornaments for your tree. Leave off the loop and you can use them as drink coasters for your holiday table.

I chose my five favorite states and created a name draft for each. Wanting more options, I also have given you three treadling patterns for each piece. This allows you to thread your loom with one warp but weave three different patterns!

Wanting fringe to be on all sides, I included a guide thread along with the warp threading and the floating selvedge. I used a heavier string for this purpose, and each time I threw the *tabby* thread I wrapped it around the guide thread to create the fringe. When I threw the shuttle with the pattern thread, I only worked with the floating selvedge, disregarding the guide thread. The placement for the guide thread is up to you; just make sure it is far enough from the weaving to give you the desired width for your fringe plus a bit extra. Giving yourself that little bit of extra allows you to adjust later if you choose.

Begin and end each piece with a narrow tabby hem. After the pieces are woven, I cut them apart and finish them with a very narrow zigzag stitch around the entire piece to keep the threads intact. You can also do a hand-stitched blind hem if you prefer. The final job is to trim the fringe evenly on all four sides and add a fabric loop to hang the ornament.

These ornaments or coasters are great for the beginner as the projects are small and quick and easy to finish. These would make wonderful gifts for friends and teachers or a special addition to a Christmas present!

Dimensions: Varies, 3 x 3 to 4 x 4 inches (7.6 x 7.6 to 10.2 x 10.2 cm)
Pattern origin: Original

Warp

Sett: 24 epi; 12-dent reed, 2 threads per dent
Length: Calculate warp length according to how many you will be making
Thread: 10/2 perle cotton, White
Floating selvedge: 10/2 perle cotton, White
Guide thread for fringe: Heavier string, kite string, or 3/2 cotton

Weft

Tabby thread: 10/2 perle cotton, White
Pattern thread: 5/2 perle cotton, Red, Green, or other color of your choice

Top left: Set up guide threads for making fringe.
Top right: You can make these coasters quickly, and three treadlings for each pattern allow you to change it up if desired.

California Threading and Tie-Up

Repeat threading 1 time.

87 ends

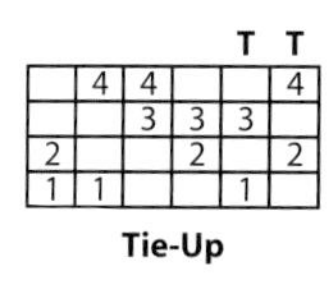

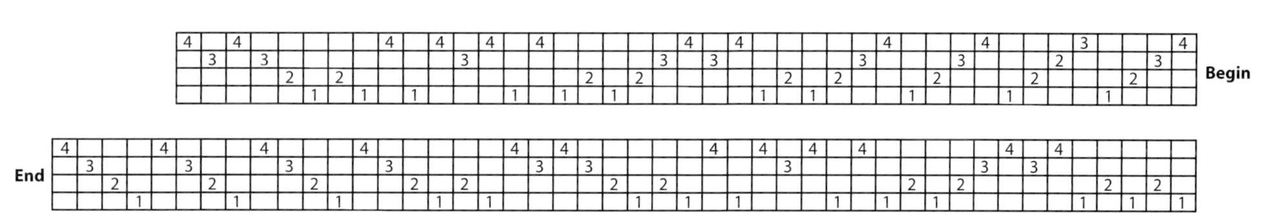

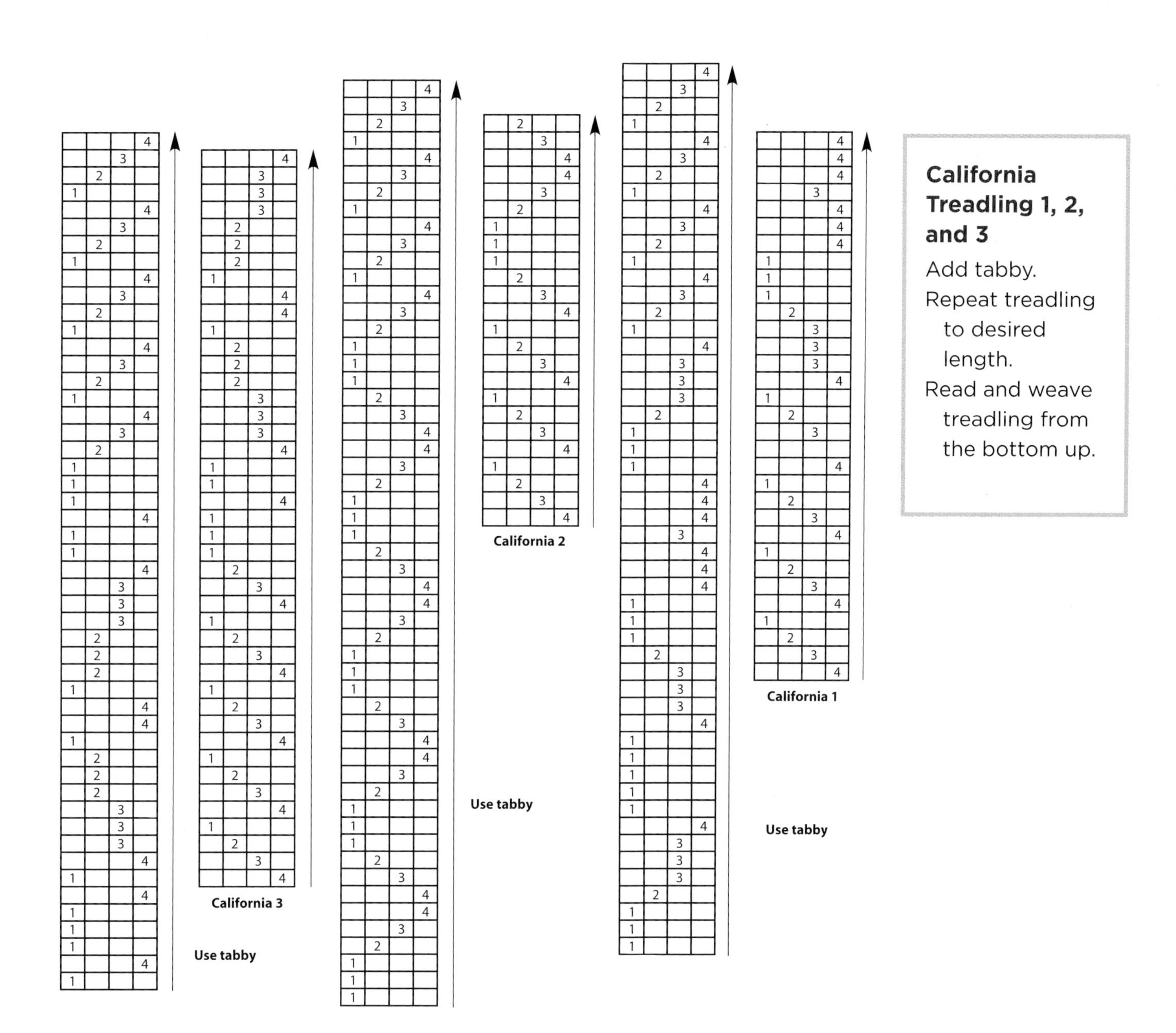

California Treadling 1, 2, and 3

Add tabby.

Repeat treadling to desired length.

Read and weave treadling from the bottom up.

Colorado Threading and Tie-Up

89 ends

Repeat threading 1 time.

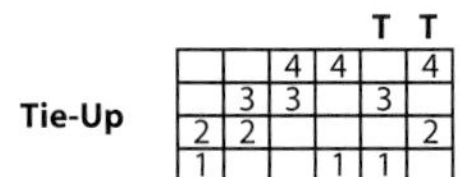

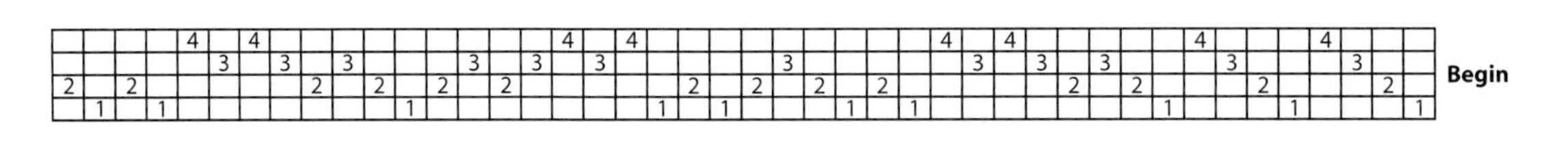

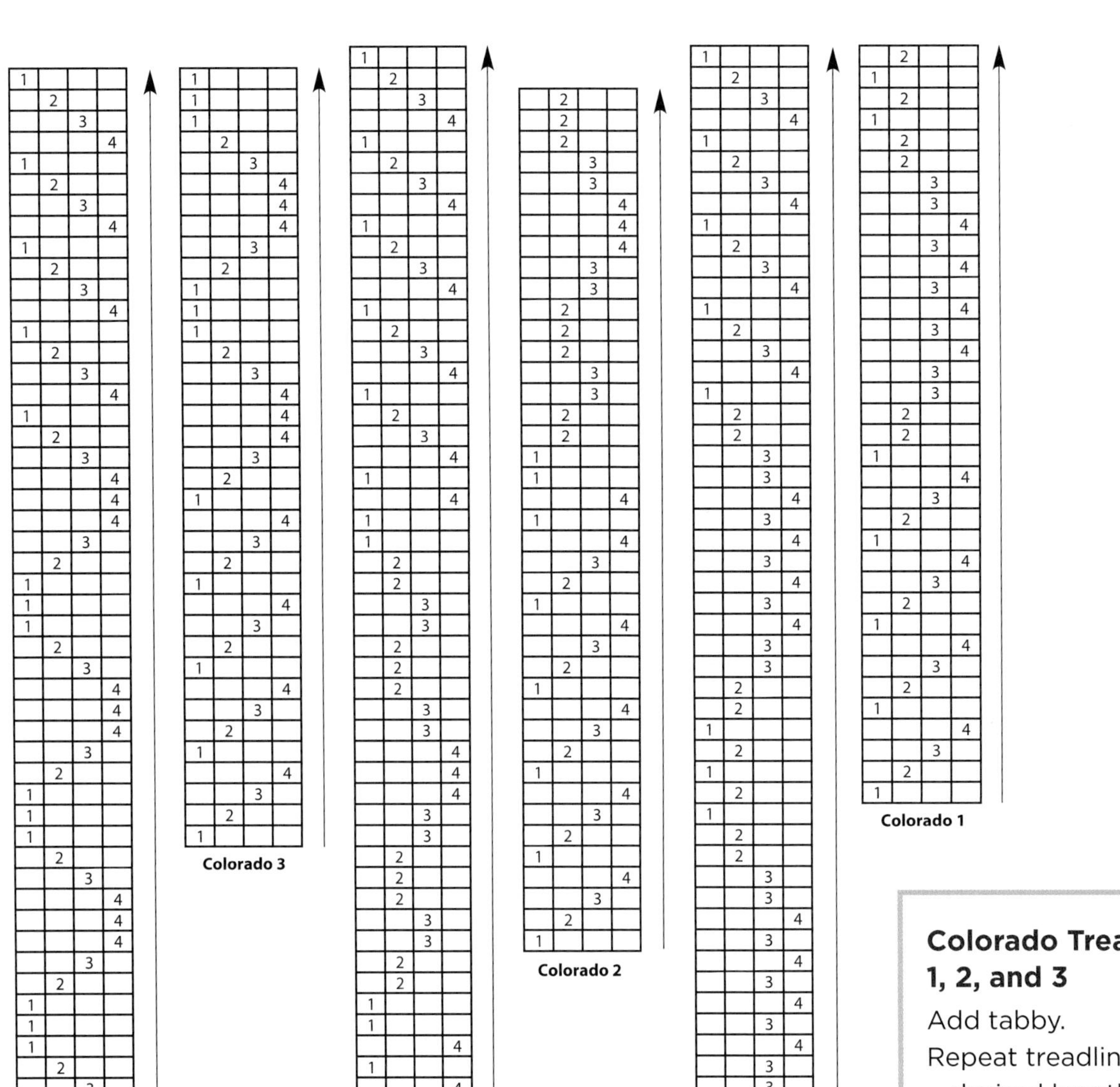

Colorado Treadling 1, 2, and 3

Add tabby.

Repeat treadling to desired length.

Read and weave treadling from the bottom up.

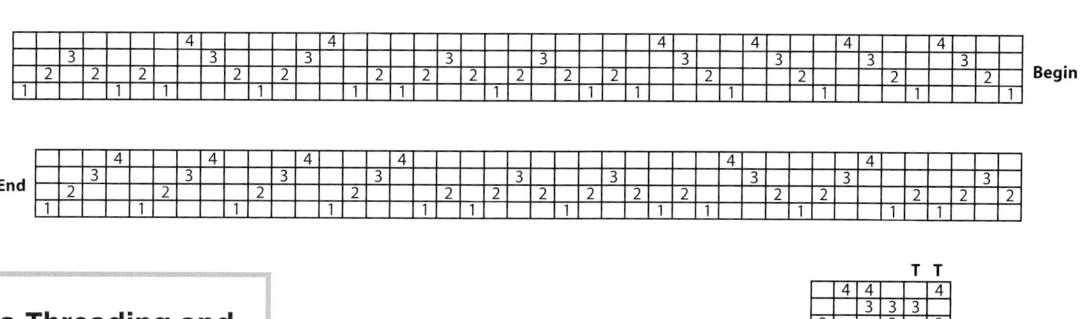

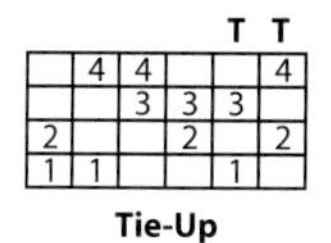

Indiana Threading and Tie-Up

Repeat threading 1 time.
85 ends

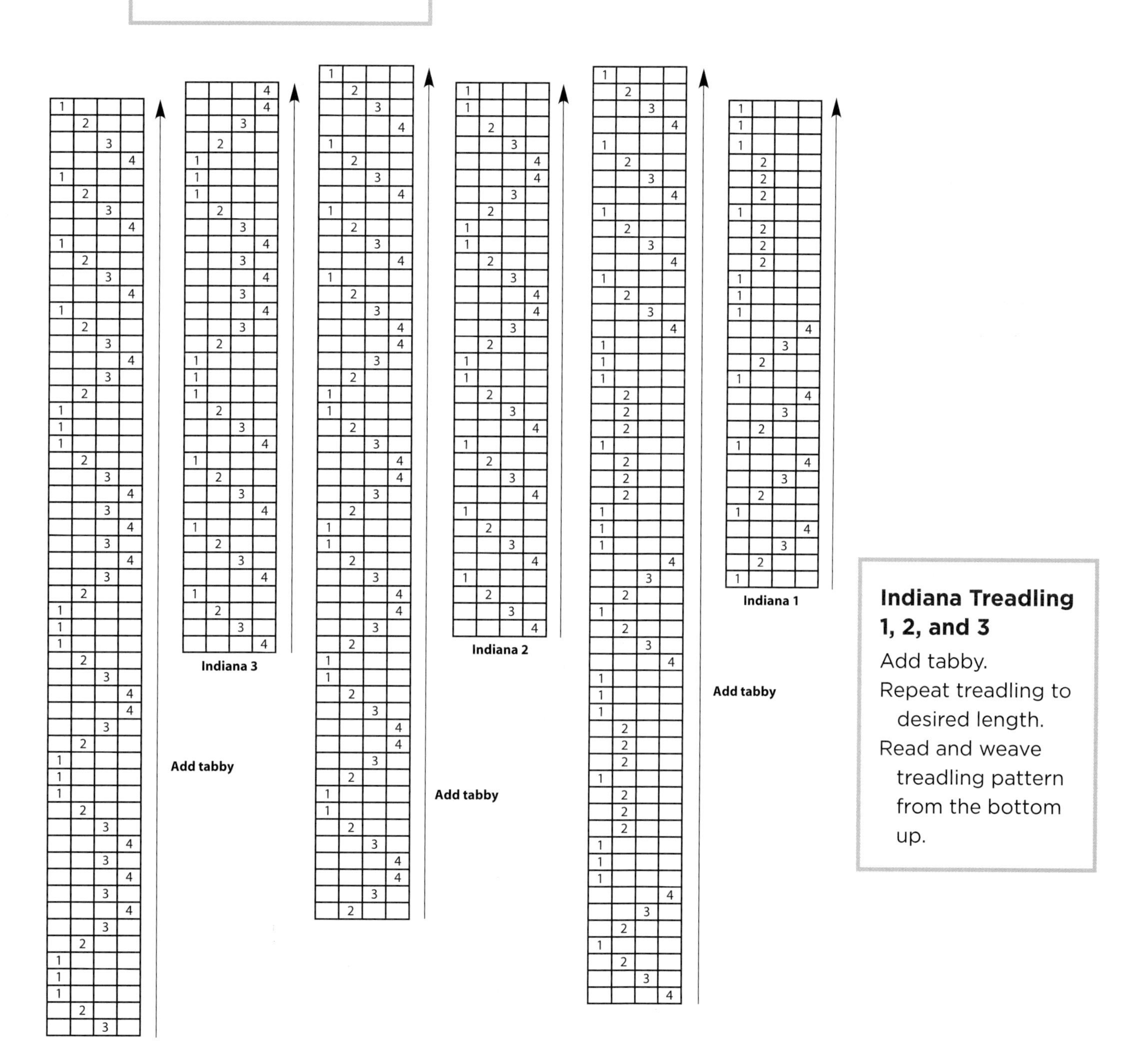

Indiana Treadling 1, 2, and 3

Add tabby.
Repeat treadling to desired length.
Read and weave treadling pattern from the bottom up.

Pennsylvania Threading and Tie-Up

Repeat threading 1 time.
89 ends

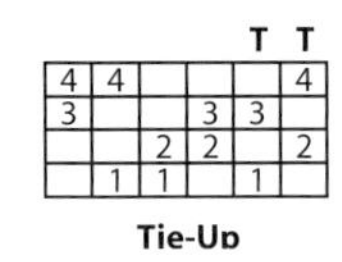

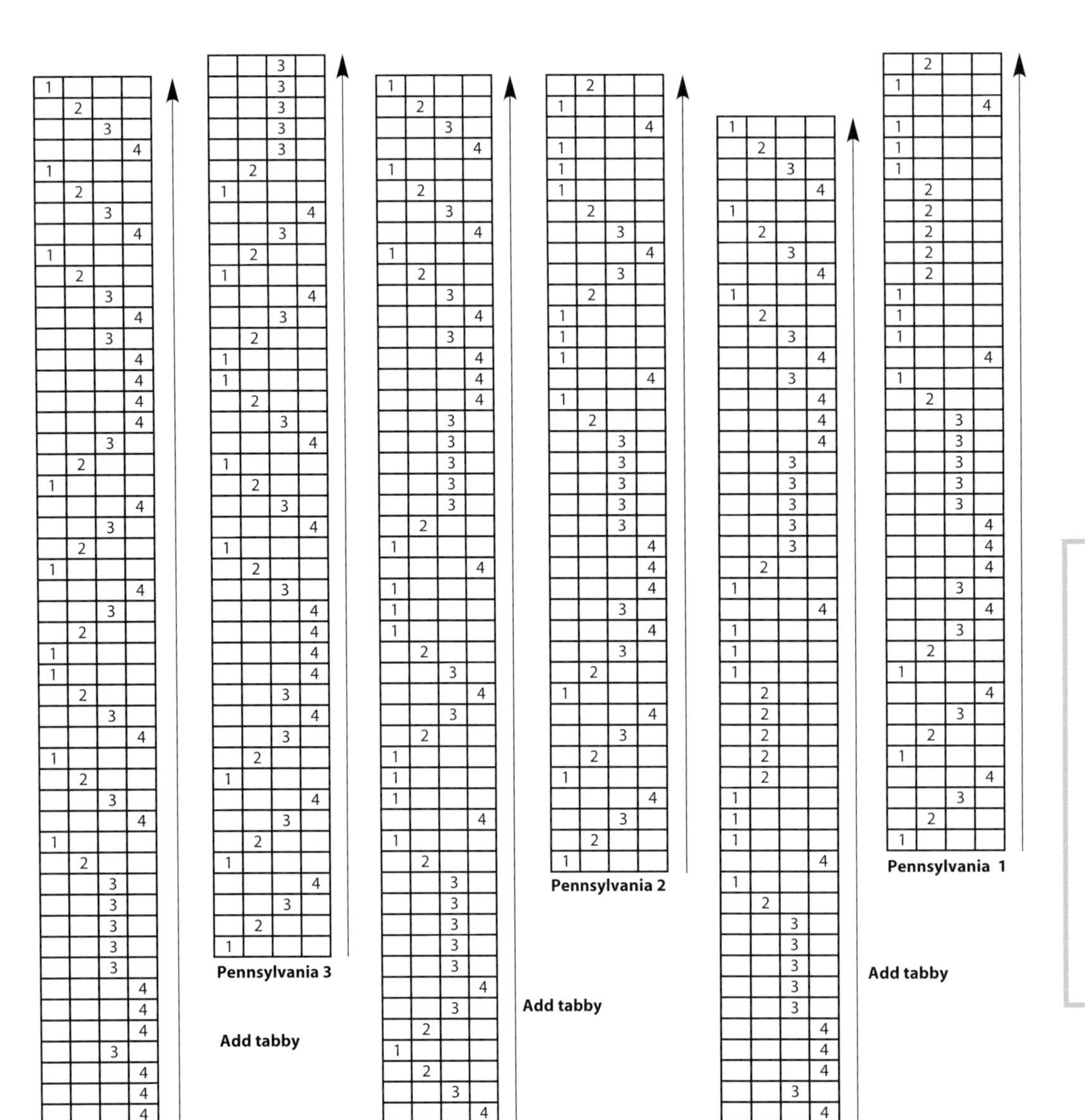

Pennsylvania Treadling 1, 2, and 3

Add tabby.
Repeat treadling to desired length.
Weave and read treadling sequence from the bottom up.

Begin

End

Nebraska Threading and Tie-Up

Repeat threading 1 time
81 ends

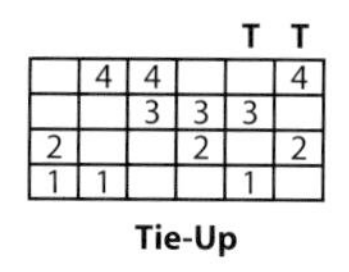

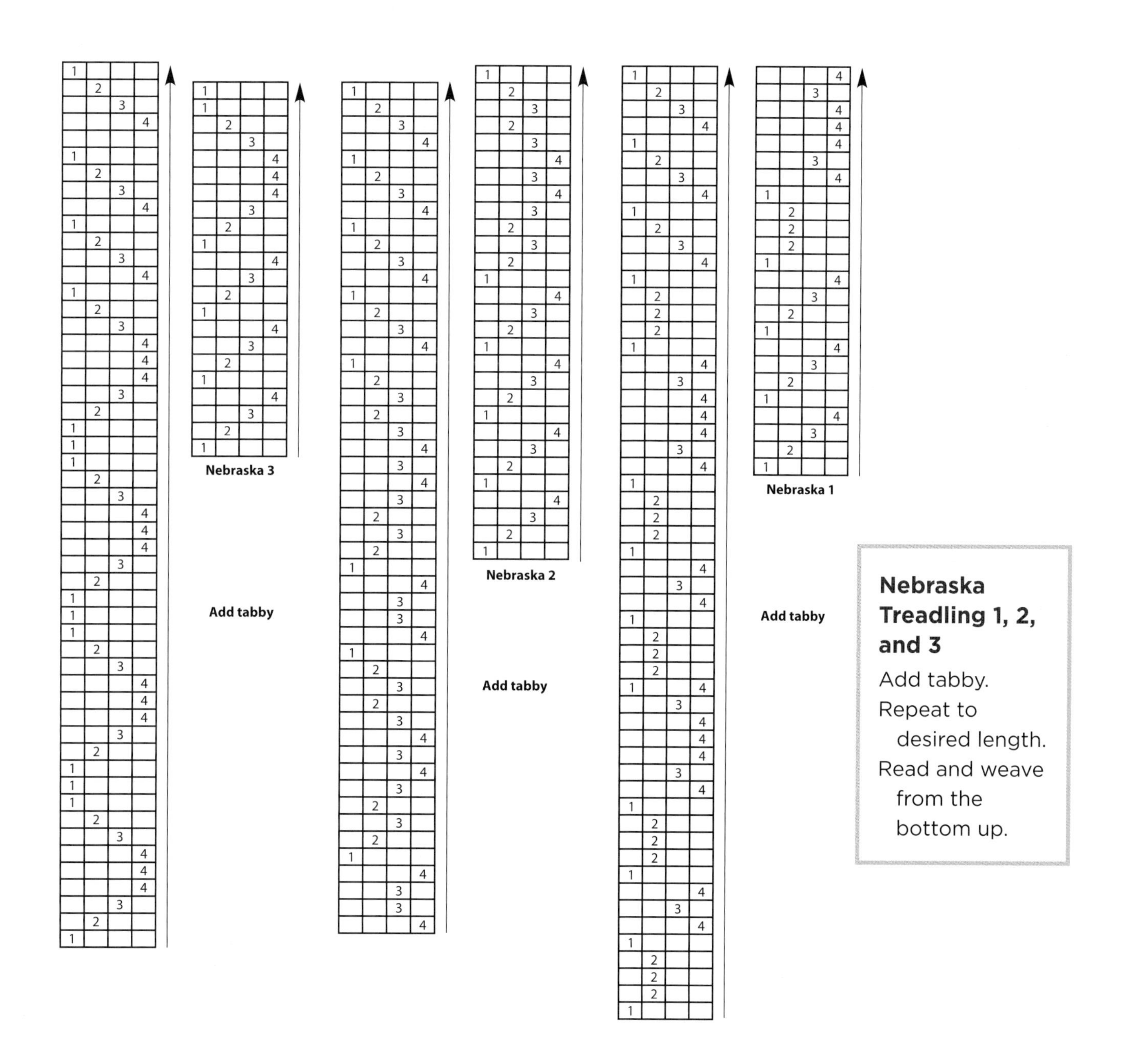

Nebraska Treadling 1, 2, and 3

Add tabby.
Repeat to desired length.
Read and weave from the bottom up.

Echo Scarf and Rainbow Vestment

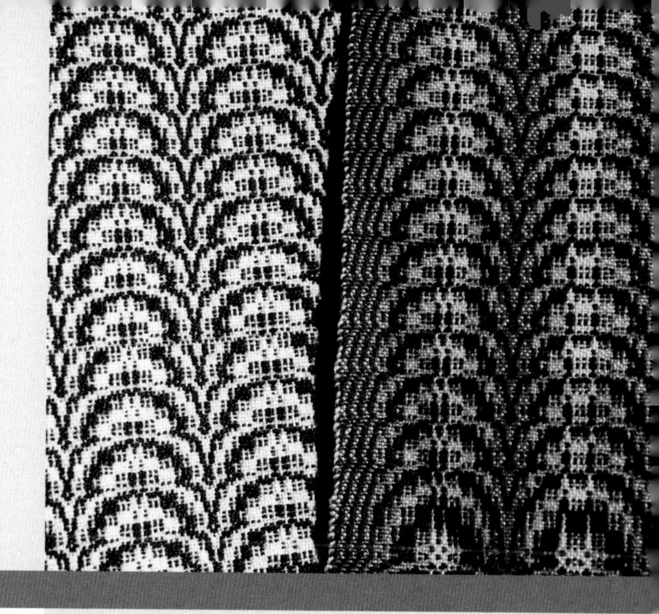

I'm a child of the sixties, and the Enigma pattern has always reminded me of the op art of that period. Rather than just repeat the full motif in the treadling, I split the motif in half, then into quarters. Using these different components, the Echo Scarf now begins with a quarter motif to a half motif, then the whole motif, and then the process reverses to the quarter motif. Once half of the scarf is woven, the whole process reverses again until you complete the opposite end. Be sure to read this pattern from the bottom up! Staying with the theme of that time period, the scarf is woven with a White warp and Black pattern thread. What fun!

The Rainbow Vestment is another version of the same pattern. This time the motif is only repeated twice in the threading instead of three times. This makes a narrower piece that is more appropriate for its use. Follow the color scheme for the vestment in the threading draft to get the proper placement of colors. As this piece is longer, you will see that there are more repeats of the quarter motifs to the center point. I used the yellow perle cotton for the tabby to keep the piece light. Any combination of colors can be used in either piece. Try gradating a color from dark to light with a contrasting pattern thread. Or you could use a variegated warp thread with a solid-pattern thread. This is a fun pattern that is sure to get lots of rave comments when worn.

ECHO SCARF

Dimensions: 9¼ x 60 inches (23.5 x 152.4 cm) with a 3-inch (7.6 cm) fringe

Pattern origin: Adapted from Enigma

Warp

Sett: 24 epi; 12 dent reed, 2 threads per dent

Length: 3-yard (2.75-m) warp

Thread: 10/2 perle cotton, White, 225 ends plus 2 floating selvedges = 227 ends, 700 yards (640 m)

Floating selvedge: 10/2 perle cotton, White

Weft

Tabby thread: 10/2 perle cotton, White, 350 yards (320 m)

Pattern thread: 5/2 perle cotton, Black, 350 yards (320 m)

Note: Weave ½ inch (1.3 cm) plain weave at beginning and end. Hem stitch to finish.

RAINBOW VESTMENT

Dimensions: 5 x 80 inches (12.7 x 203.2 cm) with 6-inch (15 cm) fringe

Pattern origin: Adapted from Enigma

Warp

Sett: 24 epi; 12-dent reed, 2 threads per dent

Length: 3½-yard (3.2-m) warp

Threads: 10/2 perle cotton, 127 ends total

- Purple, 26 ends (includes 2 for floating selvedge), 90 yards (82 m)
- Blue, 22 ends, 80 yards (73 m)
- Sapphire, 22 ends, 80 yards (73 m)
- Light Orange, 22 ends, 80 yards (73 m)
- Red, 13 ends, 80 yards (73 m)
- Light Yellow, 22 ends, 80 yards (73 m)

Floating selvedge: 10/2 perle cotton, Purple

Weft

Tabby thread: 10/2 perle cotton, Light Yellow, 200 yards (183 m)

Pattern thread: 5/2 Dragon Tale Rayon, Black, 200 yards (183 m)

Weaving: When weaving the Echo Scarf, the repeats of E and A in the body of the scarf were 40 times each. *In THIS scarf, you will increase the repeats to 60 times each.*

Note: Weave ½-inch (1.3-cm) plain weave at beginning and end. Hem stitch to finish.

COLOR SEQUENCE

Color	Ends per color
Purple	12
Blue	11
Sapphire	11
Lt. Orange	11
Lt. Yellow	11
Red	13
Lt. Yellow	11
Lt. Orange	11
Sapphire	11
Blue	11
Purple	12

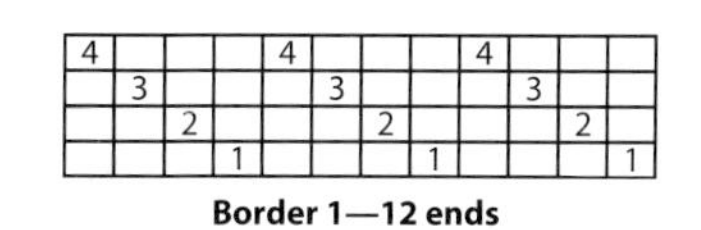
Border 1—12 ends

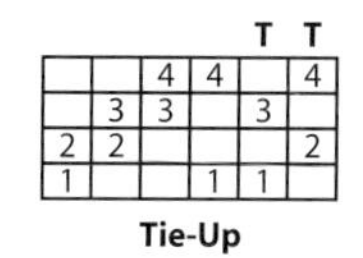

Tie-Up

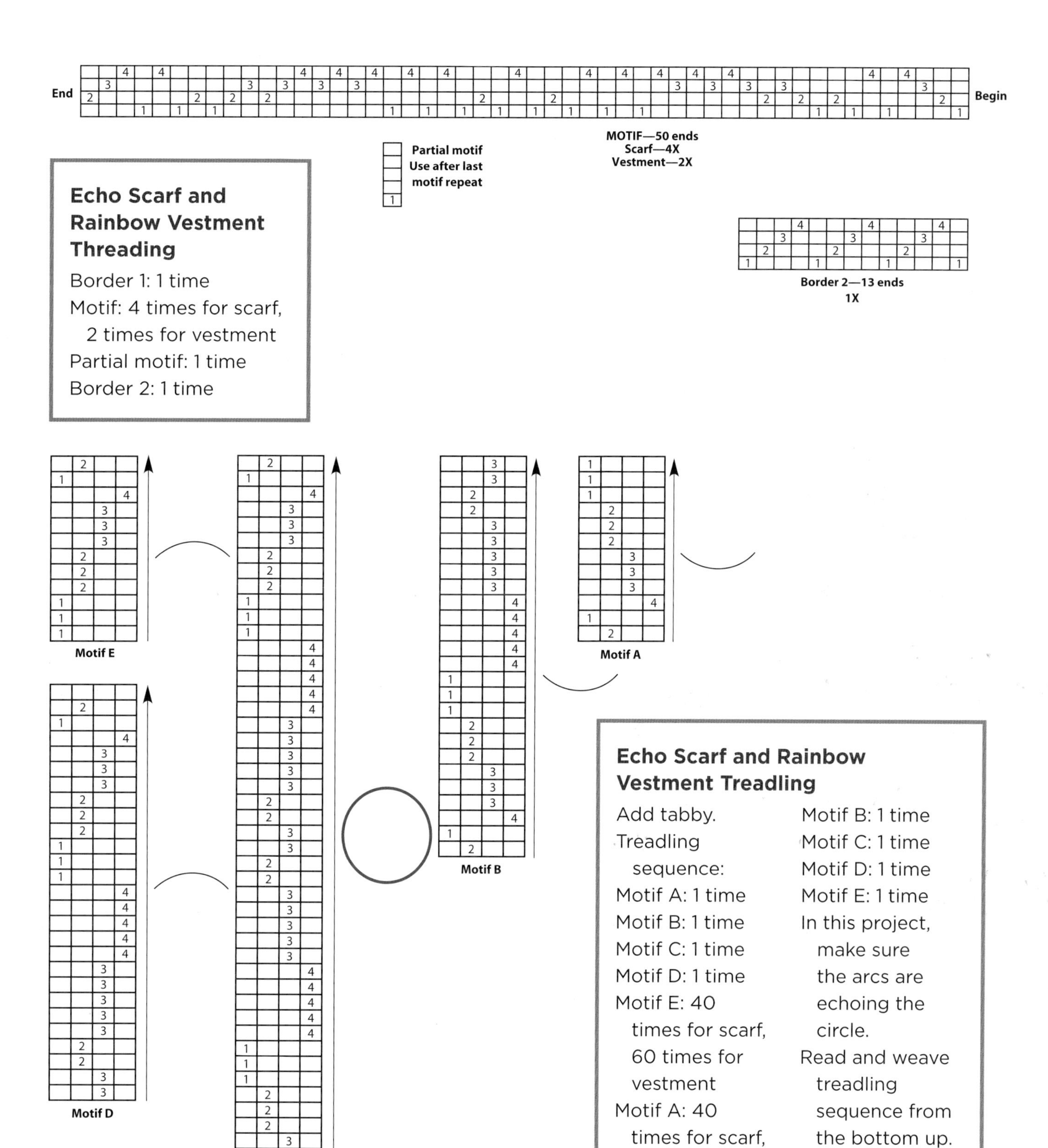

Echo Scarf and Rainbow Vestment Threading

Border 1: 1 time
Motif: 4 times for scarf, 2 times for vestment
Partial motif: 1 time
Border 2: 1 time

Echo Scarf and Rainbow Vestment Treadling

Add tabby.
Treadling sequence:
Motif A: 1 time
Motif B: 1 time
Motif C: 1 time
Motif D: 1 time
Motif E: 40 times for scarf, 60 times for vestment
Motif A: 40 times for scarf, 60 times for vestment.
Motif B: 1 time
Motif C: 1 time
Motif D: 1 time
Motif E: 1 time
In this project, make sure the arcs are echoing the circle.
Read and weave treadling sequence from the bottom up.

Elegance Tablecloth

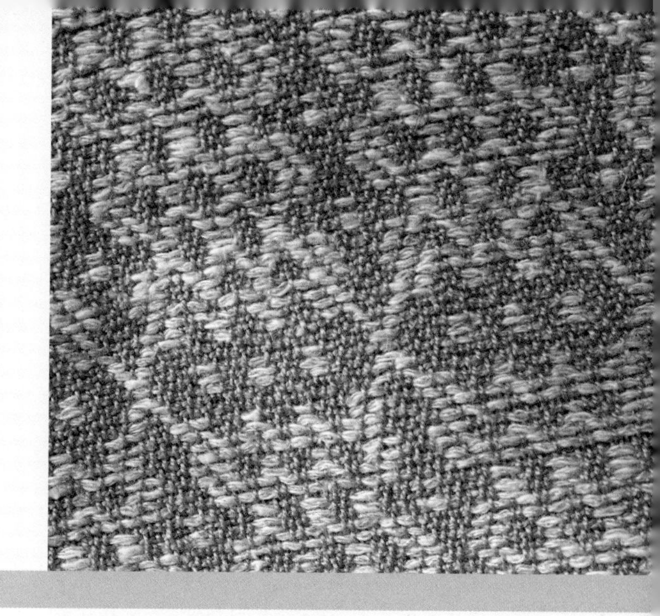

Remember those lovely linen tablecloths that our grandmothers brought out during the holidays? I wanted to make something similar but one that didn't require all that ironing! This small tablecloth would be perfect to dress up your table for the holidays, and it is wash-and-wear. I was "gifted" with a cone of thread that was a blend of linen, cotton, silk, and rayon, a truly beautiful blend. This was combined with a darker color warp thread, and this combination shows a beautiful but subtle pattern. This piece would also be lovely in a high contrast thread and the pattern would have more emphasis.

Begin and end this piece with 1½ inches (3.8 cm) of tabby weave, then do a rolled hem.

I've given you another option for this piece. If you add additional warp to your loom while threading for the tablecloth, you can also weave four napkins to make a complete set. Finish your tablecloth first, and then you can weave the napkins just using the tabby tie-up. I wove one large piece of plain fabric and then measured and cut out the napkins. I then did a rolled hem on my serger using a contrasting thread to match the pattern thread. You can easily do a hand-rolled hem or fringe if you would prefer. The napkins will give your table the finished look for that special occasion.

Dimensions: 40 x 40 inches (101.6 x 101.6 cm)

Pattern origin: Original

Warp

Sett: 24 epi; 12 dent reed, 2 threads per dent

Length: 2½-yard (2.3-m) warp if only doing table topper—2,400 yards (2,195 m); 3½-yard (3.2-m) warp if doing table topper and napkins—3,400 yards (3,110 m)

Thread: 10/2 perle cotton, Oak, 969 ends plus 2 floating selvedges = 971 ends

Floating selvedge: 10/2 perle cotton, Oak

Weft

Tabby thread: 10/2 perle cotton, Oak, 950 yards (868 m)

Pattern thread: 5/2 perle cotton or 5/2 Dragon Tale rayon, 950 yards (868 m)

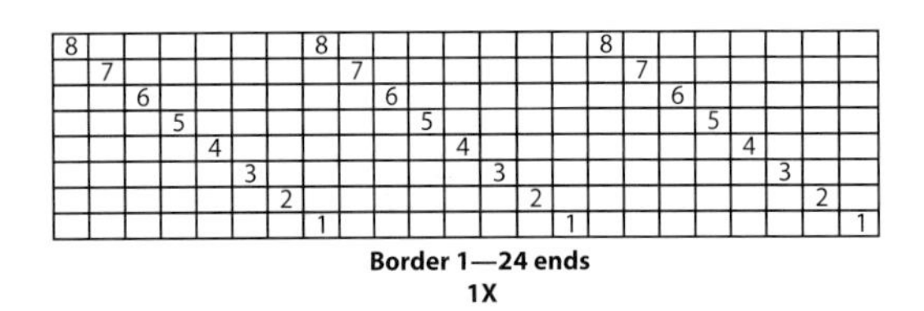
Border 1—24 ends
1X

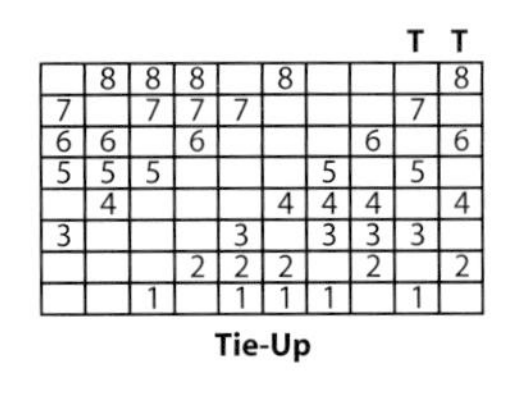
Tie-Up

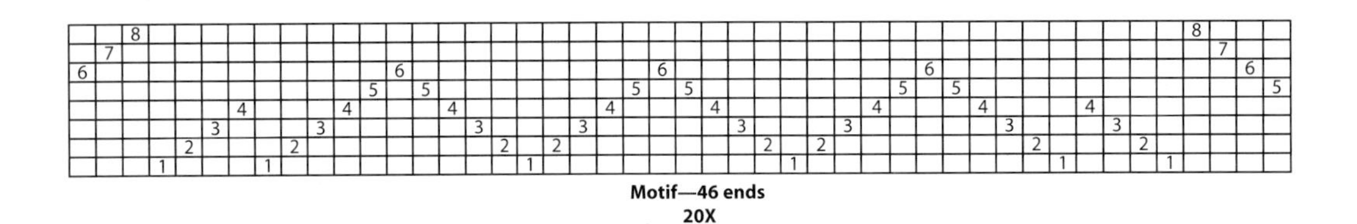
Motif—46 ends
20X

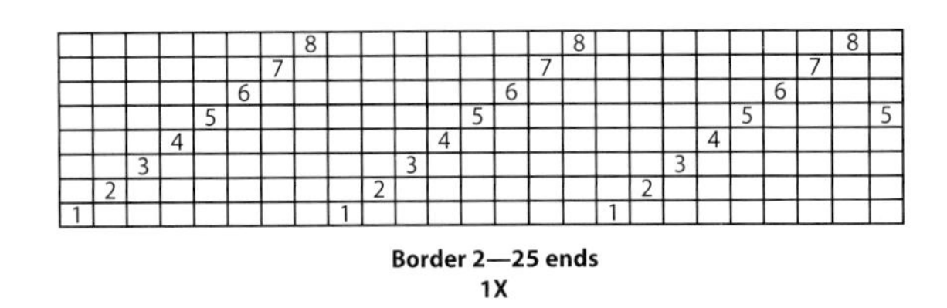
Border 2—25 ends
1X

Threading

Border 1: 1 time
Motif: 20 times
Border 2: 1 time
Border 1: 1 time

Treadling

Add tabby.
Treadling sequence:
Border 1: 1 time
Full motif: 9 times or to desired length
Partial motif: 1 time
Border 2: 1 time
Read and weave treadling from the bottom up.

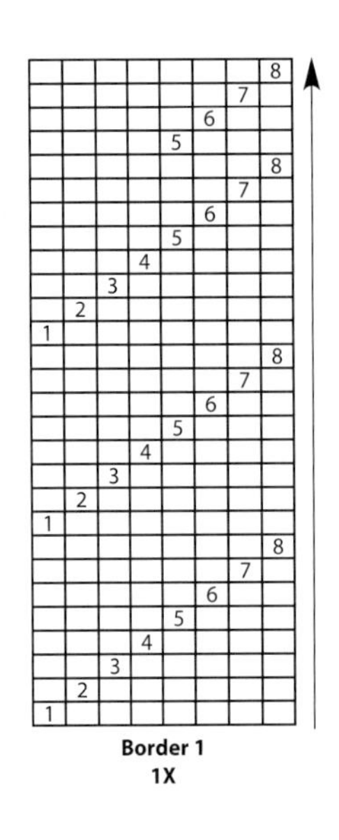
Border 1
1X

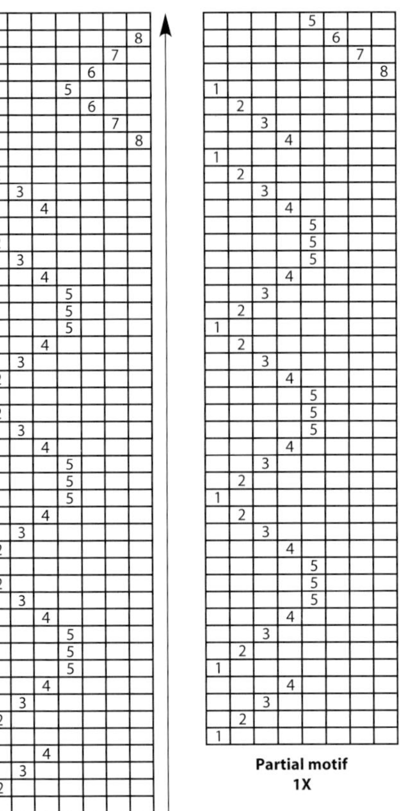
Full Motif
9X
or to desired length

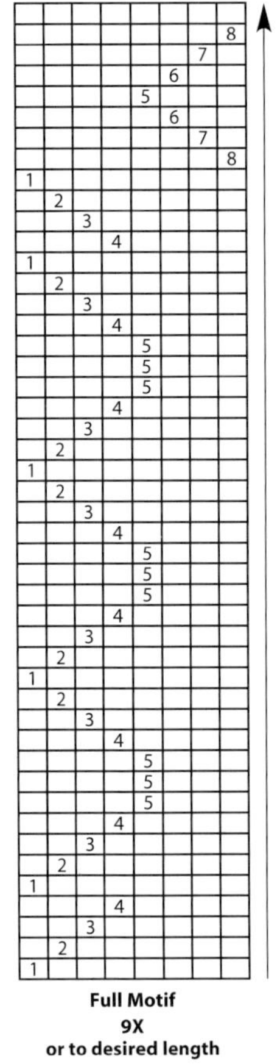
Partial motif
1X

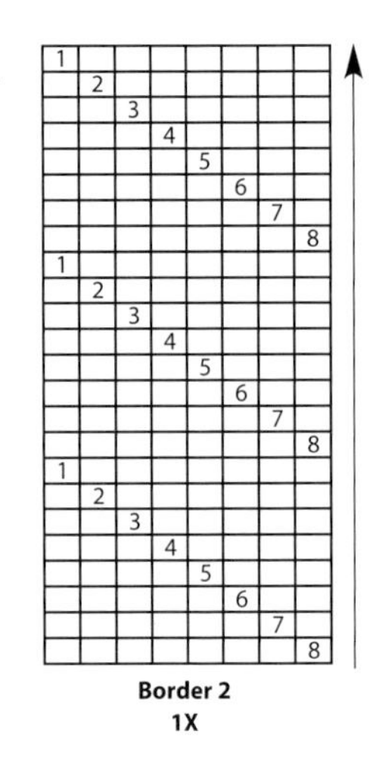
Border 2
1X

Evergreen Table Runner

Living in Pennsylvania allows me to truly enjoy all the ridges full of different species of trees. In the spring, the color green is awakening, never ceasing to amaze me with all the different hues. We see the dark rich greens, vibrant yellow green, all the way to the soft pale green of the leaves as they are just unfurling. And once all the trees have filled out, hiking through the woods is such a breath-taking experience. Looking up through the canopy that the trees have created, you can see the sun sparkling and dancing through the leaves.

This table runner is an attempt to re-create this splendor that we enjoy every year. I used three different greens in the warp to represent the leaves. I love to look for unusual yarn when I'm out and about, and I found this unique gold acrylic yarn at a local craft store. What really caught my eye was the metallic thread that was woven into it. That small piece of metallic really gave the table runner the sparkle I was looking for. Be creative . . . if you can't find the exact yarn, substitute a yarn without this thread. What about using a red perle cotton to make this a Christmas table runner? The possibilities are endless!

Begin and end this piece weaving 1½ plain tabby and making a rolled hem. You can do fringe if you would prefer by weaving just ½ inch (1.3 cm) of plain tabby and finishing with a blind hem.

Dimensions: 20 x 45 inches (50.8 x 114.3 cm)

Pattern origin: Variation of Kay's design

Warp

Sett: 24 epi; 12 dent reed, 2 threads per dent

Length: 2½-yard (2.3-m) warp

Threads: 10/2 perle cotton

- Loden Green, 600 yards (550 m), 233 ends plus 2 floating selvedges = 235 ends
- Persian Green, 350 yards (320 m), 128 ends
- Willow Green, 350 yards (320 m), 128 ends

Floating selvedge: 10/2 perle cotton, Loden Green

Weft

Tabby thread: 10/2 perle cotton, Loden Green, 500 yards (457 m)

Pattern thread: Fashion II Yarn, 95 percent acrylic, 5 percent metallic (212 yards [194 m]/ skein), 500 yards (457 m) or 3 skeins (purchased at AC Moore)

Comparable: any sport-weight yarn

COLOR SEQUENCE

Color	Motif & Border	Motif	Motif	Motif	Motif	Motif	Motif & Border
	Loden Green	Persian Green	Willow Green	Loden Green	Willow Green	Persian Green	Loden Green
	87 ends	64 ends	64 ends	64 ends	64 ends	64 ends	82 ends

Border 1—18 ends

Tie-Up

Begin

End

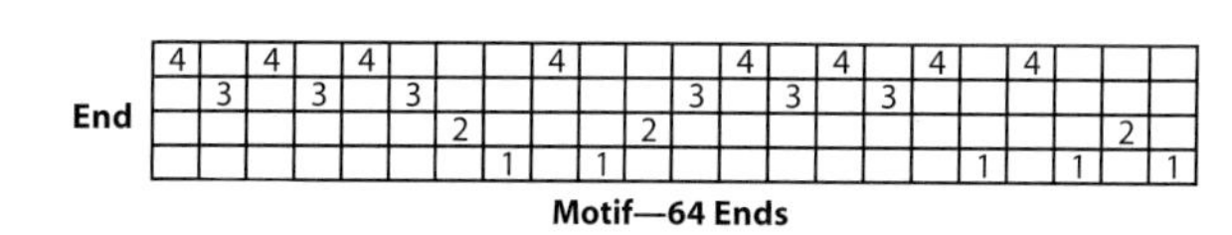

Motif—64 Ends

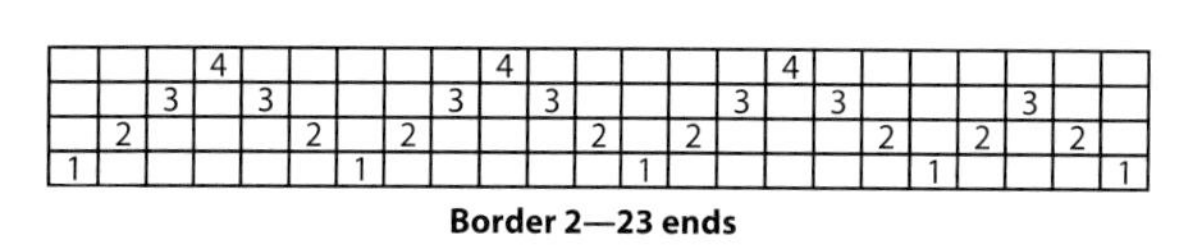

Border 2—23 ends

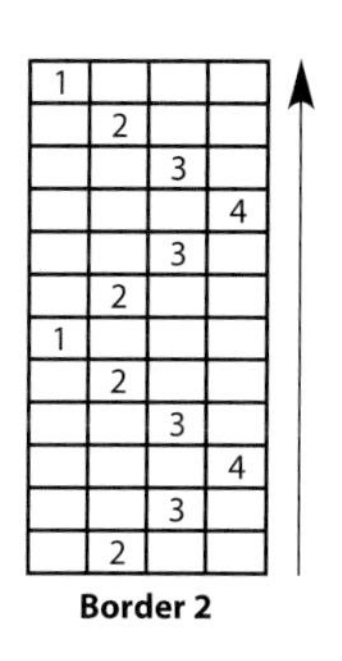

Border 2

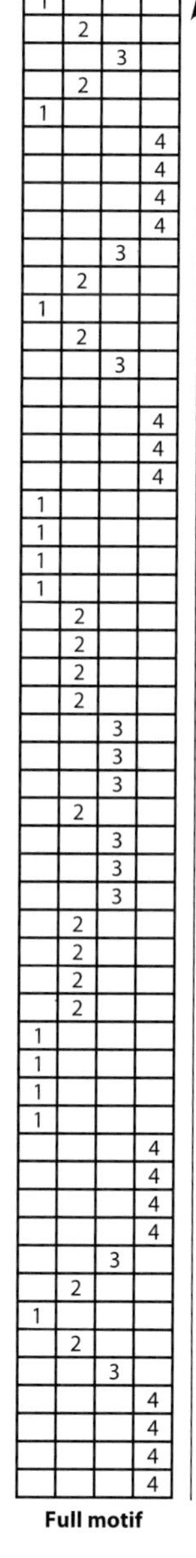

Full motif

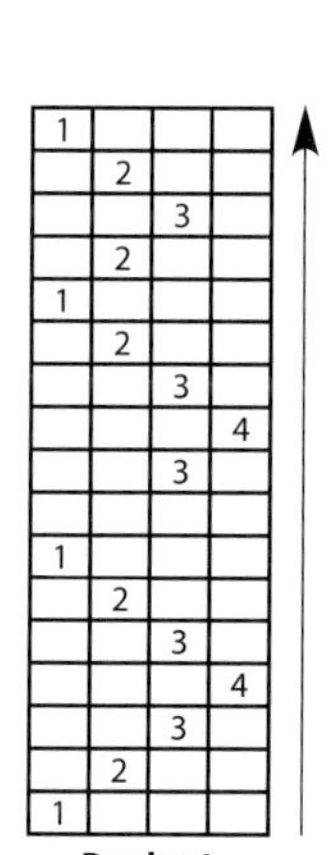

Border 1

Threading and Tie-Up

Border 1: 1 time

Motif: 7 times following color sequence chart

Border 2: 1 time

Treadling

Use tabby.

Treadling sequence:

Border 1: 1 time

Full motif: to desired length

Border 2: 1 time

Read and weave treadling sequence from the bottom up.

Inchworm Scarf

Often when I'm warping the loom to do an overshot piece, I put on enough warp to do two pieces. This gives me the option to keep one and give one away or to just change the treadling for a whole new look! For this scarf, if you look closely, you will see that the threading for this scarf is the same threading used for the Fiesta Scarf . . . still using the bright-green warp. Changing only the treadling created the undulating pattern that mimics the inchworm. For me, this is one of the great things about the overshot weave structure. Simply by changing the treadling, you can create your very own pattern!

Dimensions: 8½ x 64 inches (21.5 x 162.6 cm), 3-inch (7.6 cm) fringe

Pattern origin: Variation of Star and Rose

Warp

Sett: 24 epi; 12 dent reed, 2 threads per dent

Length: 3-yard (2.7-m) warp

Thread: 10/2 perle cotton, Lime Green, 202 ends plus 2 floating selvedges = 204 total ends, 650 yards (595 m)

Floating selvedge: 10/2 perle cotton, Lime Green

Weft

Tabby thread: 10/2 perle cotton, Lime Green, 200 yards (183 m)

Pattern thread: Aracunia, 75 percent wool, 25 percent polyamide, Pale Green Variegated

The skein has 376 yards (344 m), which is much more than needed. You will need approximately 200 yards (183 m). This is a sock-weight yarn.

Note: Weave ½ inch (1.3 cm) plain weave at beginning and end of project. Finish with hem stitch.

	4				4				4				4
3				3				3				3	
			2				2				2		
		1				1				1			

Border 1—14 ends

				T	T
		4	4		4
	3	3		3	
2	2				2
1			1	1	

Tie-Up

	4												4		4				4		4						4		4						4		4				4
3						3		3						3		3				3		3												3		3				3	
			2		2		2		2		2						2						2		2						2		2						2		
		1		1						1		1						1						1		1		1		1		1						1			

Full motif—42 ends
Repeat 4X

Threading and Tie-Up

Border 1: 1 time
Full motif: 4 times
Border 2: 1 time

			4				4				4				4				4
		3				3				3				3				3	
	2				2				2				2				2		
1				1				1				1				1			

Border 2—20 ends

Treadling

Add tabby.
Treadling sequence:
Border: 1 time
Motif: repeat to desired length
Border: 1 time
Read and weave treadling from the bottom up.

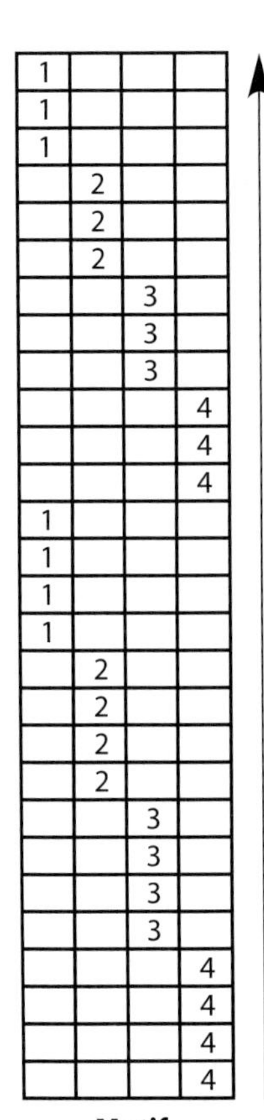

1			
1			
1			
	2		
	2		
	2		
		3	
		3	
		3	
			4
			4
			4
1			
1			
1			
1			
	2		
	2		
	2		
	2		
		3	
		3	
		3	
		3	
			4
			4
			4
			4

Motif
Repeat to desired length

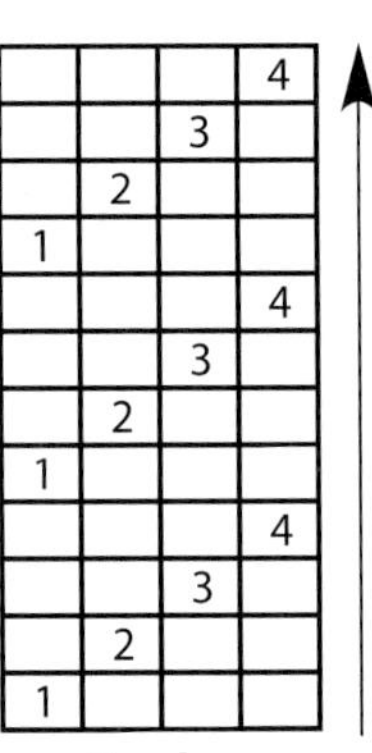

			4
		3	
	2		
1			
			4
		3	
	2		
1			
			4
		3	
	2		
1			

Border

Fiesta Scarf

Olé! This colorful scarf is a variation of the Star and Rose pattern using Mini Mochi Intense as the pattern weft. The overall effect is bright and cheery and is bound to get many comments when worn. Because there are so many colors within the piece, it can complement a number of garments in your wardrobe.

There is something you should be aware of when choosing your yarn so you can avoid a mistake that I made. You will notice that in the second multicolored scarf shown below, the pattern is nonexistent. A beautiful sock yarn was used as the pattern weft in this piece, but because the color repeats were shorter, the pattern got lost. It is still a nice scarf, but not the look I desired. This sock yarn might have worked fine with another weave structure, but it just didn't work here. Something to think about when choosing your yarn!

When you are working with yarn that changes color, it is important that the ending color on your bobbin matches the beginning color on the next bobbin. To make this happen, wind your first bobbin and then immediately rewind that bobbin onto another bobbin so that the ending color will be on the inside. Repeat this every time you wind your bobbins and your colors will match up perfectly. If you decide to do all of your bobbins at once, be sure to label them so that you pick up the right bobbin.

Dimensions: 8½ x 64 inches (21.5 x 162.6 cm), 3-inch (7.6 cm) fringe

Pattern origin: Variation of Star and Rose

Warp

Sett: 24 epi; 12 dent reed, 2 threads per dent

Length: 3-yard (2.75-m) warp

Thread: 10/2 perle cotton, Lime Green, 202 ends plus 2 floating selvedges = 204 ends, 650 yards (595 m)

Floating selvedge: 10/2 perle cotton, Lime Green

Weft

Tabby thread: 10/2 perle cotton, Lime Green, 200 yards (183 m)

Pattern thread: Mini Mochi, Intense, 1 skein, 195 yards (179 m)

Note: Weave ½-inch (1.3-cm) plain weave at beginning and end of project. Finish with hem stitch.

	4				4				4				4
3				3				3				3	
			2				2				2		
		1				1				1			

Border 1—14 ends

				T	T
		4	4		4
	3	3		3	
2	2				2
1			1	1	

Tie-Up

	4												4		4				4		4						4		4						4		4				4
3						3		3						3		3				3		3												3		3				3	
			2		2		2		2		2						2						2		2						2		2						2		
		1		1						1		1						1						1		1		1		1		1						1			

Full motif—42 ends
Repeat 4X

Threading and Tie-Up

Border 1: 1 time
Full motif: 4 times
Border 2: 1 time

			4				4				4				4
		3				3				3				3	
	2				2				2				2		
1				1				1				1			

Border 2—20 ends

			4
		3	
		3	
		3	
	2		
1			
			4
		3	
		3	
		3	
	2		
1			
1			
1			
			4
			4
			4
			4
1			
1			
1			
	2		
		3	
		3	
		3	
			4
1			
	2		
		3	
		3	
		3	
			4
1			
1			
1			
	2		
	2		
	2		
	2		
1			
1			
1			

Full motif

			4
		3	
	2		
1			
			4
		3	
	2		
1			
			4
		3	
	2		
1			

Border

Treadling

Add tabby.
Treadling sequence:
Border: 1 time
Partial motif: 1 time
Full motif: repeat to desired length
Border: 1 time
Weave and read treadling from the bottom up.

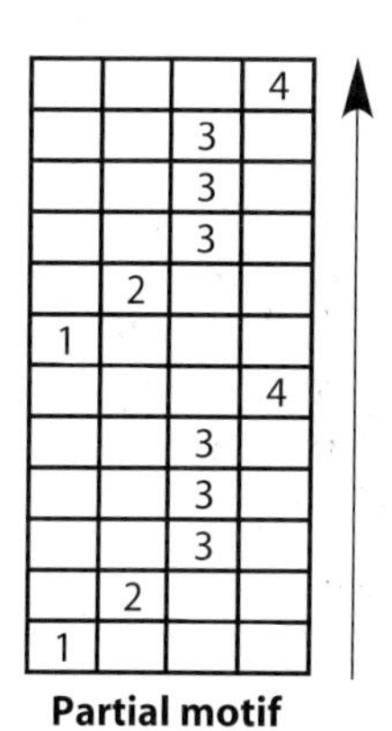

			4
		3	
		3	
		3	
	2		
1			
			4
		3	
		3	
		3	
	2		
1			

Partial motif
Use before starting the full motif repeat

A Touch of Green Cape

This unusual cape, created from three flat pieces, is the perfect accessory for a cool spring morning. It is easy to weave and assemble and breaks away from the traditional long shawl. The weft thread for this cape was a lovely hand-spun yarn from a friend. I have given you a comparable yarn that can be purchased. It would be a lovely cape in any combination of colors . . . so be creative!

Begin and end the long piece with ½ inch (1.3 cm) of plain tabby weave. The long piece is woven to 68 inches (172.7 cm). Allow for a 4-inch (10.2-cm) fringe on each end. After the tabby and border, you will weave 21 full motifs and then the partial finishing motif, followed by the border and tabby. Advance your warp to start the next piece.

The next two pieces are identical. Allowing for the 4-inch (10.2-cm) fringe, begin by weaving ½-inch (1.3-cm) plain tabby weave. Then weave Border 1 followed by 5 repeats of the full motif, and then the partial finishing motif. Border 2 follows this. Now, instead of a ½-inch (1.3-cm) plain tabby, you will weave 1 inch (2.5 cm) of plain tabby. (This will allow for ½ inch [1.3 cm] to be turned under when attaching to the main piece.) Repeat this process for the second piece. Be sure to keep your beat the same, as these two pieces have to match. It is a good idea to measure as you go. I hem-stitch all my ends so that they lie flat and are smooth.

After you have removed your weaving from the loom, you will assemble them as such:

Lay the two small pieces side by side and hand-sew them together using the warp thread. I serged the raw edge of this piece. If you don't have a serger, it would be best to either machine-zigzag or hand-whip the edge to keep it from unraveling. Next, fold the long piece in half to find the midway point and mark this point with a pin. The seam on the smaller piece will line up with this halfway point. Fold the 1-inch (2.5-cm) plain tabby in half, and with the raw edge toward the inside, pin this piece to the long piece on the wrong side. Now, using the warp thread, hand-sew this to the long piece. You will want to do this from both the front and the back so that the piece is securely attached.

Trim your fringes and wet-finish, and you now have a unique cape to wear for many occasions.

Dimensions: 3 pieces total:
1 piece 68 x 14 inches (172.7 x 35.6 cm), 2 pieces 18 x 14 inches (45.7 x 35.6 cm)

Pattern origin: Leaves

Warp

Sett: 12 epi; 12 dent reed, 1 thread per dent

Length: 4½-yard (4.1-m) warp

Thread: Harrisville Shetland, Pebble, 800 yards (732 m), 172 ends plus 2 floating selvedges = 174 ends

Floating selvedge: Harrisville Shetland, Pebble

Weft

Tabby thread: Harrisville Shetland, Pebble, 600 yards (550 m)

Pattern thread: Harrisville Highland, your choice of comparable color, 600 yards (550 m)

- Project used hand-spun and hand-dyed yarn

4			
	3		
		2	
			1

Border 2—20 ends
Repeat 5X

4		4				4		4			
	3		3				3		3		
				2						2	
					1						1

Partial motif—12 ends
Repeat 1X

Begin

4		4				4		4			
	3		3				3		3		
				2						2	
					1						1

End

4		4												4		4		4		4		4					
	3		3		3		3												3		3		3		3		
				2		2		2		2		2												2		2	
									1		1		1		1		1										1

Full motif—120 ends
Repeat 3X

4			
	3		
		2	
			1

Border 1—20 ends
Repeat 5X

				T	T
		4	4		4
	3	3		3	
2	2				2
1			1	1	

Tie-Up

Threading

Border 1: 5 times
Full motif: 3 times
Partial motif: 1 time
Border 2: 5 times

1			
	2		
		3	
			4

Border 1
Repeat 3X
at beginning and end

1			
	2		
		3	
			4
1			
	2		
		3	
			4
1			
	2		
		3	
			4
		3	
		3	
			4

Border 2
Repeat 1X

1			
	2		
	2		
	2		
		3	
		3	
		3	
		3	
			4
			4
			4
			4
			4
1			
1			
1			
1			
1			
	2		
	2		
	2		
	2		
	2		
		3	
		3	
		3	
			4
			4
			4
1			
	2		
		3	
			4
		3	
		3	
			4

Full motif
Repeat to desired length

Treadling

Border 1: 3 times
Full motif:
repeat to
desired length
Border 2: 1 time
Read and weave
from the
bottom up

Garden Lights Place Mat and Napkins

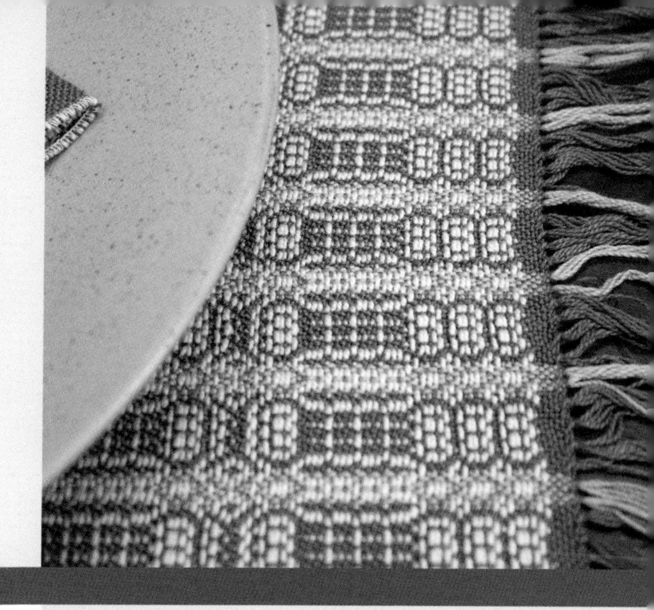

This place mat and napkin set would be lovely for that outdoor picnic or as a gift for someone special. These motifs remind me of the bright solar lights that brighten my garden in the summer. Follow the colorway provided with the warp tie-up. The full motif is done in the Avocado green, and the partial motif is done in the Willow Green.

Or, if you would prefer, use a totally different set of colors to match your dinnerware.

The napkins are easily woven with just a plain tabby weave. I used the Avocado green for my napkins and rethreaded the loom. If you prefer, just add some extra warp and you will have napkins with a stripe. I used my serger to make a rolled hem with a contrasting thread. If you do not have access to a serger, weave the place mats 2 inches (5.1 cm) longer and do a hand-rolled hem.

Dimensions:

- 4 place mats, 12 x 16 inches (30.5 x 40.6 cm), 2-inch (5.1 cm) fringe
- 4 napkins, 12 x 12 inches (30.5 x 30.5 cm)

Pattern origin: Original

Warp

Sett: 24 epi; 12 dent reed, 2 threads per dent

Length: 3½-yard warp

Threads: 10/2 perle cotton

- Willow Green, 77 ends, 280 yards (256 m)
- Avocado, 230 ends plus 2 floating selvedges = 232 ends, 850 yards (777 m)

Floating selvedge: 10/2 perle cotton, Avocado

Weft

Tabby thread: 10/2 perle cotton, Avocado, 650 yards (595 m)

Pattern thread: 5/2 perle cotton, Flaxon, 500 yards (457 m)

Border 1—20 ends

Tie-Up

Partial motif—7 ends

Full motif—26 ends

Threading

Threading sequence:
Border 1: 1 time
Full motif: 10 times
Partial motif: 1 time
Border 2: 1 time

Border 2—20 ends

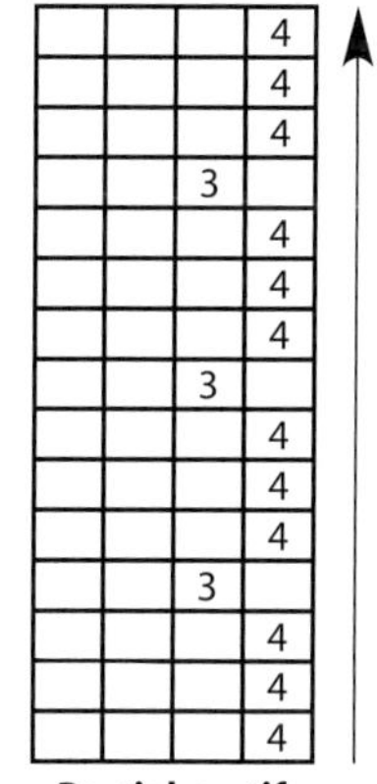

Partial motif

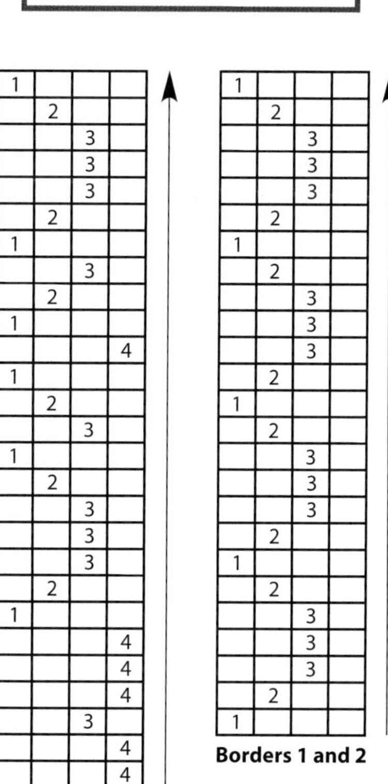

Full motif
Repeat 6X or to desired length

Borders 1 and 2

Treadling

Add tabby.
Treadling sequence:
Borders 1–2: 1 time
Full motif: repeat 6 times or to desired length
Partial motif: 1 time
Borders 1–2: 1 time
Read and weave treadling from the bottom up.

Napkins

Tabby weave structure

- Set loom at 12½ inches to allow for any draw in
- 10/2 perle cotton, your choice of color
- 300 ends, you do not need a floating selvedge
- 12 dent reed, 2 threads per dent
- If you are serging your napkins, you can use a 2½-yard (2.3 m) warp. If you need to hem your napkins, be safe and use a 2¾- (2.5 m) or 3-yard (2.75 m) warp.

Ghost Eyes Table Runner

A perfect table runner for a ghostly celebration! Every little circle looks like a pair of eyes that . . . maybe . . . could belong to a ghost! The contrast of the Black, White, and bright Tangerine thread makes this runner a real standout for the holiday. Add a pumpkin and a bowl of candy corn and your table is ready to go.

Begin and end this runner with ½ inch (1.3 cm) of plain tabby and a hem stitch. If you don't like the fringe, you can weave 1½ inches (3.8 cm) of tabby and make a rolled hem.

Dimensions: 16 x 50 inches (40.6 x 127 cm), 3-inch (7.6 cm) fringe

Pattern origin: Original

Warp

Sett: 24 epi; 12 dent reed, 2 threads per dent

Length: 2½-yard (2.3-m) warp

Thread: 10/2 perle cotton

- White, 246 ends, 500 yards (458 m)
- Black, 136 ends plus 2 floating selvedges = 138 ends, 325 yards (297 m)

Floating selvedge: 10/2 perle cotton, Black

Weft

Tabby thread: 10/2 perle cotton, White, 450 yards (412 m)

Pattern thread: 5/2 perle cotton, Tangerine, 450 yards (412 m)

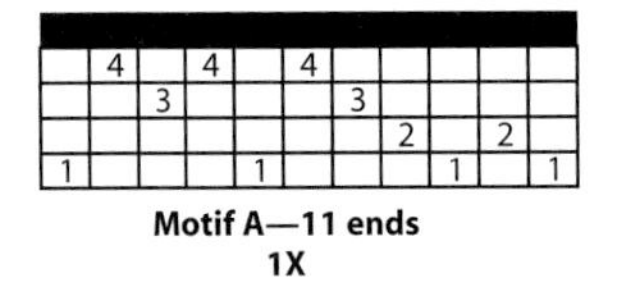

Motif A—11 ends
1X

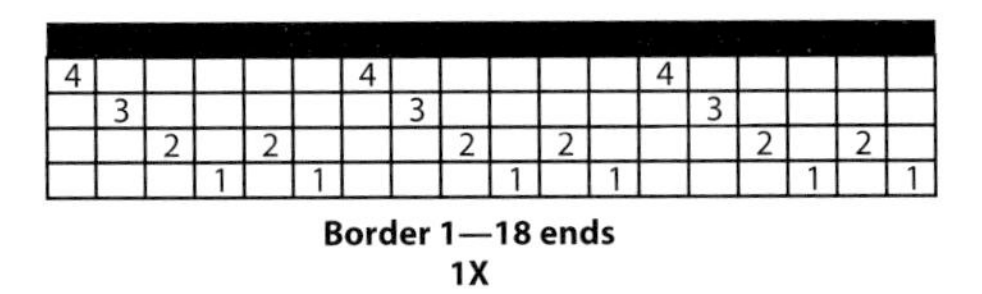

Border 1—18 ends
1X

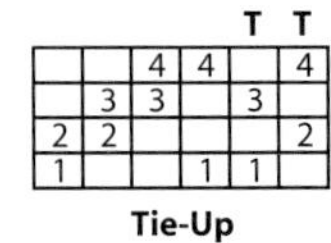

Tie-Up

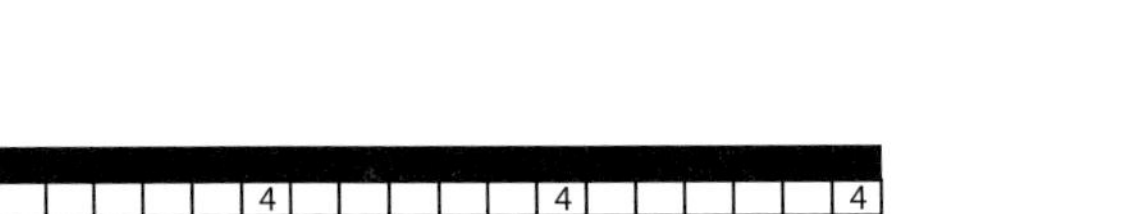

Motif B—use 2 times in total—41 ends

Threading and Tie-Up

Border 1: 1 time
Motif A: 1 time
Motif B: 1 time
Motif C: 1 time
Motif B: 1 time
Motif D: 1 time
Border 2: 1 time

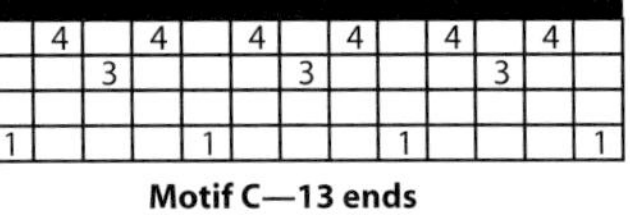

Motif C—13 ends

Border 2—18 ends
1X

Motif D—11 ends
1X

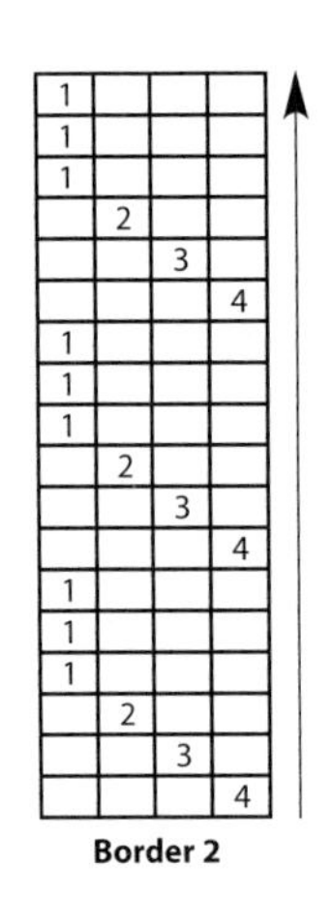

Border 2

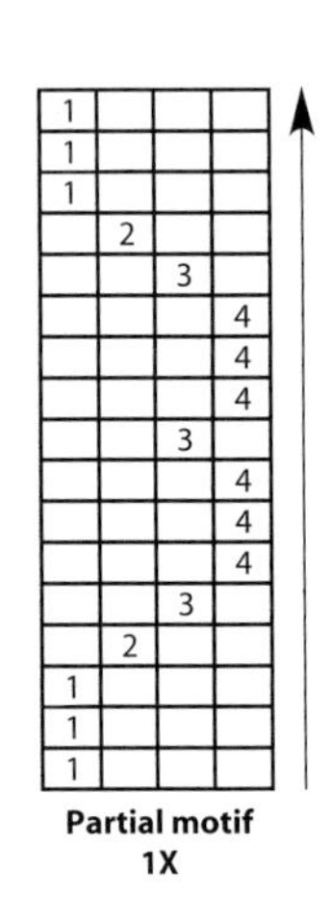

Partial motif
1X

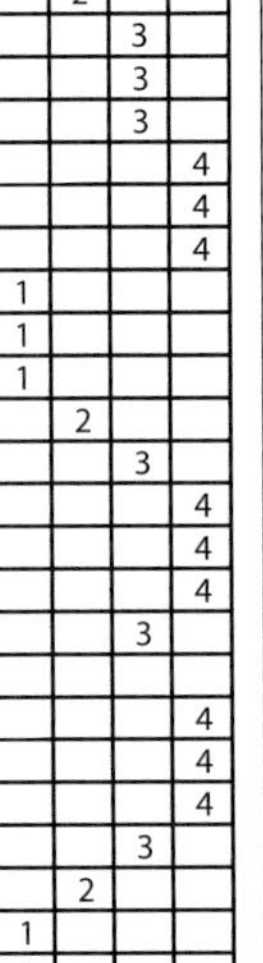

Main motif

Repeat 18X
or to desired length

Border 1

Treadling

Add tabby.
Treadling sequence:
Border 1: 1 time
Main motif: repeat 18 times or to desired length
Partial motif: 1 time
Border 2: 1 time
Read and weave from the bottom up

Cotton Candy Scarf (faux ikat)

Picnics, carnivals, and street fairs are events we look forward to all year. And this scarf portrays the colors of that favorite summertime treat we eat on those occasions, cotton candy!

This scarf was hand-dyed using Cushing's Direct Dyes. The warp was wound, then the dyes were applied in stripes and processed. Be sure to add some extra warps so that you have enough for the floating selvedge and any warp threads that might break. Cushing's Dyes are very easy to use! Just follow the directions and you will have success. Choose the colors that *you* want for your scarf.

I use the lark's head knot method to tie on to the back beam, but instead of the loops all being the same size, I make them varying sizes. Then as I begin to beam the warp on, the striped colors separate, giving the appearance of an ikat dyed warp. Very easy and creative!

Dimensions: 9½ x 66 inches (24.1 x 167.6 cm), 3-inch (7.6 cm) fringe

Pattern origin: Original

Warp

Sett: 24 epi; 12 dent reed, 2 threads per dent

Length: 3-yard (2.75-cm) warp

Thread: 10/2 perle cotton, White dyed with Cushing's Direct Dyes, 231 ends required, add 7 ends to allow for floating selvedge or breakage, for a total of 238 ends, 750 yards (686 cm)

Floating selvedge: 10/2 perle cotton, White, dyed

Weft

Tabby thread: 10/2 perle cotton, White, 350 yards (320 m)

Pattern thread: 5/2 perle cotton, White, 350 yards (320 m)

Note: See page 85 for instructions on dyeing warp and page 87 for instructions on tying on with lark's head knots.

Dyeing for Faux Ikat

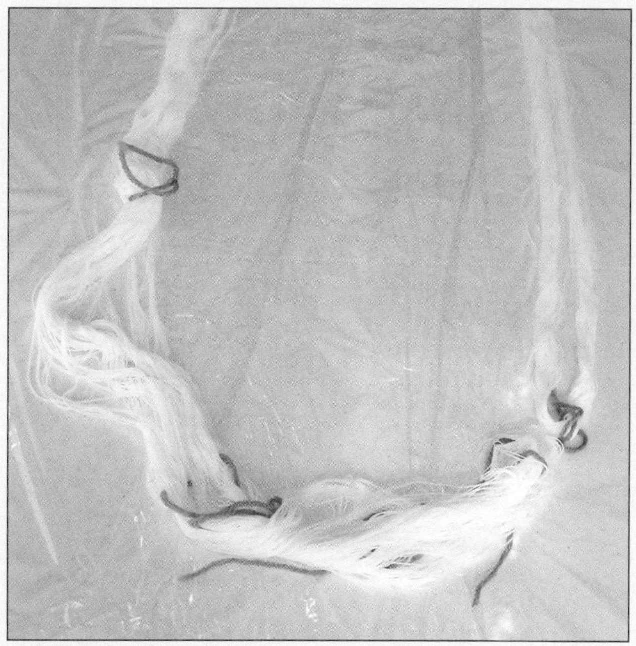

1. Start with undyed yarn in loose bundles and follow the instructions on the dye. Place your yarn on plastic to protect your work surface.

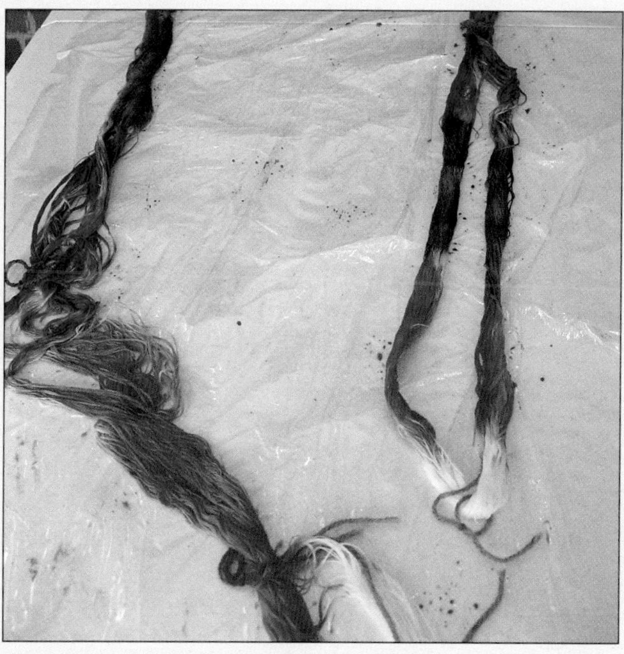

2. Add the dye in sections as desired.

3. Allow to dry thoroughly.

4. Use the lark's head knot method of tying on your warp, varying the length of the loops (see sidebar on page 87), to achieve a faux ikat look.

Threading and Tie-Up

Border 1: 1 time

Full motif: 6 times

Partial motif: 1 time

Border 2: 1 time

4				4				4			
	3				3				3		
		2				2				2	
			1				1				1

Border 1—12 ends

				T	T
	4	4			4
		3	3	3	
2			2		2
1	1			1	

Tie-Up

4		4								4		4				4				4		4							
	3						3																		3				
				2		2		2						2				2						2		2		2	
			1		1				1		1		1		1		1		1		1		1				1		1

Full motif—30 ends
6X

							4		4				4				4		4							
				3																		3				
	2		2		2						2				2						2		2		2	
1		1				1		1		1		1		1		1		1		1				1		1

Partial motif—27 ends
1X

			4				4				4
		3				3				3	
	2				2				2		
1				1				1			

Border 2—12 ends

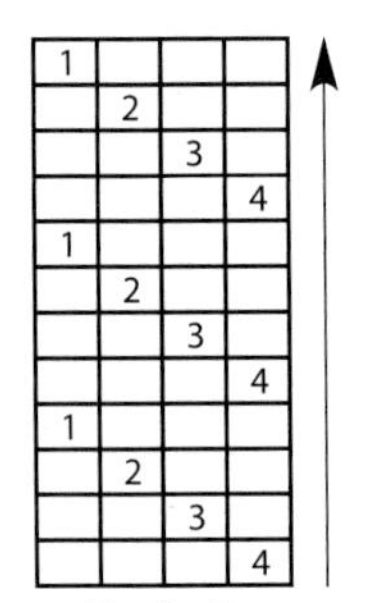

Border 2

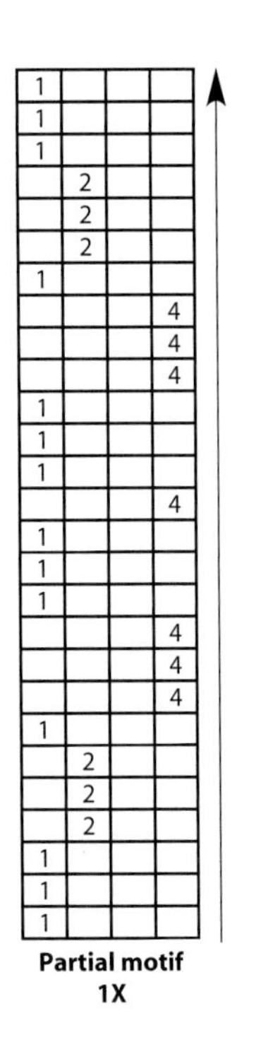

Partial motif
1X

			4
		3	
			4
1			
1			
1			
	2		
	2		
	2		
1			
			4
			4
			4
1			
1			
1			
			4
1			
1			
1			
			4
			4
			4
1			
	2		
	2		
	2		
1			
1			
1			

Full motif
Repeat to desired length

			4
		3	
	2		
1			
			4
		3	
	2		
1			
			4
		3	
	2		
1			

Border 1

Treadling

Add tabby.

Treadling sequence:

Border 1: 1 time

Full motif: to desired length

Partial motif: 1 time

Border 2: 1 time

Read and weave treadling from the bottom up.

Lark's Head Knot Method of Tying On

When I tie on to the back apron, I use the lark's head knot method. I find that it is the most efficient use of my warp, plus I can knot my thread bundles as I thread the heddles. Normally my loops are all the same size, but as you can see in the photo below, to achieve the faux ikat look I have made the loops varying sizes. The differences are about 1 inch (2.5 cm), but you can use any length that you want. The string used to make these loops must be a non-stretchy string. You will need the same number of loops as you have knots.

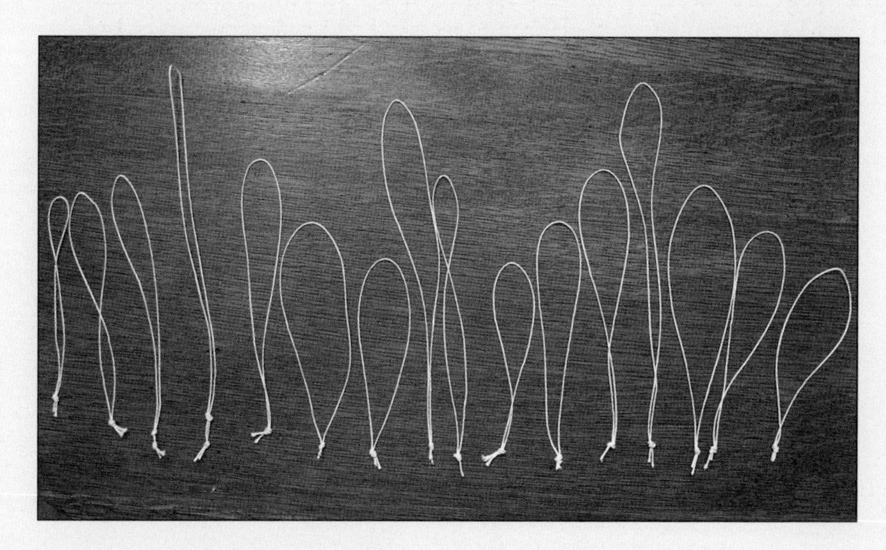

First you will need to attach the loops to the apron rod. Wrap the loop around the rod and pull the end through, as shown below. Be sure to have the knot close to the apron rod so it doesn't interfere with the warp threads.

To attach your warp, make a lark's head knot, put the knotted end of the warp through this, and pull tight to secure the warp.

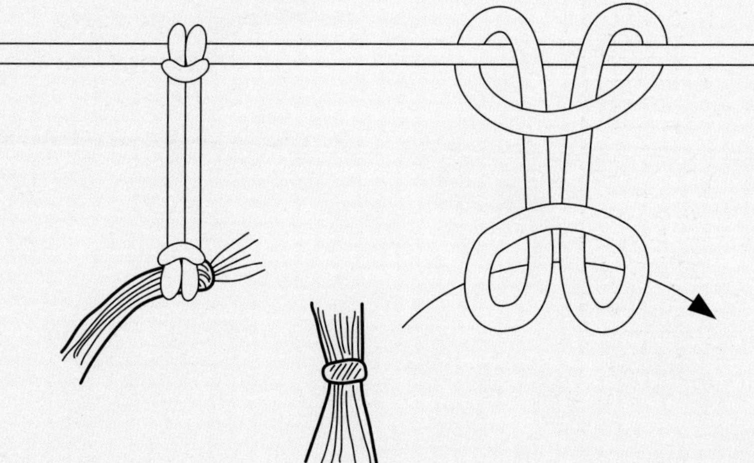

Now your warp is securely attached to the apron rod and you are ready to finish beaming on your warp.

If you are creating the faux ikat, the different lengths of the loops will separate the colors, creating the look that you want!

Nature Speaks Scarf

Nature provides a multitude of colors for us to enjoy—green, pink, and blue being just the basics . . . grass, flowers, and sky. This original pattern would be the perfect addition to your spring wardrobe.

I began with a White warp and dyed this using Cushing's Direct Dyes. These dyes are very easy to use . . . follow directions and you will be successful. As you can see in the example, the colors were painted on in stripes and then processed. Any number of colors could be used. There are 253 ends to the scarf, but be sure to dye extra so that you have enough for the floating selvedges and any warp threads that might break.

I use the Lark's Head Knot method to tie on to the back beam, but instead of the loops all being the same size, I make them varying sizes (see sidebar on page 87). Then as I begin to beam the warp on, the striped colors separate, giving the appearance of an ikat dyed warp.

Dimensions: 10½ x 66 inches (26.7 x 167.6 cm), 3-inch (7.6-cm) fringe

Pattern origin: Original

Warp

Sett: 24 epi; 12 dent reed, 2 threads per dent

Length: 3-yard (2.75-cm) warp

Thread: 10/2 perle cotton, White dyed with Cushing's Direct Dyes, 253 ends required, add 7 ends to allow for floating selvedge or breakage, for a total of 260 ends, 800 yards (732 m)

Floating selvedge: 10/2 perle cotton, White, dyed

Weft

Tabby thread: 10/2 perle cotton, White, 385 yards (352 m)

Pattern thread: 5/2 perle cotton, White, 385 yards (352 m)

Note: See page 85 for instructions on dyeing warp.

Threading

Border 1: 1 time
Full motif: 7 times
Partial motif: 1 time
Border 2: 1 time

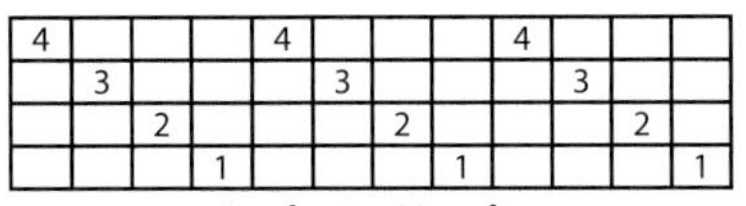

Border 1—12 ends

				T	T
	4	4			4
		3	3	3	
2			2		2
1	1			1	

Tie-Up

4				4						4						4		4						4					
									3						3		3		3						3				
		2				2		2				2		2						2		2				2		2	
	1		1		1		1				1		1								1		1				1		1

Full motif—30 ends
7X

					4		4						4					
				3		3		3						3				
	2		2						2		2				2		2	
1		1								1		1				1		1

Partial motif—19 ends
1X

			4				4				4
		3				3				3	
	2				2				2		
1				1				1			

Border 2—12 ends

1			
	2		
		3	
			4
1			
	2		
		3	
			4
1			
	2		
		3	
			4

Border 2

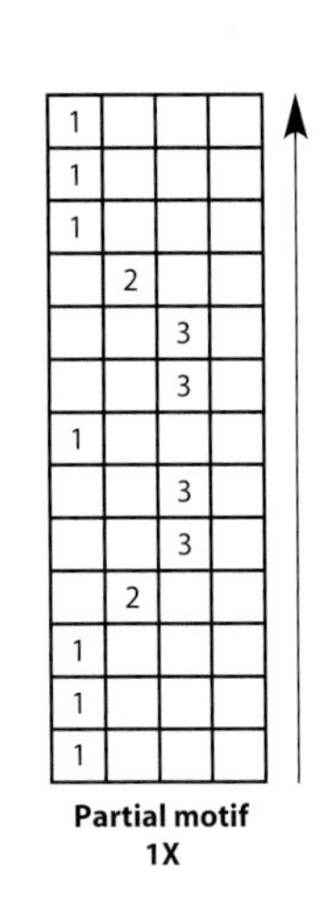

Partial motif
1X

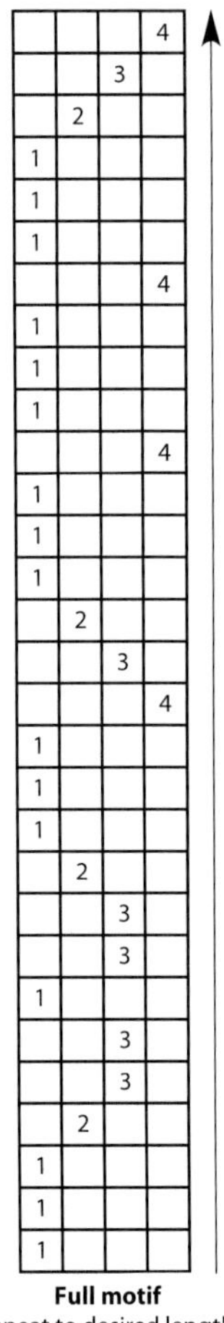

Full motif
Repeat to desired length

			4
		3	
	2		
1			
			4
		3	
	2		
1			
			4
		3	
	2		
1			

Border 1

Treadling

Add tabby.
Treadling sequence:
Border 1: 1 time
Full motif: repeat to desired length
Partial motif: 1 time
Border 2: 1 time
Read and weave from the bottom up.

Irish Pathways Ruana

Keeping warm is important, but it is always best to do it in style! A trip to Ireland was the inspiration for this piece, seeing the huge varieties of the color green! This ruana uses Harrisville Shetland Light for the warp and Harrisville White Highland Lite for the pattern weft. You could also double your Shetland Light for the pattern weft if you chose.

The tabby weave is the major portion of this piece, saving the overshot pattern for the trim and giving emphasis to the pattern it creates. It is very important to keep good measurements as you are weaving so your overshot pattern lines up in the back when sewing the two pieces together.

Allowing for a 4-inch (10.2-cm) fringe, weave 4 inches (10.2 cm) of plain tabby. Then weave two repeats of the overshot motif. You could weave more or less if you prefer. Next you will weave 35 inches (88.9 cm) of plain tabby for the main part of the ruana. Again, weave two repeats of the overshot pattern and finish with 4 inches (10.2 cm) of plain tabby. Wind your warp forward approximately 10 inches (25.4 cm), which allows for fringes, and repeat this process for the second panel. It will be your choice as to whether you prefer to do a hem stitch or knots. If you want a hem stitch, be sure to do it as you are weaving the piece.

You will notice that there is only one border in the threading draft. This was so the pattern motif would match in the back without a border interruption. *If* you want to use this motif for a different project and need a border on both sides, I have included an optional second border to use at the beginning of the threading draft.

COLOR SEQUENCE										
B	DG	B	S	B	L	B	S	B	DG	B
5	50	5	33	5	75	5	33	5	50	5
Number of Ends per Color										
Total of 271 ends										

B: BLACK; DG: DARK GREEN; S: SAGE; L: LIME GREEN

Dimensions: 23 x 60 inches (58.4 x 152.4 cm), 2 pieces of equal dimensions

Pattern origin: Original

Warp

Sett: 12 epi; 12 dent reed, 1 thread per dent

Length: 5¼-yard (4.8-cm) warp

Thread: Harrisville Shetland Light, 100 percent wool

- Dark Green, 100 ends, 530 yards (485 m)
- Black, 30 ends plus 2 floating selvedges = 32 ends, 160 yards (146 m)
- Sage, 66 ends, 360 yards (330 m)
- Lime, 75 ends, 400 yards (366 m)

Floating selvedge: Harrisville Shetland Light, 100 percent wool, Black, warp color position

Weft

Tabby thread plus plain weave: Harrisville Shetland Light, 100 percent wool, Sage, 1,025 yards (938 m)

Pattern thread: Harrisville Highland, 100 percent wool, White, 115 yards (106 m)

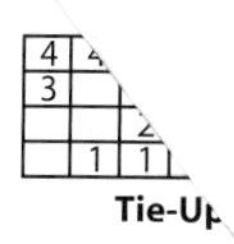

Tie-Up

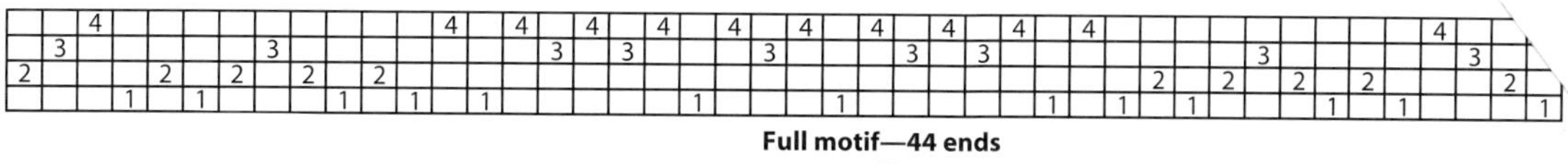

Full motif—44 ends
6X

Threading and Tie-Up

Full motif: 6 times

Border: 1 time

If using optional border, it will go before the motif.

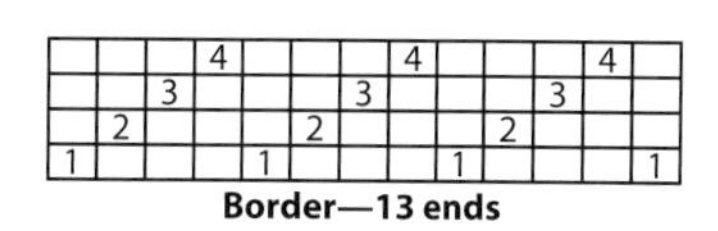

Border—13 ends

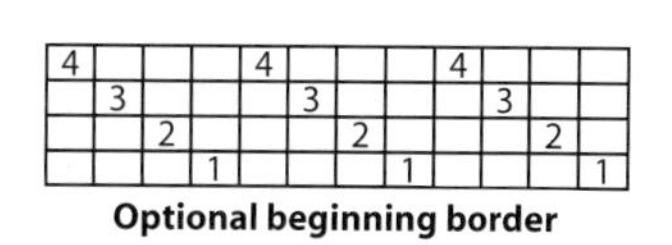

Optional beginning border

	2		

After second repeat treadle "2" to balance motif

Treadling for Overshot Pattern Only

Add tabby.

Weave full motif 2 times. After last repeat, treadle 2 to balance the motif.

Read and weave treadling from the bottom up.

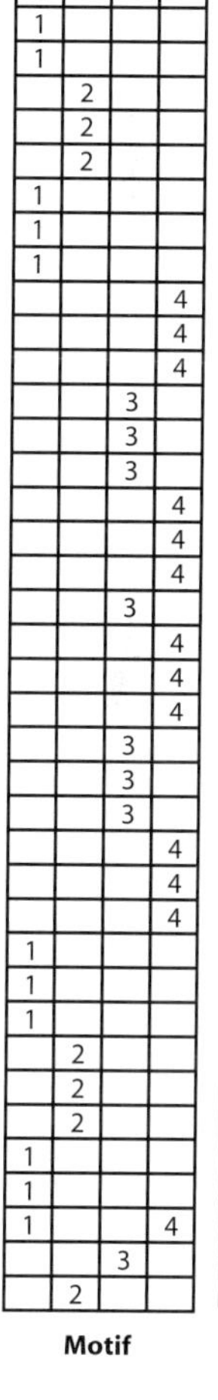

Repeat 2X

Motif

Carefully line up the two panels and mark the halfway point. Then put another marker 3 inches (7.6 cm) away from the halfway point. You will hand-sew these pieces to the 3-inch (7.6-cm) mark, which gives room for your neck.

A piece of faux leather was used in the back where the two pieces are joined, to eliminate the natural stress in this area. The constant pull on this spot could cause the fibers to pull apart. Here is a nifty hint for applying this piece of faux leather or any small piece: Cut a piece of the faux leather larger than needed; draw your triangle on the leather with a piece of chalk. Position this piece, and then sew on that line. Once it is attached, then you can trim close to the sewn edge. You will get a piece that looks much better than trying to sew a small triangle onto your woven piece. If you want to use a thin piece of real leather, maybe one you salvaged from an old purse, be sure to use a leather needle. These needles have sharp edges to cut the leather as they sew.

I've Got the Blues Wrap

One of the wonderful things about belonging to a guild is sharing our talents with other members. This was the inspiration for this sideways wrap. One of our members opened her home to us for a dyeing workshop. We had a wonderful time. While most of the participants made multicolored skeins of yarn, I just had to be different! I wanted to do some pot dyeing!

We used the dye color Peacock from PRO Chemical & Dye for this project. The warp fiber was put in a less concentrated dye pot and only stirred minimally. For the weft fiber we used a much heavier concentration of the same color with just a touch of Black. I chose the blue color because, as you know, trying to match blues in different weights and brands of fibers can be a huge problem. And I knew that I would have the same color blue if I dyed it myself. Not only was it a wonderful day with friends, but some beautiful yarn was created.

This wrap is made from two pieces that are woven separately and then hand-sewn together, leaving an opening for the head. Allowing for a 4-inch (10.2-cm) fringe, weave the first piece to 60 inches (152.4 cm), then wind your warp forward 10 inches (25.4 cm). This will allow for the 4-inch (10.2-cm) fringe for both pieces. Weave the second piece exactly as the first, measuring the motifs as you go. This will ensure they match up later. Pin the two pieces together, matching the motif. Find the center point and measure 6 inches (15.2 cm) on each side. This will give you a 12-inch (30.5 cm) opening for your head. It would be a good idea to try the wrap on to make sure that the opening fits you properly.

Adding the undyed stripe adds interest to the cape as well as an area that emphasizes the pattern.

You will begin and end with ½-inch (1.3-cm) plain tabby and blind hem if desired. The motif is repeated fifteen times and then balanced with the last partial motif. It is important that you measure as you go and keep your beat consistent so that the motifs match when the two pieces are sewn together. This stunning piece will look good for dressy occasions or with blue jeans!

Dimensions: 19 x 60 inches (48.3 x 152.4 cm), plus 4-inch (10.2-cm) fringe, 2 pieces of equal dimensions

Pattern origin: Original

Warp

Sett: 12 epi; 12 dent reed, 1 thread per dent

Length: 5-yard (4.6-m) warp

Thread: Knit Picks Bare Dyeable Yarn, Peruvian Highland Wool, fingering weight

- Dyed variegated yarn with PRO Chemical & Dye color Peacock Blue, 151 ends plus 2 floating selvedges = 153 ends, 800 yards (732 m)
- Undyed yarn, 44 ends, 250 yards (229 m)

Floating selvedge: Dyed Knit Picks Bare Dyeable Yarn, Peruvian Highland Wool, fingering weight

Weft

Tabby thread: Dyed Yarn, Knit Picks Peruvian Highland Wool, fingering weight, 800 yards (732 m): This yarn is dyed a solid blue, no variation.

Pattern thread: Knit Picks Bare Dyeable Yarn, Superwash Wool, nylon, sport weight; dyed with Pro Chemical Dyes, Peacock Blue and Black; 800 yards (732 m)

THREADING SEQUENCE

Border 2	Partial motif	Motif	Motif	Motif	Border 1
Variegated	Variegated	Variegated	White	Variegated	Variegated
12 ends	39 ends	44 ends	44 ends	44 ends	12 ends

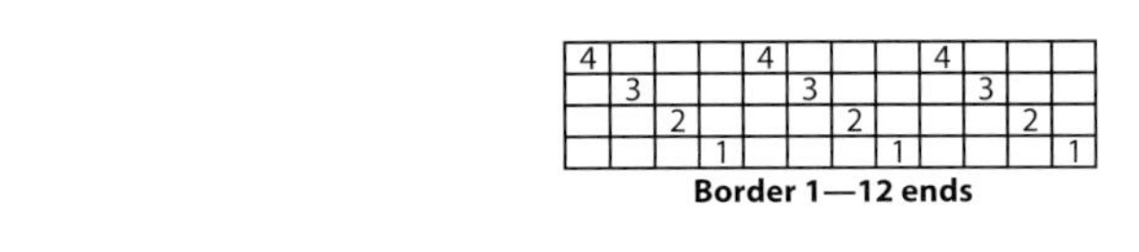

Border 1—12 ends

Tie-Up

Full motif—44 ends

Partial motif—39 ends

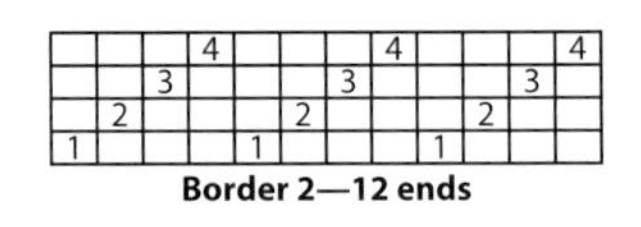

Border 2—12 ends

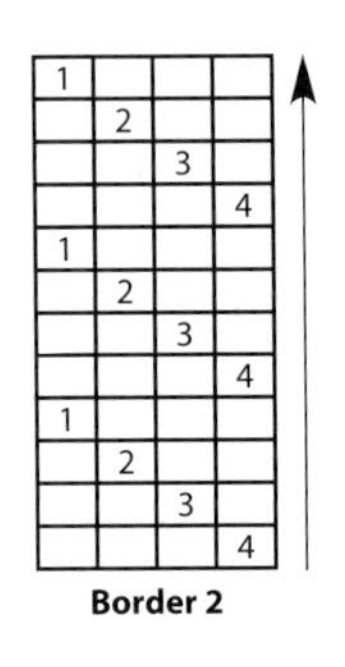

Border 2

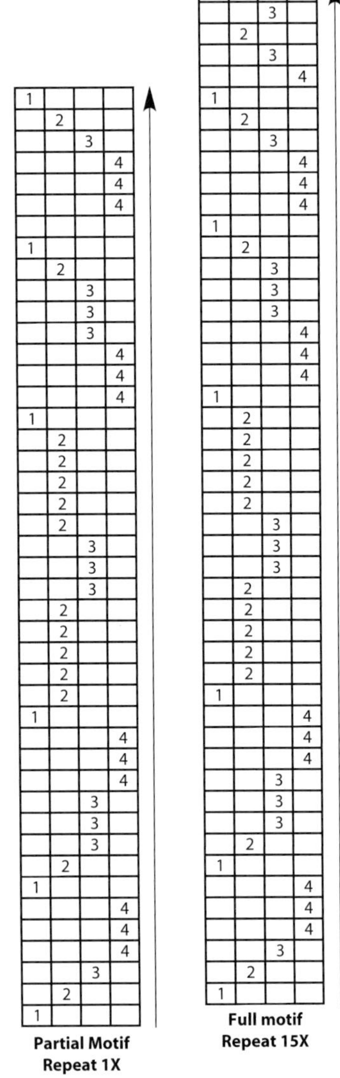

Partial Motif Repeat 1X

Full motif Repeat 15X

Border 1

Threading and Tie-Up

Border 1: 1 time, variegated

Motif: 3 times, 2 variegated, 1 white

Partial motif: 1 time, variegated

Border 2: 1 time, variegated

Treadling

Add tabby.

Treadling sequence:

Border 1: 1 time

Full motif: 15 times

Partial motif: 1 time

Border 2: 1 time

Read and weave treadling from the bottom up.

Mardi Gras Table Runner

Table runners are both beautiful and useful. The same can be said for rag rugs. So why not combine these techniques to create a new and unusual table runner? This piece takes the rug warp and torn fabric model that we use to make rugs into the concept of a table runner. However, instead of tearing the cloth into 2-inch (5.1-cm) strips, the fabric is torn into 3/4-inch (1.9-cm) strips, which gives the table runner a more delicate appearance. My fabric choice is multicolored with a silver thread in it, which adds some extra sparkle! Changing up the fabric choice and the warp color choice will give you unlimited options for your piece. Be sure to use a firm beat just as you would when you make a rug.

Weave a 1/2-inch (1.3-cm) plain tabby at both the beginning and end of the piece before beginning the pattern. I suggest that you blind-hem the piece, as knots will create lumps and bumps on your table. Begin with Border 1. Next weave Block A then Block B to within 5 inches (12.7 cm) of your desired length, then repeat Block A to finish. End with Border 2 and your fringe.

Dimensions: 13 x 43 inches (33 x 109.2 cm), 3-inch (7.6-cm) fringe

Pattern origin: Original

Warp

Sett: 12 epi; 12 dent reed, 1 thread per dent

Length: 2½-yard (2.3-m) warp, 450 yards (412 m)

Thread: 8/4 cotton rug warp, Black, 171 ends plus 2 floating selvedges = 173 ends

Floating selvedge: 8/4 cotton rug warp, Black

Weft

Tabby thread: 8/4 cotton rug warp, Black, 150 yards (138 m)

Pattern thread: 1½-yard (1.4-m), 45-inch (1.2-m) wide cotton fabric torn into ¾-inch (1.9 cm) strips

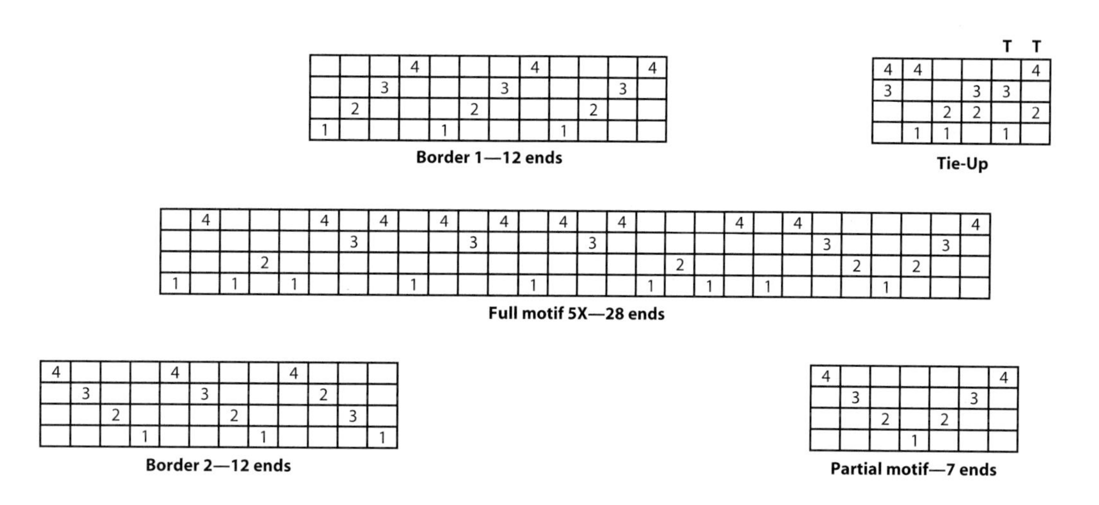

Threading and Tie-Up

Border 1: 1 time
Full motif: 5 times
Partial motif: 1 time
Border 2: 1 time

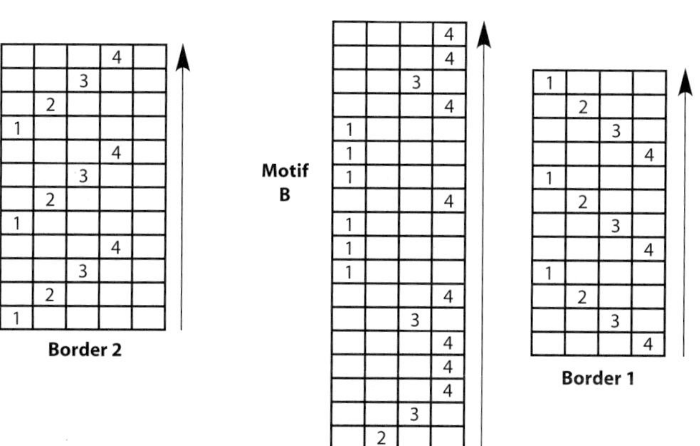

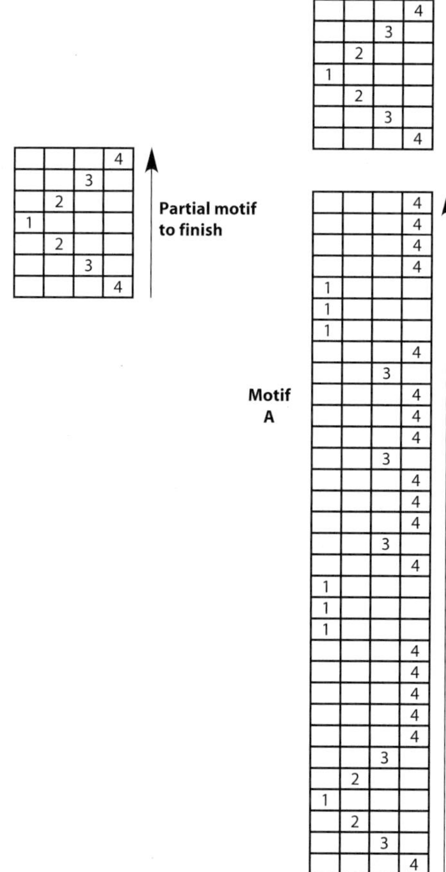

Treadling

Add tabby.
Treadling sequence:
Border 1: 1 time
Alternate Motifs A and B to desired length, ending with Motif A.
Partial motif: 1 time
Border 2: 1 time
Read and weave treadling from the bottom up.

Merry Christmas Runner

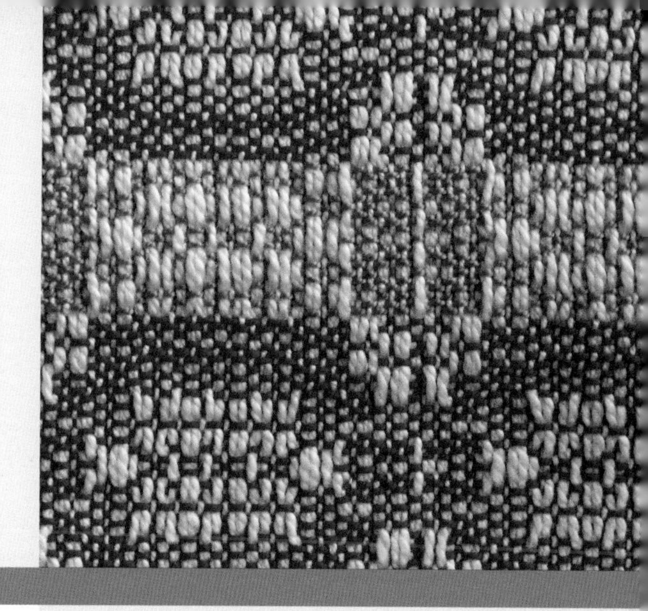

Everyone should have that special table runner for the Christmas holidays! This runner reflects the green Christmas tree and the shiny red bulbs that decorate it. Add this to your Christmas table along with your Christmas table setting, and you are sure to get lots of compliments.

When threading this runner, begin with Border 1, then Motifs A and B—each four times—and then one more Motif A, finally threading Border 2. This will balance your runner.

Begin and end the runner with ½ inch (1.3 cm) plain tabby and hem-stitch rather than create knots. You could also do twisted fringe if you would prefer.

I added an additional 18 inches (45.7 cm) to the warp, making the total warp 3 yards (2.75 m) so I would have a bit extra to play with. From this extra piece I was able to make four Christmas stockings. Red and green fleece was used for the stocking. You can find the stocking patterns online, use a purchased pattern, or just trace around a Christmas stocking you already have. I added some bells and a ribbon loop to finish.

Dimensions: 15½ x 48 inches (39.4 x 121.9 cm), 3-inch (7.6-cm) fringe

Pattern origin: Original

Warp

Sett: 24 epi; 12 dent reed, 2 threads per dent

Length: 2½ yard (2.3 m) warp

Thread: 10/2 perle cotton

- Red, 185 ends, 500 yards (457 m)
- Sapphire, 188 ends plus 2 floating selvedges = 190 ends, 500 yards (457 m)

Floating selvedge: 10/2 perle cotton, Sapphire

Weft

Tabby thread: 10/2 perle cotton, White, 400 yards (366 m)

Pattern thread: 5/2 perle cotton, White, 400 yards (366 m)

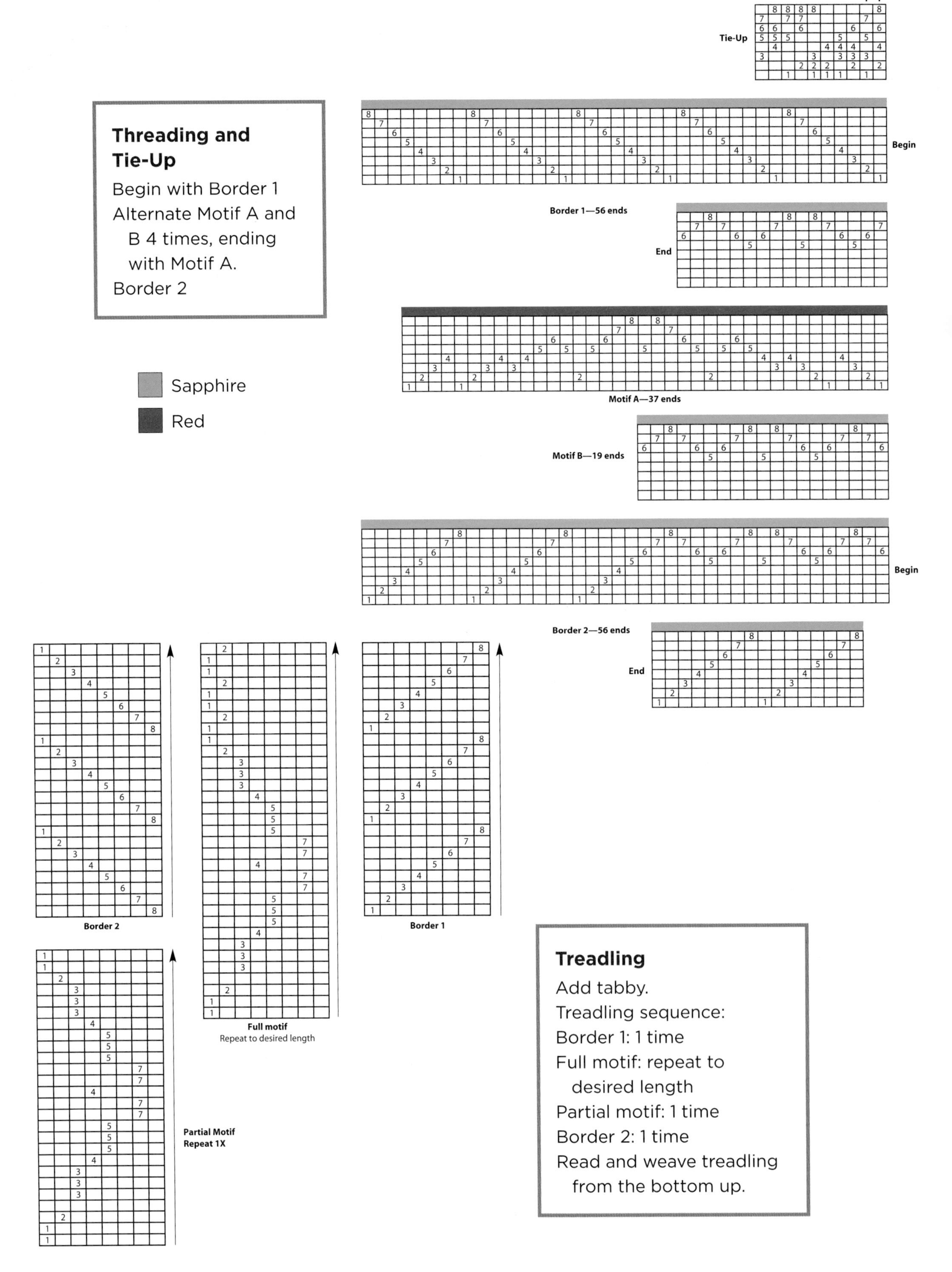
Threading and Tie-Up
Begin with Border 1
Alternate Motif A and B 4 times, ending with Motif A.
Border 2
Sapphire
Red
Tie-Up
T T
Begin
Border 1—56 ends
End
Motif A—37 ends
Motif B—19 ends
Begin
Border 2—56 ends
End
Border 2
Full motif
Repeat to desired length
Border 1
Partial Motif
Repeat 1X
Treadling
Add tabby.
Treadling sequence:
Border 1: 1 time
Full motif: repeat to desired length
Partial motif: 1 time
Border 2: 1 time
Read and weave treadling from the bottom up.

Overshot Rug

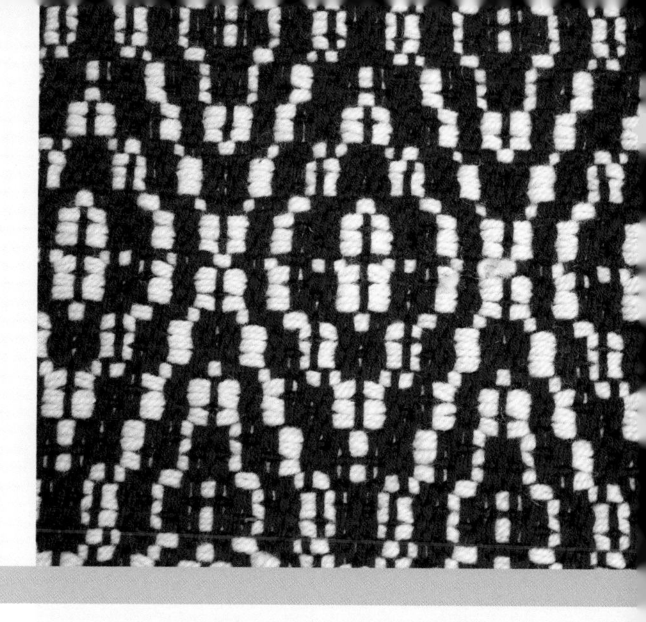

Overshot is a wonderful weave structure for rugs! What a statement this rug would make in your entranceway, kitchen, or bathroom. By doubling the warp thread, the rug is sturdier and will withstand a lot of use. You also need to double the floating selvedge, being sure to match the warp threads. I used a double shuttle when weaving, so I laid two wool threads at a time when creating the pattern. I was given a huge cone of 3-ply wool rug yarn, which is what I used in this project. I've listed a comparable yarn for you.

This rug weaves up quickly and would make a great housewarming gift for a friend or family member. Weave 1 inch (2.5 cm) of tabby at the beginning and end of the rug when leaving fringe, or if you prefer to roll the hem, then you will want to weave 1½ inches (3.8 cm). If you are leaving fringe, I advise that you twist the fringe, as it will fray out over time. The twisted fringe keeps its appearance longer.

Dimensions: 27 x 45 inches (68.6 x 114.3 cm), with 4-inch (10.2-cm) twisted fringe
Pattern origin: Original

Warp

Sett: 12 epi; 12 dent reed, 2 threads per dent
Length: 2¾-yard (2.5-m) warp
Thread: 8/4 cotton rug warp, Purple, 1,800 yards (1,646 m), 318 ends, doubled so the total number of ends is 636 ends plus 4 floating selvedges = 640 ends
Floating selvedge: 8/4 cotton rug warp, Purple
Use 2 threads for each floating selvedge (the same as for the regular warp threads).

Weft

Tabby thread: 8/4 cotton rug warp, Purple, 400 yards (366 m)
Pattern thread: rug wool, Natural (doubled), 900 yards (823 m)
Comparable: 3-ply rug wool

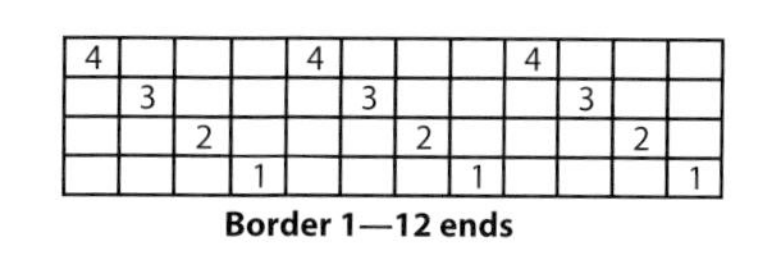

Border 1—12 ends

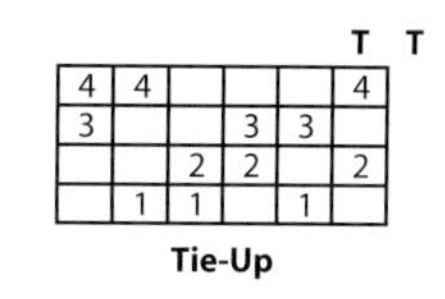

Tie-Up

	4		4										4		4		4								4		4					
		3						3						3				3		3						3		3				
					2		2		2		2								2		2		2						2		2	
1				1		1				1		1				1						1		1						1		1

Begin

Full motif—49 ends
Repeat 6X

End

					4		4								4
				3		3						3		3	
	2		2						2		2		2		
1		1						1		1					

Border 2—12 ends

			4				4				4
		3				3				3	
	2				2				2		
1				1				1			

Threading and Tie-Up

Border 1: 1 time
Full motif: 6 times
Border 2: 1 time

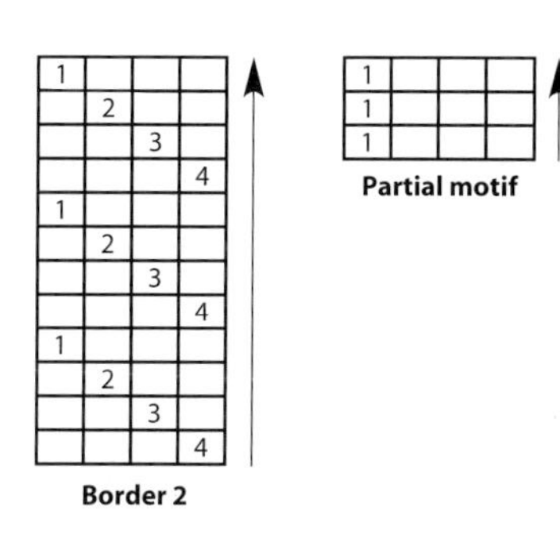

Border 2

Partial motif

	2		
		3	
		3	
		3	
			4
1			
1			
1			
	2		
	2		
	2		
		3	
			4
			4
			4
		3	
			4
1			
1			
1			
	2		
	2		
	2		
1			
1			
1			
			4
		3	
			4
			4
			4
		3	
	2		
	2		
	2		
1			
1			
1			
			4
		3	
		3	
		3	
	2		
1			
1			
1			

Full motif
Repeat to desired length

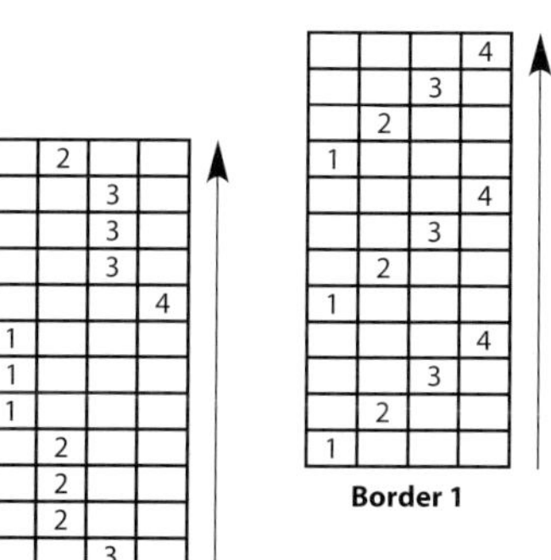

Border 1

Treadling

Add tabby.
Treadling sequence:
Border 1: 1 time
Full motif: repeat to desired length
Partial motif: 1 time
Border 2: 1 time
Read and weave treadling from the bottom up.

Treadling 1

Treadling 2

Treadling 3

Pillows

Pillows are a wonderful way to liven up any room. These pillows have the same threading, just different treadling patterns, making each pillow unique. Make your warp as long as you need for the size and number of pillows you want to make. Using a neutral warp will allow you to use multiple colors for the weft. What wonderful Christmas or housewarming presents these would make!

You can finish the pillows with piping, trim, or a plain edge, using a complementary fabric for the backing. Or if you prefer, you can weave fabric for both sides. I've included the colors used for the pillows shown, although any color you choose would be perfect!

There were no borders on the threading draft, but if you use the instructions on making a border, you can easily add one and make a table runner, place mats, or any other project.

Dimensions: 14 x 14 inches (35.6 x 35.6 cm) and 12 x 12 inches (30.5 x 30.5 cm)

Pattern origin: Original

Warp

Sett: 24 epi; 12 dent reed, 2 threads per dent

Length: Warp length and amount determined by number of pillows you will be creating. I use a minimum warp of 2 yards (1.8 m) for one 18-inch (45.7 cm) pillow.

If you are adding a border, be sure to add the 2 extra threads in your calculation for a floating selvedge.

Thread: 10/2 perle cotton, White

Be sure to include your floating selvedge.

Weft

Tabby thread: 10/2 perle cotton, White

Pattern thread: 5/2 perle cotton; Willow Green, Bali, and Dark Green were used for these projects. The amount needed will be determined by how many pillows you are creating.

				T	T
		4	4		4
	3	3		3	
2	2				2
1			1	1	

Tie-Up

		4		4				4		4						4		4						4		4						4		4				4		4			
	3						3		3						3		3								3		3						3		3						3		3
2						2						2		2						2		2						2		2						2						2	
			1		1						1		1						1		1		1						1		1						1		1				

Full motif—44 ends

Threading and Tie-Up

Repeat threading to desired width.

	2		
		3	
			4
			4
			4
1			
	2		
		3	
		3	
		3	
			4
1			
1			
1			
	2		
		3	
		3	
		3	
			4
1			
1			
1			
1			
1			
			4
		3	
		3	
		3	
	2		
1			
1			
1			
			4
		3	
		3	
		3	
	2		
1			
			4
			4
			4
		3	
	2		
	2		

Treadling #3

1			
1			
1			
			4
			4
			4
1			
1			
1			
			4
			4
			4
		3	
		3	
	2		
	2		
1			
1			
	2		
	2		
		3	
		3	
			4
			4
			4

Treadling #2

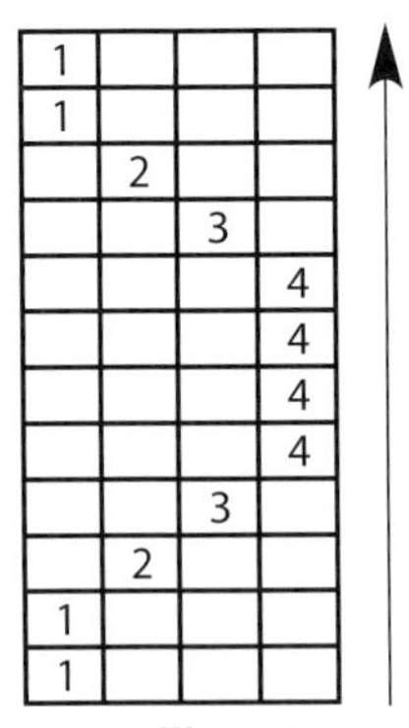

1			
1			
	2		
		3	
			4
			4
			4
			4
		3	
	2		
1			
1			

Treadling #1

Treadling

Add tabby.

Choose a treadling pattern and repeat to the desired length.

Weave and read treadling from the bottom up.

Pink-a-licious Blanket

What a fun blanket for that new baby in the family! Made from an original design, this blanket highlights the use of three different shades of pink, two in the warp and a vivid pink for the pattern weft. Made from perle cotton, it has a wonderful drape and will withstand numerous washings. A change in the color palette to blues could make it appropriate for a boy, and it could just as easily be made gender neutral. It would also be great to drape over the back of your couch for those cold winter nights.

In threading this draft you will begin with Border 1. Then Motif A and Motif B, repeating this sequence fifteen times before ending with Motif A. Last you will thread Border 2. Follow the color sequence that is shown.

When you are weaving this piece, begin and end with 1½ inches (3.8 cm) of plain tabby weave and do a rolled hem once your piece is complete. Begin weaving with Border 1 using White for the tabby thread. You will also use White for the tabby for Border 2. Additionally, all of the Motif A treadling patterns will use White for the tabby thread.

As you begin to weave Motif B, you will follow the same color sequence for the tabby thread that was used for the threading. The first Motif B will use Petal Pink for the tabby thread. The second Motif B will use Poplin for the tabby thread. Continue in this manner until the last Motif B, which should be using Petal Pink for the tabby. The color changes are subtle but definitely make your piece more interesting. This is a fun piece to make, but be sure to keep track of where you are in the color sequence.

If this gets too complicated, just pick one color for the tabby and use it throughout your piece.

Dimensions: 37 x 42 inches (94 x 106.7 cm)

Pattern origin: Original

Warp

Sett: 24 epi; 12 dent reed, 2 threads per dent

Length: 2½-yard (2.3-m) warp

Thread: 10/2 perle cotton

- White, 512 ends plus 2 floating selvedges = 514 ends, 1,300 yards (1,190 m) (Borders and Motif A)
- Petal Pink, 216 ends, 550 yards (503 m) (Motif B)
- Poplin, 189 ends, 500 yards (457 m) (Motif B)

Floating selvedge: 10/2 perle cotton, White

Weft

Tabby thread: 10/2 perle cotton

- White, 525 yards (480 m)
- Petal Pink, 150 yards (138 m)
- Poplin, 150 yards (138 m)

Pattern thread: 5/2 perle cotton, Dark Pink (Webs), 825 yards (755 m)

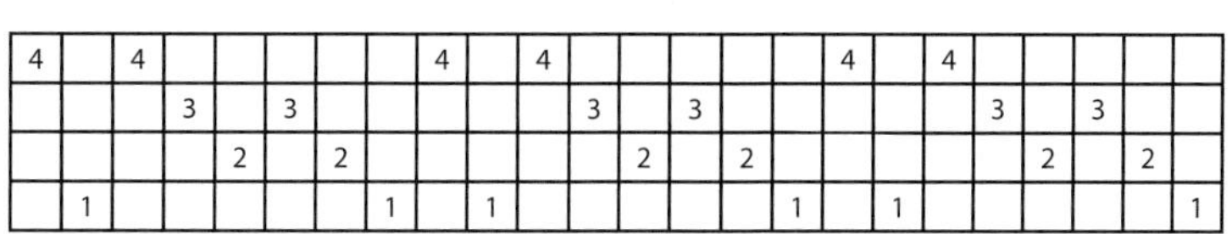

Border 1—24 ends

				T	T
	4	4			4
		3	3	3	
2			2		2
1	1			1	

Tie-Up

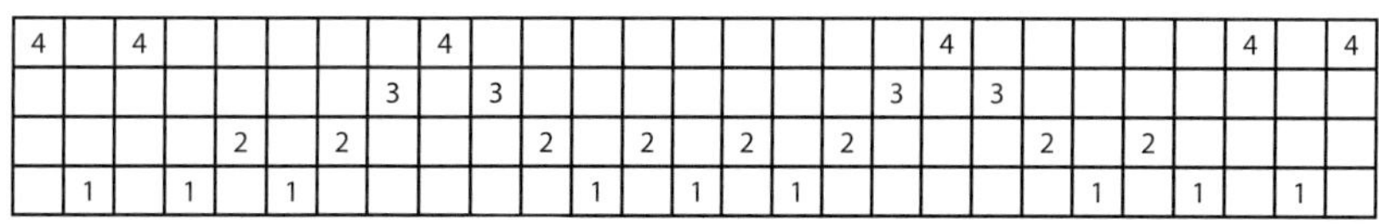

Motif A—29 ends

Threading and Tie-Up

Border 1: 1 time

Alternate Motifs A and B 7 times

Then repeat Motif A, Motif B, Motif A 1 time

Border 2: 1 time

Follow chart for color sequence.

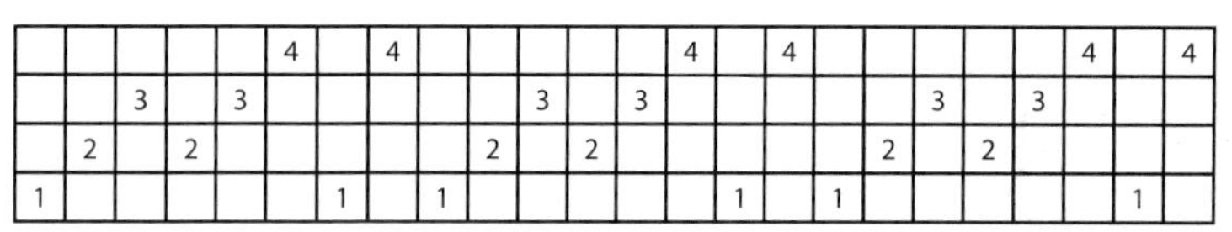

Motif B—27 ends

					4		4						4		4						4		4
		3		3						3		3						3		3			
	2		2						2		2						2		2				
1						1		1						1		1						1	

Border 2—24 ends

Border 2	Motif A	Motif B	Motif A	Motif B	Motif A	Motif B	Motif A	Border 1
White	White	Petal Pink	White	Poplin	White	Petal Pink	White	White
1X	1X	1X	1X	← This section repeated 7 times →				1X
	← This section balances piece →							

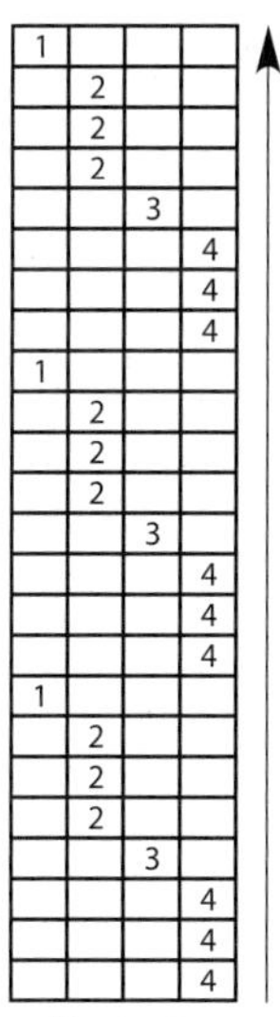

Border 2

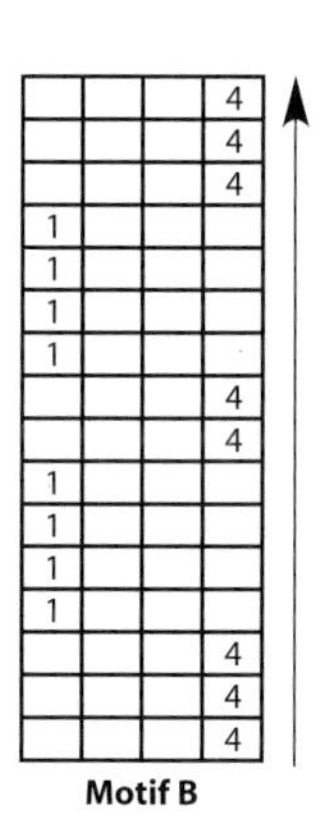

Motif B

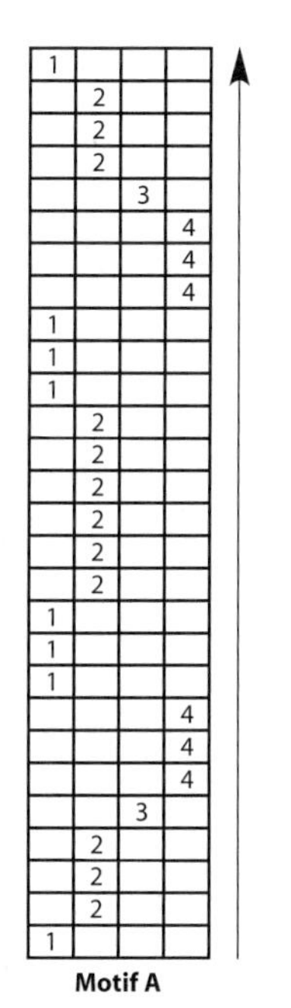

Motif A

			4
			4
			4
		3	
	2		
	2		
	2		
1			
			4
			4
			4
		3	
	2		
	2		
	2		
1			
			4
			4
			4
		3	
	2		
	2		
	2		
1			

Border 1

Treadling

Add tabby following color sequence of warp thread.

Treadling sequence:

Border 1: 1 time

Alternate Motifs A and B to desired length, ending with Motif A.

End with Border 2

Read and weave treadling from the bottom up.

Prayer Shawl

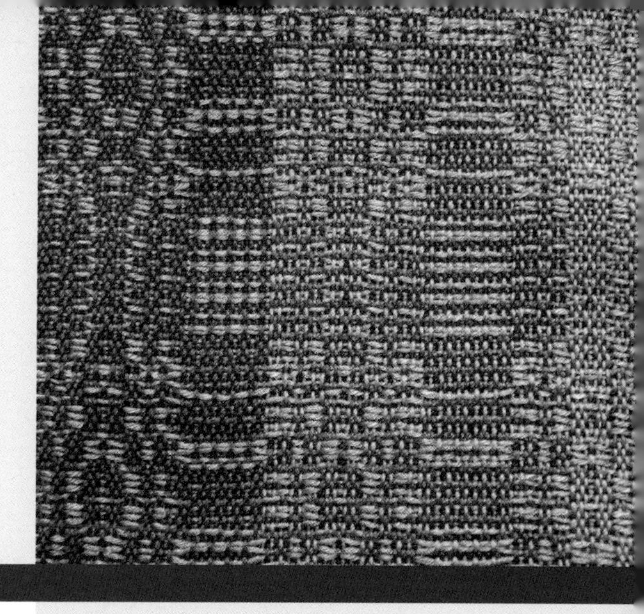

Prayer shawls are that special gift made for someone who needs some extra-special care and love. This beautiful shawl has a prayer woven right into it, as the pattern is a name draft of "The Lord is my Shepherd." I chose the colors most often associated with churches, purple and gold. What a comfort this would be to someone who is hurting.

Looking at the color scheme for the warp threads, you will see that some sections are made of one solid color and the adjoining section is a 50/50 blend of two colors. This helps to make the color blend from section to section. I did a random pickup when threading the two colors for the warp. Please note that the color sequence does not correspond to the width of the weaving motif.

I used the Purple for the tabby thread throughout the piece. Feel free to change this and use one of the other colors if you prefer. Begin and end the piece with ½-inch (1.3-cm) plain tabby and a blind hem and a lovely fringe.

This shawl would be beautiful in many different colorways, whether they be monochromatic or many different colors. Choose your colors and make this piece your own!

Dimensions: 21½ x 84 inches (66 x 213.4 cm), with 4-inch (10.2-cm) fringe

Pattern origin: Original

This is a name draft for "The Lord is my Shepherd."

Warp

Sett: 24 epi; 12 dent reed, 2 threads per dent

Length: 3½-yard (3.2 m) warp

Thread: 10/2 perle cotton

- Purple, 193 ends plus 2 for floating selvedge = 195 ends, 700 yards (640 m)
- Sheer Lilac (Webs), 216 ends, 800 yards (732 m)
- Lilac Snow (Webs), 108 ends, 400 yards (366 m)

Floating selvedge: 10/2 perle cotton, Purple

Weft

Tabby thread: 10/2 perle cotton, Purple, 900 yards (823 m)

Pattern thread: 6-ply rayon, Gold (Mill End), 900 yards (823 m)

Comparable: 5/2 perle cotton or 5/2 Dragon Tale rayon

Threading and Tie-Up

Border 1: 1 time
Motif: 9 times
Border 2: 1 time
Follow color chart for color placement.

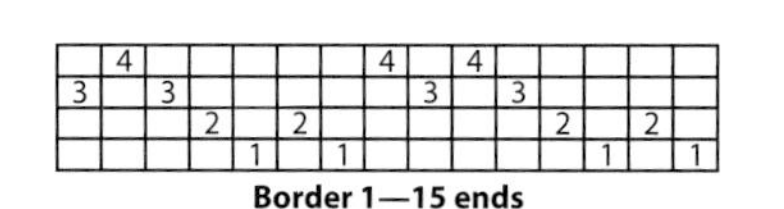

Border 1—15 ends

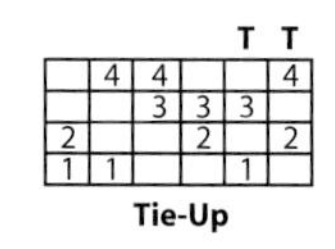

Tie-Up

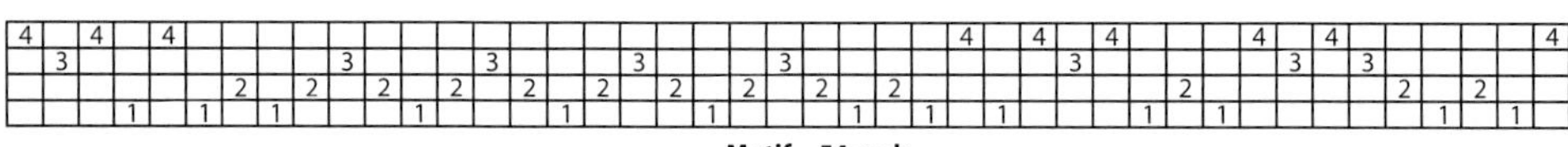

Motif—54 ends
Repeat 9X

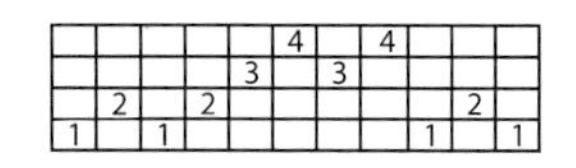

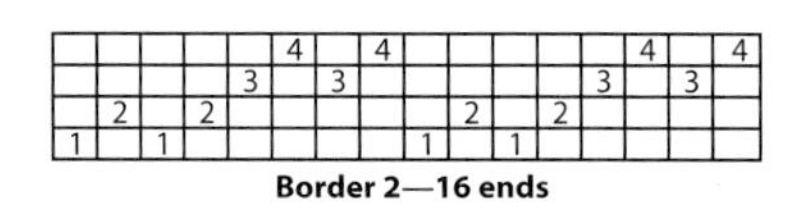

Border 2—16 ends

Border 2		50/50		50/50		50/50		50/50		Border 1
Purple	Purple	Purple/Sheer Lilac	Sheer Lilac	Sheer Lilac/Lilac Snow	Lilac Snow	Sheer Lilac/Lilac Snow	Sheer Lilac	Purple/Sheer Lilac	Purple	Purple
16 ends	54 ends	54 ends	54 ends	54 ends	54 ends	54 ends	54 ends	54 ends	54 ends	15 ends

Treadling

Add tabby.
Treadling sequence:
Border 1: 1 time
Full motif: 20 times
Partial motif: 1 time
Border 2: 1 time
Read and weave treadling from the bottom up.

Border 2
1X

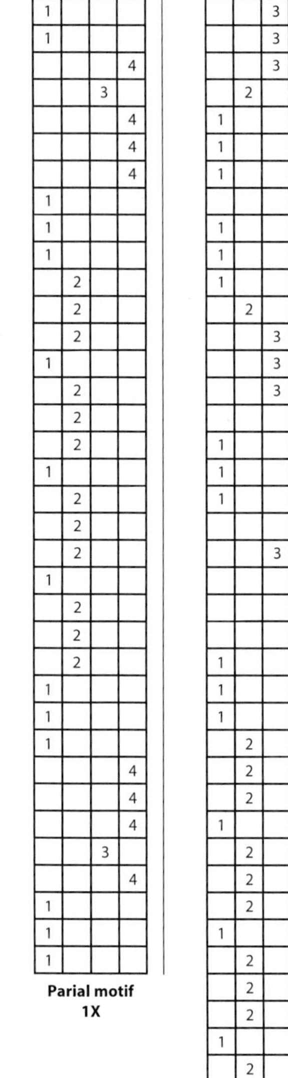

Parial motif
1X

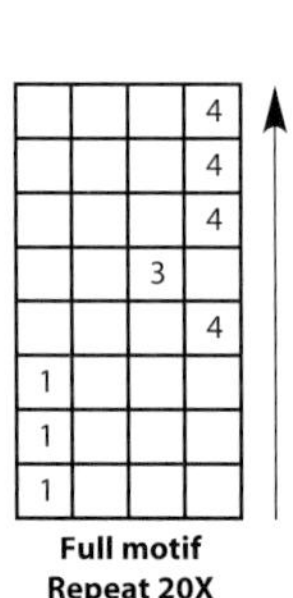

Full motif
Repeat 20X
or to desired length

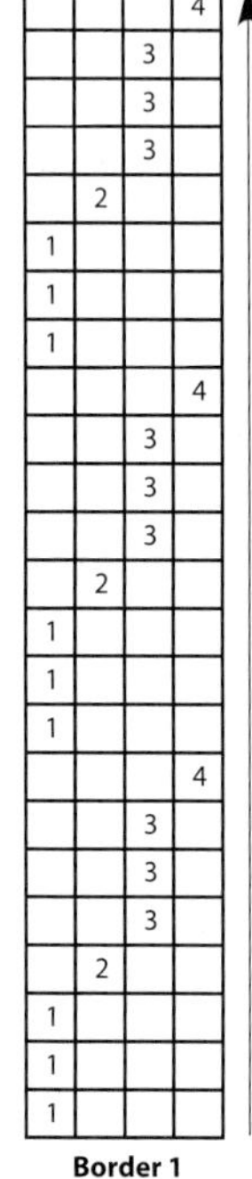

Border 1
1X

Pretty in Pink Dress

When my girls were young, I loved dressing them in pink frilly dresses for Sunday mornings. A trip to the fabric store usually resulted in something new for each of them. One of the best parts of weaving is that now I can create my own fabrics and not be limited to what is on the market.

A few things you must consider when making a dress or garment of this type: Purchased fabric is generally a much lighter weight than the fabric we weave. The pattern for the skirt of this dress requires twice as much fabric as the width of the bodice. This would be gathered in to fit to the bodice. However, this would not work well with a heavier handwoven fabric. Because of the weight difference, you would only want to have a maximum of one and one-half the width of the bodice.

Also, whenever possible, eliminate the seams. Overlap the pattern pieces at the sewing line, pin together, and treat this as one piece. This will solve the problem of bulk at the side seams and under the arms. I eliminated the side seams, keeping only the back seam, where the zipper was inserted.

I have also found that it is better to do a hand-picked understitching at the neck and armholes. This will help the lining of the bodice to lay better and eliminate the problem of the lining rolling to the outside.

When estimating the yardage needed, I add 20 percent to both the length and width. The last thing I want to happen is to not have enough fabric to complete my project. Any extra fabric can be made into toys, purses, or a variety of other smaller projects.

When using this pattern, you will notice that there is one motif and two borders. *I've included the borders if you decide you want to use this pattern for a table runner or another project. You do not need to include the borders if you are creating yardage.*

You will want to determine where to place the motif in your garment and then measure to the sides of the pattern pieces to determine how many times you will repeat the Straight Twill Before

Dimensions: Determined by project

Pattern origin: Original

Warp

Sett: 24 epi; 12 dent reed, 2 threads per dent

Length: Determined by project; you'll need to weave fabric the width of the widest pattern piece and as long as the total length of all pattern pieces.

Thread: 10/2 perle cotton, yardage determined by project

- White
- Fuchsia (or color of choice)

Floating selvedge: 10/2 perle cotton, White

Weft

Tabby thread: 10/2 perle cotton, White

Pattern thread: 5/2 perle cotton, White

Note: I used McCall's pattern M5791 for this dress.

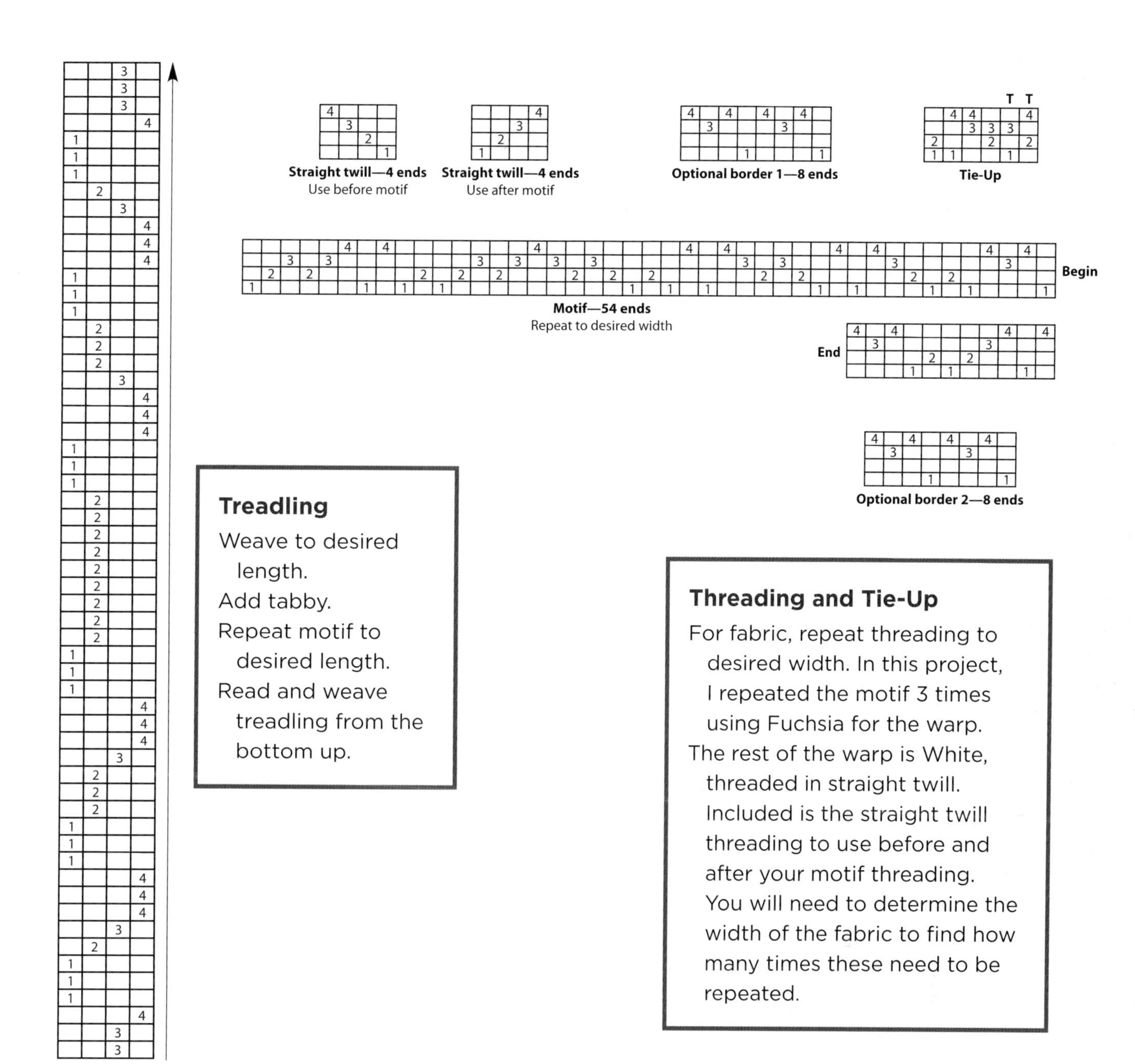

Motif and Straight Twill After Motif to get the width required. It will take a bit of figuring, but it is worth the effort. Just be patient! If you are really struggling with this idea . . . purchase some inexpensive muslin and cut out the pattern. Then roughly outline on the muslin where you want your motif to be. This will help you to visualize how wide your fabric will need to be. Be sure to make fabric for all the required pattern pieces.

There are a multitude of children's clothing patterns that you could use for your handwoven fabric. Think about the placement of the pattern and how you can make it the emphasis of the design. Have fun, and you will definitely be making a one-of-a-kind garment.

Purple Passion Throw

Purple is such a rich, vibrant color, and it makes most everyone smile! So naturally, to create a lap robe or a small throw would be the perfect use of this wonderful color. The Mary Ann Ostrander weaving motif is an elegant pattern and exactly what was needed for this project. Borders were added to the sides, beginning, and end to frame out the throw.

I used two colors of cotton in the warp, White and Orchid. If you wind these two threads at the same time, you can really speed up the process. When I threaded the heddles, I chose the colors randomly rather than in the order of White–Orchid, etc. Feel free to be more precise if that is more comfortable for you. However, a word of warning: If you make a mistake, it will really show up. I like the use of the two colors, as I believe it softens the contrast between the pattern weft thread and the background. I used a "found" wool yarn for the pattern thread but have given you a comparable thread that can be purchased. Remember, this is your throw so if you would prefer to use one color, then do it! This would be a wonderful gift for a family member who is housebound!

Begin the throw with ½-inch (1.3-cm) plain tabby and a hem stitch. If the fringe bothers you, then weave 1½-inch (1.3-cm) of tabby and do a rolled hem.

Dimensions: 36 x 60 inches (91.4 x 152.4 cm), with 4-inch (10.2-cm) fringe

Pattern origin: Mary Ann Ostrander

Warp

Sett: 24 epi; 12 dent reed, 2 threads per dent

Length: 3-yard (2.75-m) warp

Thread: 10/2 perle cotton

- White, 419 ends, 1,300 yards (1,190 m)
- Orchid, 418 ends, 1,300 yards (1,190 m)

Add 1 thread of each color for the floating selvedges.

Random pickup

Floating selvedge: 10/2 perle cotton, White or Orchid

Weft

Tabby thread: 10/2 perle cotton, Orchid, 1,200 yards (1,100 m)

Pattern thread: Comparable to "found" wool: 2/8 Maine Line Jaggerspun, Deep Purple, 1,200 yards (1,100 m)

Threading

Border 1: 6 times

Full motif: 11 times

Partial motif: 1 time

Border 2: 6 times

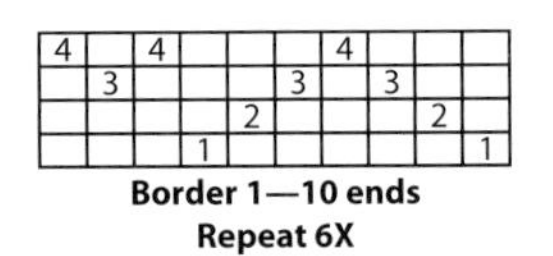

Border 1—10 ends
Repeat 6X

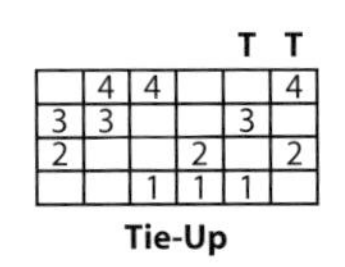

Tie-Up

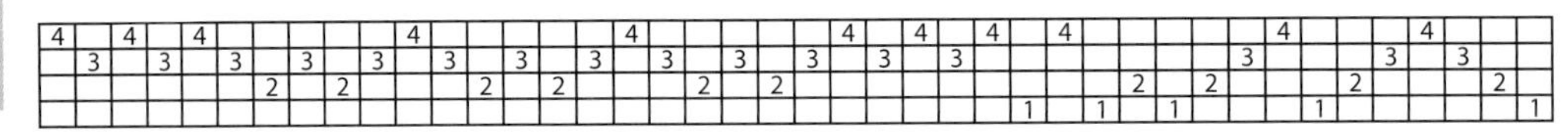

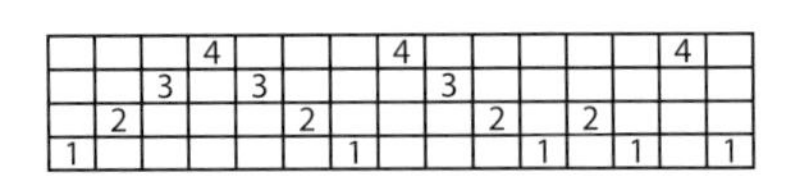

Full motif—60 ends
Repeat 11X

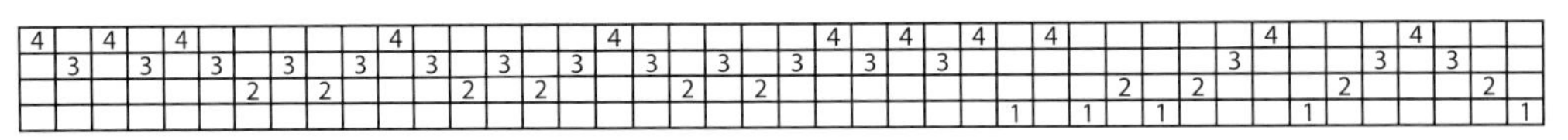

Partial motif—57 ends
Repeat 1X

Border 2—10 ends
Repeat 6X

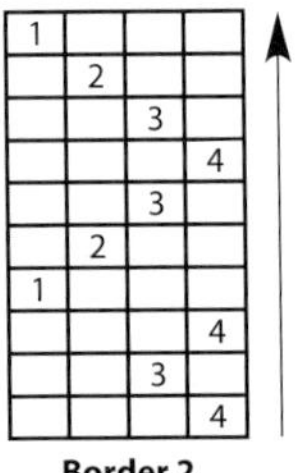

Border 2
Repeat 6X

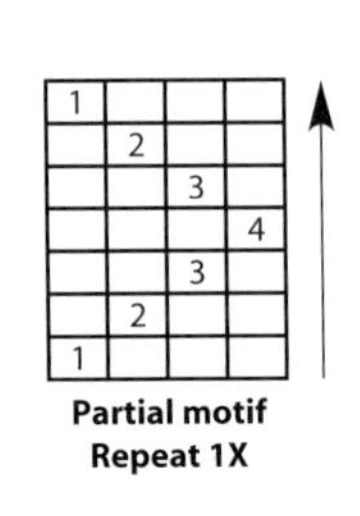

Partial motif
Repeat 1X

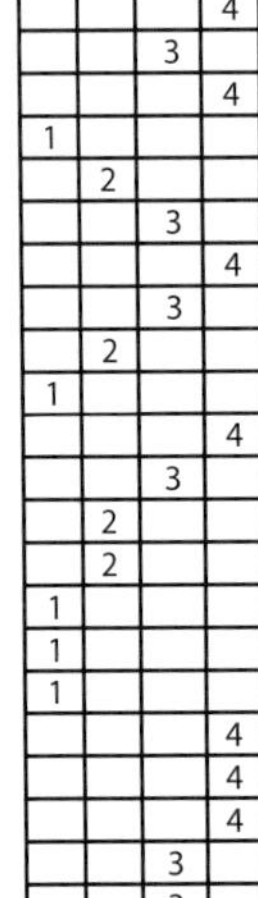

Full motif
Repeat 12X
or to desired length

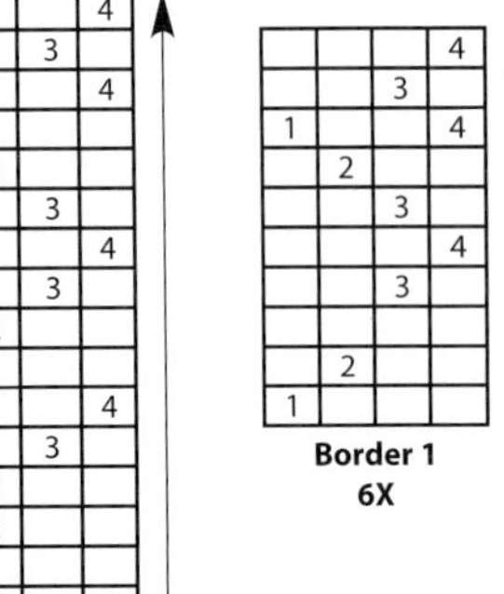

Border 1
6X

Treadling

Add tabby.

Treadling sequence:

Border 1: 6 times

Full motif: 12 times or desired length

Partial motif: 1 time

Border 2: 6 times

Read and weave treadling sequence from the bottom up.

Rose Path Shawl

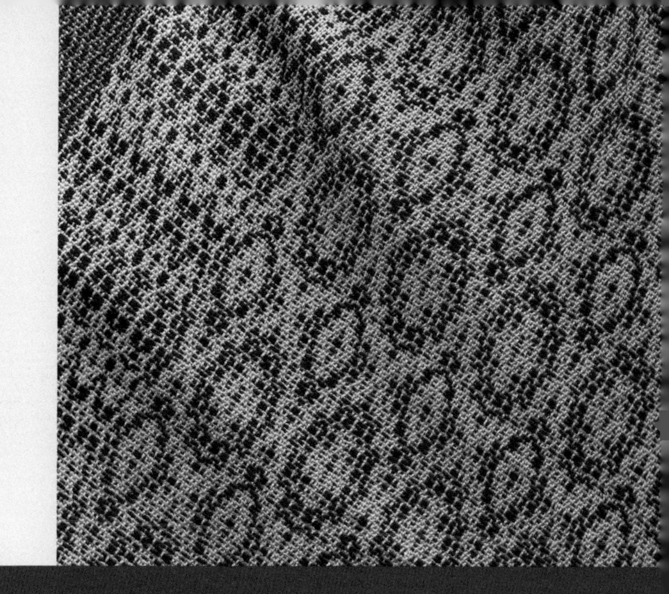

Spring is such a beautiful season! The grass is turning green, and the flowers are starting to bloom, putting behind us the cold, harsh winter weather. As I sit at my loom and weave, I enjoy looking out the window and seeing my rosebush bursting into vibrant colors of pink. Such was the inspiration for this shawl.

I used two different colors of pink for the center of the shawl to give a bit of variation, just as my roses have a variety of hues. Where the pink and green colors mix, the colors blend, almost creating brown tones, which is indicative of the stems and thorns of the rosebush. This shawl could easily be changed to represent a rosebush of any color. Change the pinks to yellows, oranges, or purples, and you will have your own special handiwork.

Begin and end the shawl with ½ inch (1.3 cm) of plain tabby and finish with a hem stitch and a beautiful fringe!

Dimensions: 24 x 85 inches (61 x 215.9 cm), with 5-inch (12.7 cm) fringe

Pattern origin: Original

Warp

Sett: 24 epi; 12 dent reed, 2 threads per dent

Length: 3½-yard (3.2-m) warp

Thread: 10/2 perle cotton

- Loden Green, 104 ends plus 2 floating selvedges = 106 ends, 375 yards (343 m)
- Scarab, 146 ends, 525 yards (480 m)

Center warp: 10/2 perle cotton

- Wisteria, 159 ends, 575 yards (526 m)
- Electric, 160 ends, 575 yards (526 m)

The center warp is a random pickup.

Floating selvedge: 10/2 perle cotton, Loden Green

Weft

Tabby thread: 10/2 perle cotton, Wisteria, 1,200 yards (1,100 m)

Pattern thread: 5/2 Dragon Tale Rayon, Burgundy, 1,200 yards (1,100 m)

Threading and Tie-Up

Border 1: 1 time
Motif A: 2 times
Motif B: 6 times
Partial Motif B: 1 time
Motif C: 7 times
Partial Motif C: 1 time
Motif D: 6 times
Partial Motif D: 1 time
Motif E: 2 times
Border 2: 1 time

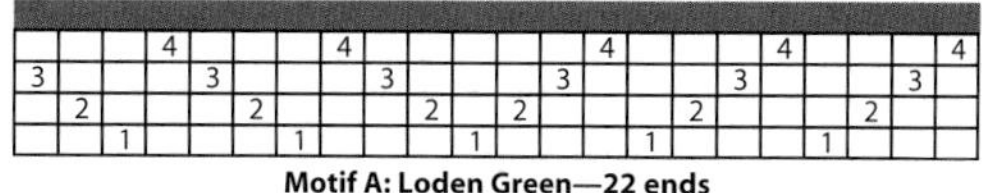
Motif A: Loden Green—22 ends
Repeat 2X

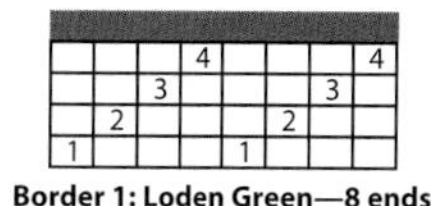
Border 1: Loden Green—8 ends
Repeat 1X

Tie-Up

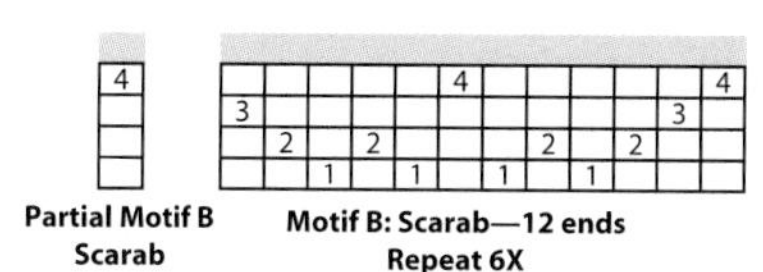
Partial Motif B
Scarab

Motif B: Scarab—12 ends
Repeat 6X

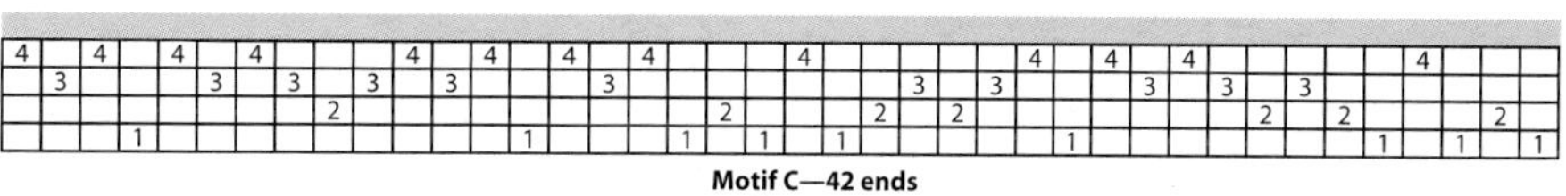
Motif C—42 ends
Repeat 7X
Color blend of Wisteria and Electric

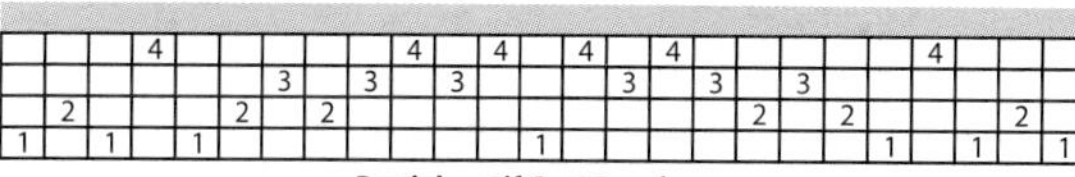
Partial motif C—25 ends
Repeat 1X
Color blend of Wisteria and Electric

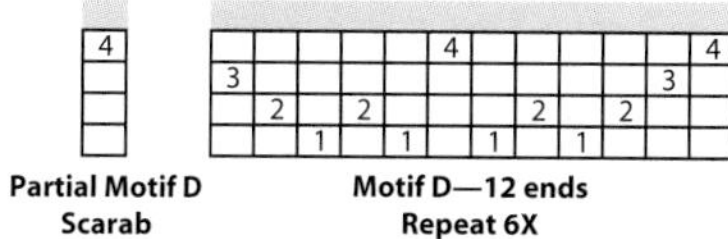
Partial Motif D
Scarab

Motif D—12 ends
Repeat 6X

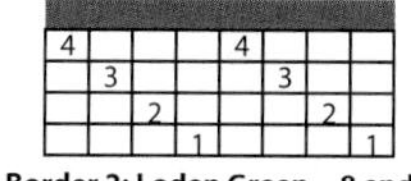
Border 2: Loden Green—8 ends
Repeat 1X

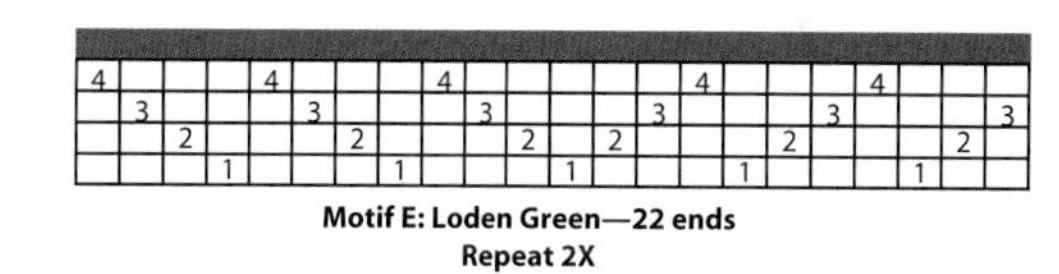
Motif E: Loden Green—22 ends
Repeat 2X

Treadling

Add tabby.
Treadling sequence:
Border 1: 1 time
Full motif: to desired length
Partial motif: 1 time
Border 2: 1 time

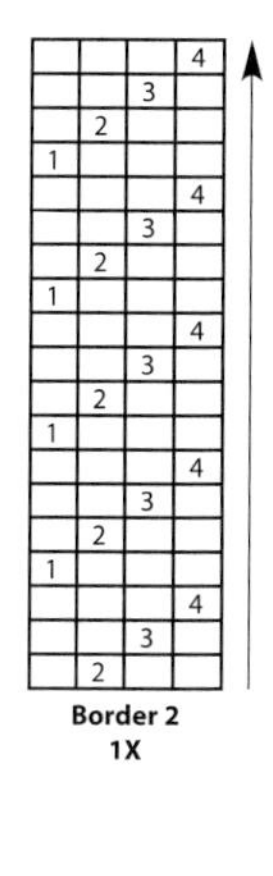
Border 2
1X

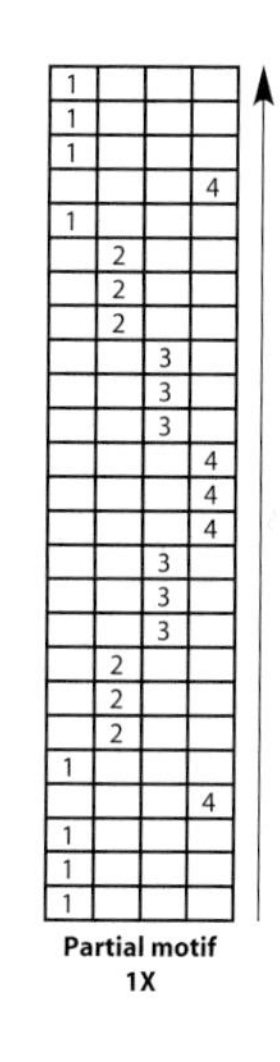
Partial motif
1X

Full motif
Repeat to desired length

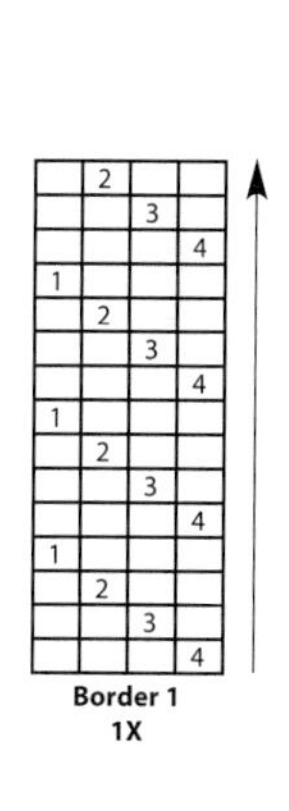
Border 1
1X

Whig Rose Shawlette

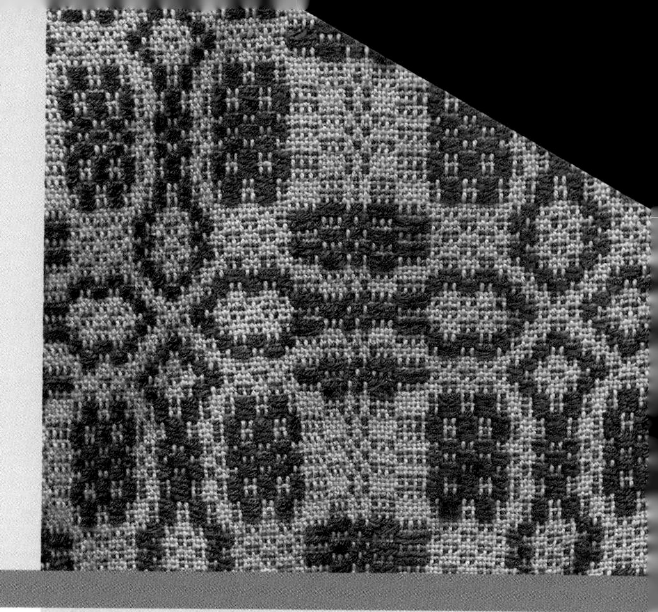

So often we look at our weaving, and it is always square or rectangular. This can be so repetitive after a while, and we want to do something different. Small shawls for wearing just over our shoulders have become very popular. They are wonderful for keeping you warm and not getting in the way. So, this was a challenge for me . . . how to create this small shawl but woven instead of knitted. I chose the Whig Rose pattern, as it is a nice-sized symmetrical pattern and the decreases at the sides can be proportional.

For the widest areas of the weaving, it will be best to use a temple to keep the piece at the proper size. Weave a tabby border at the beginning. I planned to use a serged edge, so I kept this border narrow. If you do not have this option, still plan to do the smallest rolled edge that you can to keep the edge from being too heavy and cumbersome.

After weaving your first motif, blind hem stitch the two outside motifs, then cut away enough of the warp threads for the two outside motifs so you can get your shuttle through. Don't stress over this. You want to be as close as possible, but one or two threads will not make a big difference. Pull the cut threads back through the heddles to get them out of your way. You will continue in this manner after every repeat. This will decrease the width by two motifs each time. *If you cut all of the threads, you can mess up the tension so do use caution.*

A floating selvedge will not work with this shawlette as you will be cutting warp threads after each repeat, so you will need to twist your shuttle around the outer threads at each end. When you get your piece off the loom at the end, check your edges. If you missed some areas and you see loose loops, it is easy to go back and catch the threads, using the same thread as your warp.

You can be as creative as you like with this shawlette, adding beads within the weaving or in the fringe. Kreamer Yarns Sterling Silk & Silver would make a lovely pattern thread with the silver thread adding sparkle to the piece. So many ideas . . . so little time!

Dimensions: 40½ x 14½ inches (102.9 x 35.6 cm)
Pattern origin: Whig Rose

Warp

Sett: 24 epi; 12 dent reed, 2 threads per dent
Length: 2-yard (1.8-m) warp
Thread: 10/2 perle cotton, Deep Beige, 981 ends, 2,000 yards (1,829 m)
Floating selvedge: none

Weft

Tabby thread: 10/2 perle cotton, Deep Beige, 200 yards (183 m)
Pattern thread: 6-ply rayon, Chocolate, Mill End, 200 yards (183 m)
Comparable: 5/2 perle cotton or 5/2 Dragon Tale Rayon, 200 yards (183 m)

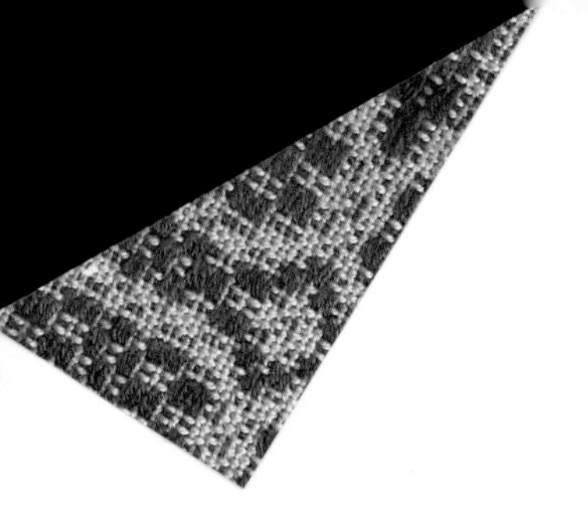

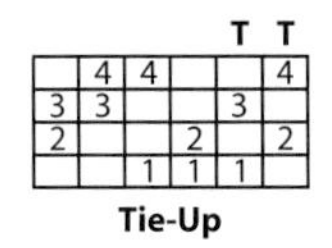

Tie-Up

Full motif—90 ends
Repeat 10X

Partial motif—81 ends
Repeat 1X

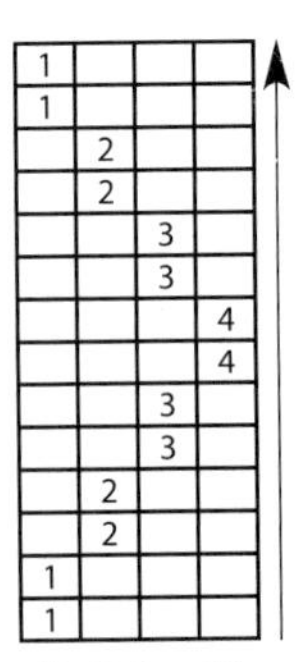

Partial motif

Full motif

Threading and Tie-Up

Full motif: 10 times
Partial motif: 1 time

Treadling

Add tabby.
Treadling sequence:
Repeat Full Motif, reducing each edge after each repeat.
Finish piece with Partial Motif for balancing.
Read and weave from the bottom up.

Snakeskin Scarf

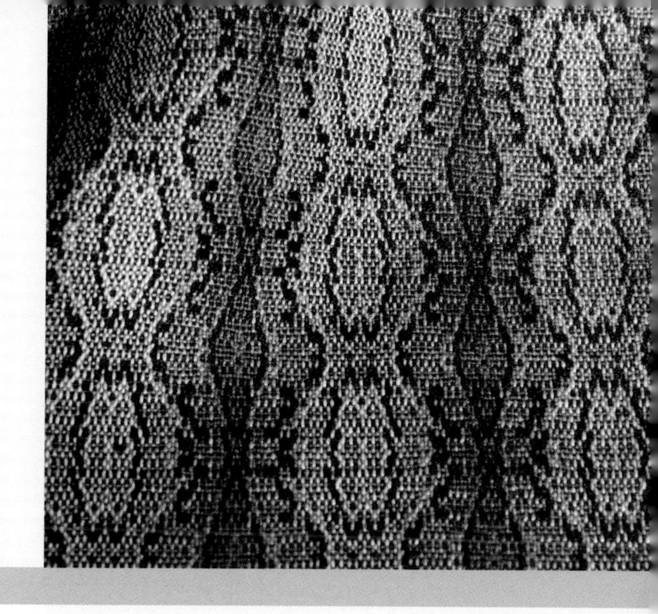

Not for the faint of heart! This overshot pattern was created quite by happenstance, and yet it is as beautiful as it is unusual. One of the features that I particularly like about overshot is the creativity in developing new patterns. As I worked with the tie-up and treadling for this piece, I could see that it began to morph into a snakeskin design. Moving ahead with that idea, and adding color, it looked even more like a snake. Definitely an unusual piece, but quite striking!

Begin and end this piece with ½ inch (1.3 cm) of tabby and a hem stitch. Follow the threading color chart, repeating the motif three times to get the full width of the scarf.

Dimensions: 10 x 64 inches (25.4 x 162.6 cm), with 3-inch (7.6-cm) fringe

Pattern origin: Original

Warp

Sett: 24 epi; 12 dent reed, 2 threads per dent

Length: 3-yard (2.75-m) warp

Thread: 10/2 perle cotton

- Mead, 100 ends plus 2 floating selvedges = 102 total, 325 yards (298 m)
- Deep Beige, 66 ends, 225 yards (206 m)
- Light Beige, 81 ends, 275 yards (252 m)

Floating selvedge: 10/2 perle cotton, Mead

Weft

Tabby thread: 10/2 perle cotton, Mead, 375 yards (343 m)

Pattern thread: 5/2 Dragon Tale Rayon, Black, 375 yards (343 m)

Begin and end the project with ½ inch (1.3 cm) of plain tabby.

Threading and Tie-Up

Border 1: 1 time

Full motif: 3 times

Border 2: 1 time

Follow color sequence at the top of threading chart.

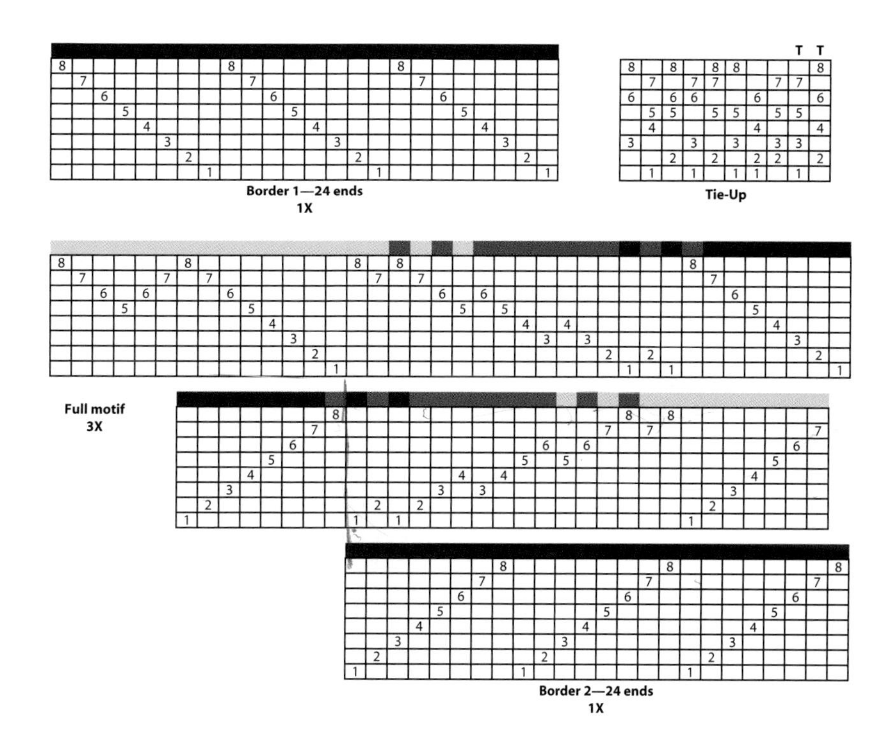

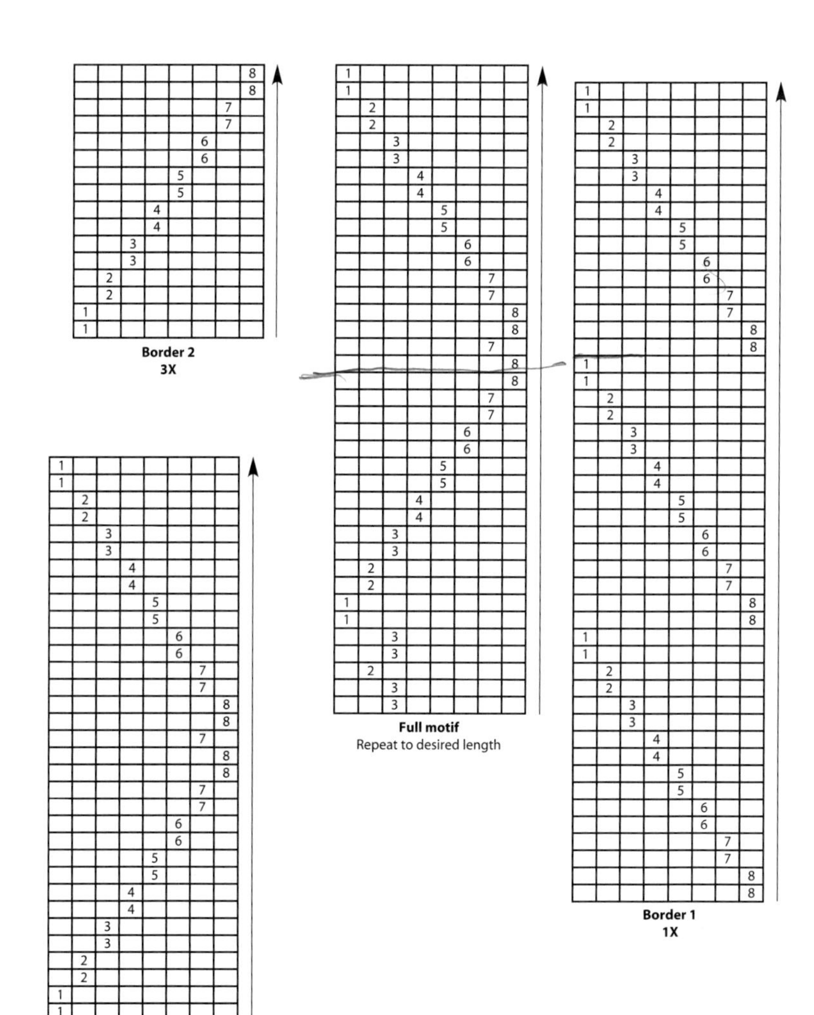

Treadling

Add tabby.

Treadling sequence:

Border 1: 1 time

Full motif: repeat to desired length

Partial motif: 1 time

Border 2: 3 times

Read and weave from the bottom up.

Winter Snowflakes Shawl

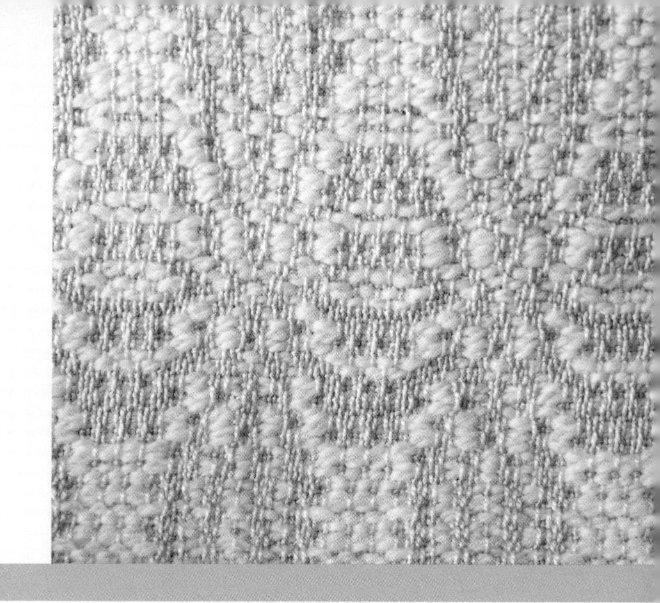

There is nothing quite like a cold, crisp winter day. I remember, as a child, watching the ice crystals form on the window and becoming quite upset when my older brothers would wipe them off. This shawl is a name draft . . . winter snowflake . . . and so I chose the silvery gray warp that reminds me of the icy cold winter. I wanted to be able to use this shawl on a cool day, so the pattern weft is luscious White wool, the color of freshly fallen snow! This resulted in an elegant, refined shawl that would work for many occasions. Use White perle cotton in place of the wool, and you have a winter table runner perfect for the holiday season! This would also make a lovely shawl for a bride!

Allow for your fringe as you begin weaving this piece. Secure the beginning and end by weaving ½ inch (1.3 cm) of plain tabby. I prefer the hem stitch for this piece instead of knots, but the choice is yours. For a table runner you may want to eliminate the fringe altogether!

Dimensions: 23 x 80 inches (58.4 x 203.2 cm), with 4-inch (10.2 cm) fringe

Pattern origin: Original

Warp

Sett: 24 epi; 12 dent reed, 2 threads per dent

Length: 3½-yard (3.2-m) warp

Thread: 10/2 perle cotton, Stone, 559 ends plus 2 floating selvedges = 561 ends, 2,000 yards (1,829 m)

Floating selvedge: 10/2 perle cotton, Stone

Weft

Tabby thread: 10/2 perle cotton, Stone, 1,000 yards (915 m)

Pattern thread: 2/8 Jaggerspun Maine Line, White, 1,000 yards (915 m)

Begin and end the project with ½ inch (1.3 cm) of plain tabby.

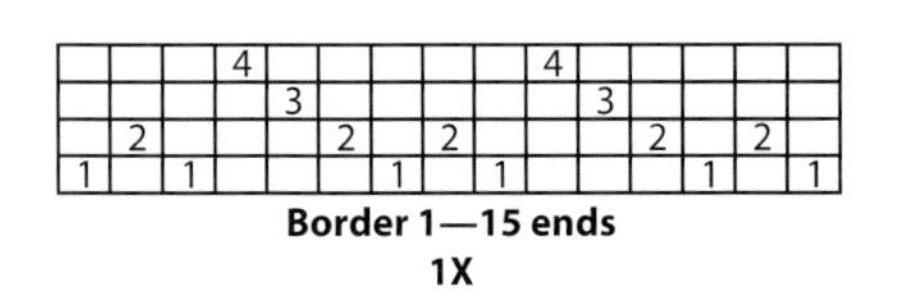
Border 1—15 ends
1X

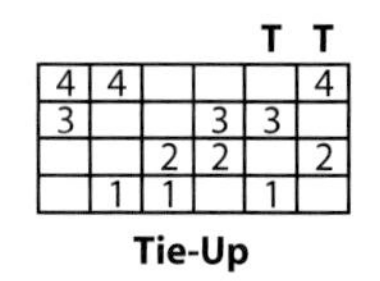
Tie-Up

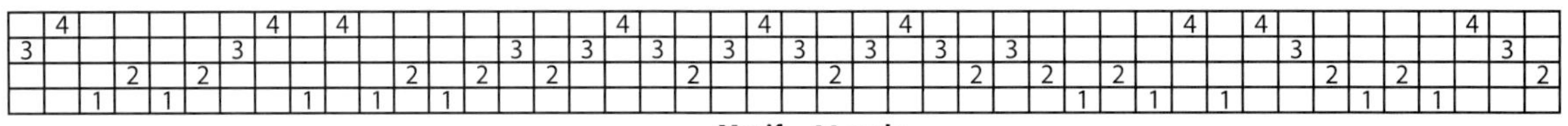
Motif—44 ends
12X

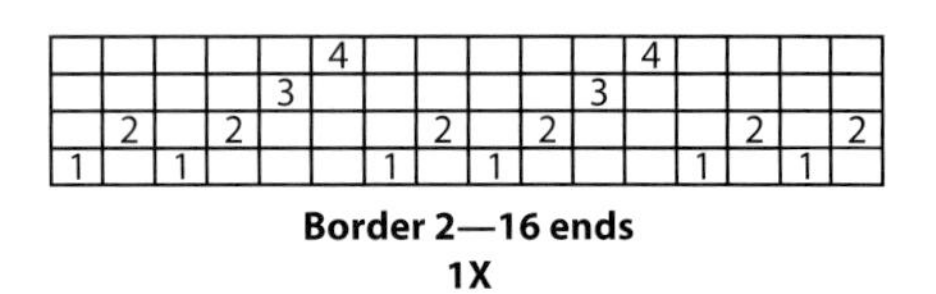
Border 2—16 ends
1X

Threading and Tie-Up

Border 1: 1 time
Motif: 12 times
Border 2: 1 time

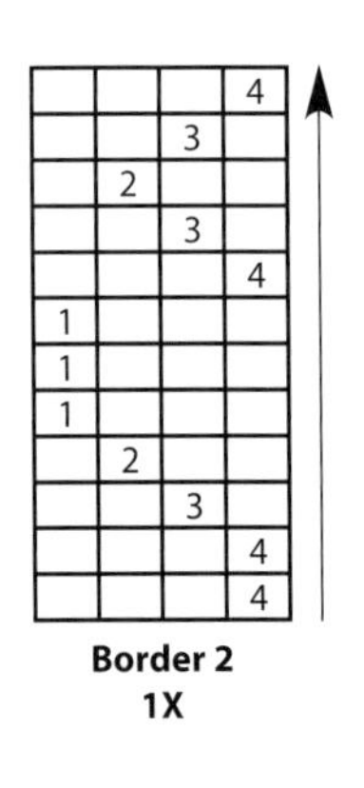
Border 2
1X

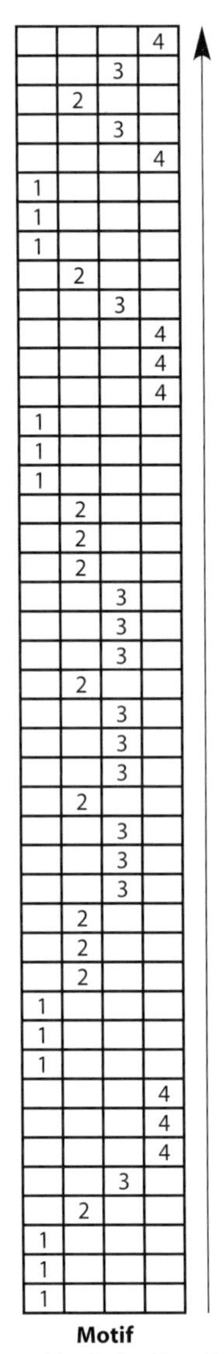
Motif
Repeat to desired length

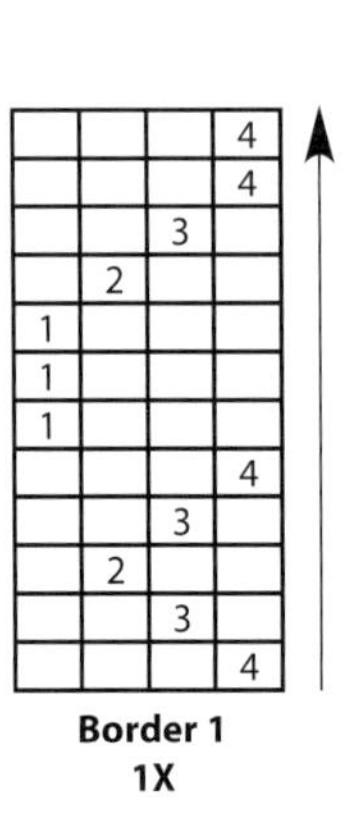
Border 1
1X

Treadling

Add tabby.
Treadling sequence:
Border 1: 1 time
Motif: to desired length
Border 2: 1 time

Springtime Place Mats

Springtime for your table! This set of place mats and napkins is not only a beautiful collection to have but also will teach you some things about overshot. Notice that each place mat and napkin has a *different* look. This is because a different color tabby thread was used in each set . . . blue, yellow, pink, and lavender. Yet they all work together, because the overshot pattern is the same with each place mat along with one color for the warp.

Now look closely at the napkins. Because you are using a tabby as a tie-down thread after every pattern weft, it is easy to create a large section of tabby for the napkins. Weave the tabby for the first half of the napkin, and then weave one repeat of your overshot pattern. After that, return to the tabby and finish the napkin. Be sure to use each of the colors so that your napkins coordinate with the place mats. What a wonderful table setting you will have created!

I finished the edges of the napkins with a rolled hem on a serger using a dark green thread that matches the pattern weft. If you do not have this option, you can simply do a rolled hem on each end. If you like the appearance of the dark green thread, you could do a simple buttonhole stitch with embroidery floss.

And, as always, be creative. Use a red tabby and you have a Christmas set. Change the warp to white, use black for your tabby and orange for the pattern weft, and now you can celebrate Halloween. Isn't weaving fun?

Dimensions:

- Place mats: 14½ x 21 inches (36.8 x 53.3 cm)
- Napkins: 14½ x 14½ inches (36.8 x 36.8 cm)

Pattern origin: Original

Warp

Sett: 24 epi; 12 dent reed, 2 threads per dent

Length: 6-yard (5.5-m) warp

Thread: 10/2 perle cotton, Scarab, 359 ends plus 2 floating selvedges = 361 ends, 2,250 yards (2058 m)

Floating selvedge: 10/2 perle cotton, Scarab

Weft

Tabby thread: 10/2 perle cotton

- Violet, 350 yards (320 m)
- King Blue, 350 yards (320 m)
- Wisteria, 350 yards (320 m)
- Gold, 350 yards (320 m)

Pattern thread: 5/2 perle cotton, Dark Green, 800 yards (732 m)

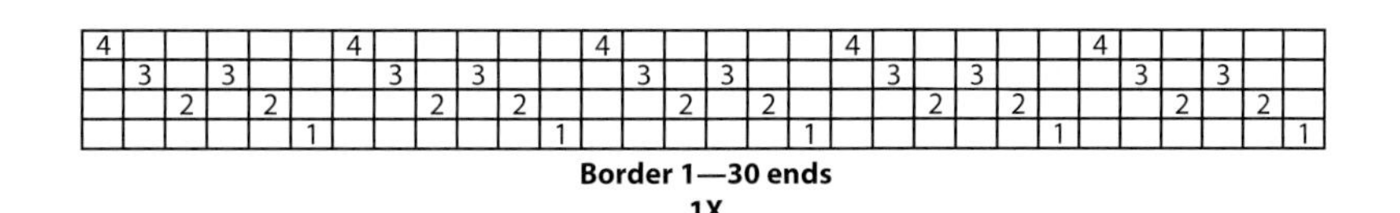

Border 1—30 ends
1X

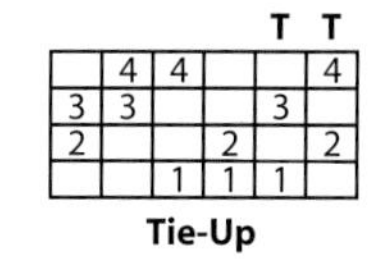

Tie-Up

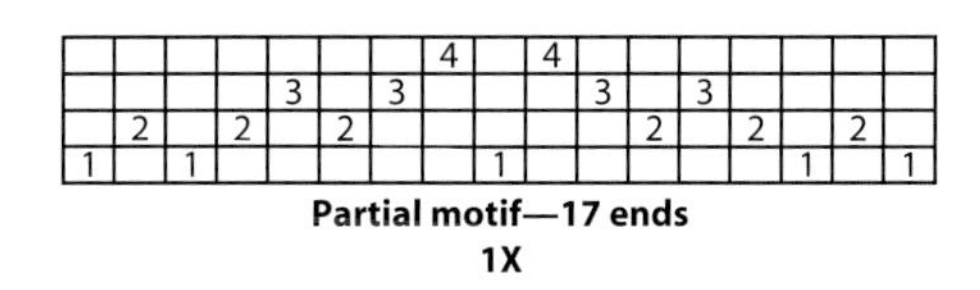

Partial motif—17 ends
1X

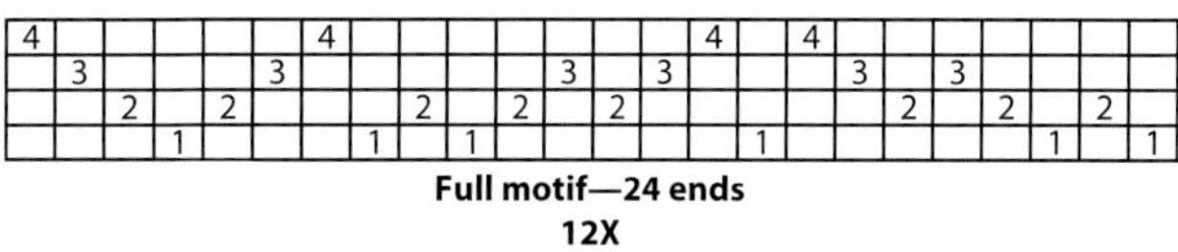

Full motif—24 ends
12X

Threading and Tie-Up

Border 1: 1 time
Full motif: 12 times
Partial motif: 1 time
Border 2: 1 time

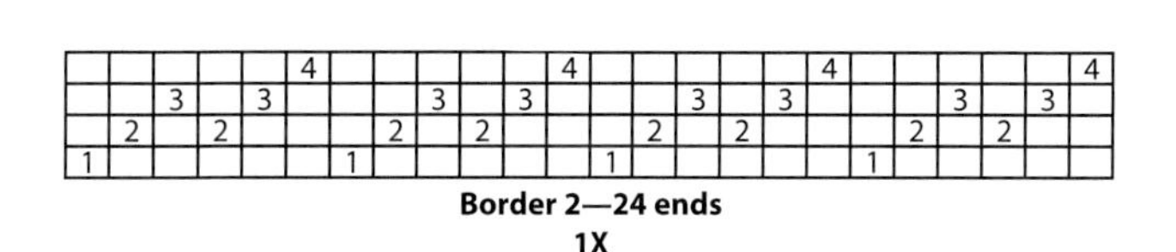

Border 2—24 ends
1X

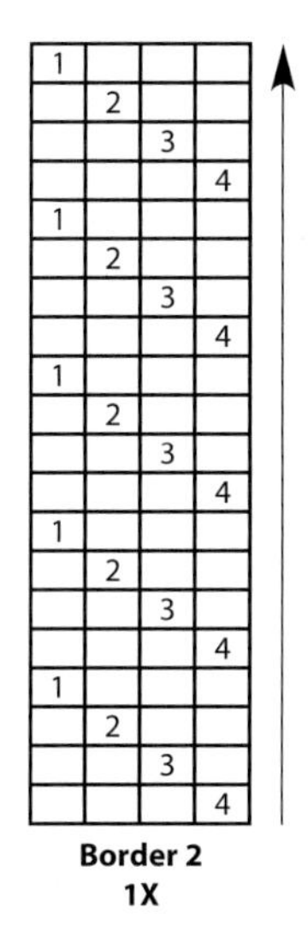

Border 2
1X

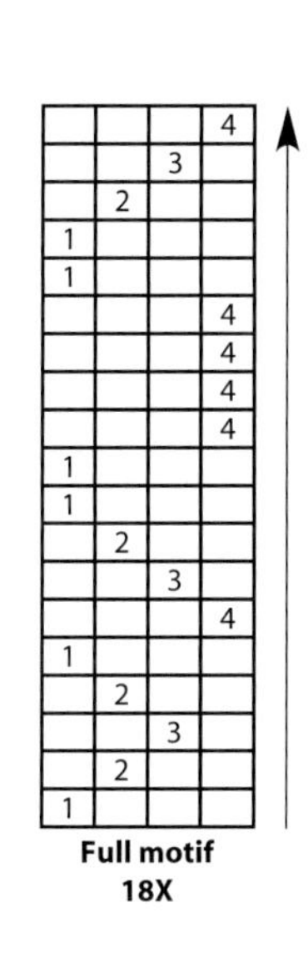

Full motif
18X

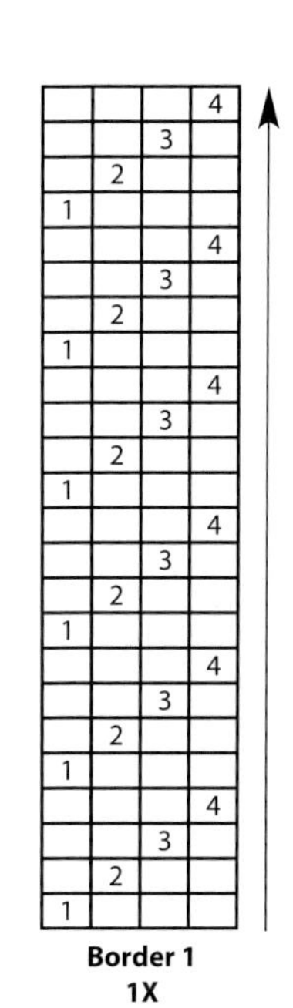

Border 1
1X

Treadling

Add tabby.
Treadling sequence:
Border 1: 1 time
Full motif: 18 times
Partial motif: 1 time
Border 2: 1 time
Weave and read treadling from the bottom up.

1			
	2		
		3	
	2		
1			

Partial motif
1X

Starburst Scarves and Pouch

Modernizing some of the traditional patterns is a great way to create some new and unique drafts. These pieces were designed using that idea. The original pattern is the Maltese cross, which has been a staple of weavers for years. Adding threads in the treadling created new shapes, giving the scarves a distinctive look.

For the red and white scarf, I added beads as I did the twisted fringe. This is easily done by threading the beads onto one of the strands and then doing the twisting. It gives the scarf a bit of sparkle!

The gold scarf has a wonderful drape as a multicolored tencel was used in the warp. The rich colors make this the perfect scarf for that dressier occasion.

Because of the different size weft thread, the motif repeats for the two scarves are different. For the red scarf, the treadling motif was repeated seven times. For the gold scarf, it was repeated six times. Of course, you can weave to your desired length and then finish with the partial motif and border. Thread size does make a difference!

Begin and end the scarf with ½ inch (1.3 cm) of tabby weave and a hem stitch.

I've included an additional treadling for the purses. I love to add extra warp so that I can experiment. This treadling is just a smaller portion of the scarf treadling. This allowed me to make the small purses and still have the pattern fit the project. These purses are lined, and a cording is attached so that they can be worn around the neck. Perfect to carry that cell phone in a fashionable way!

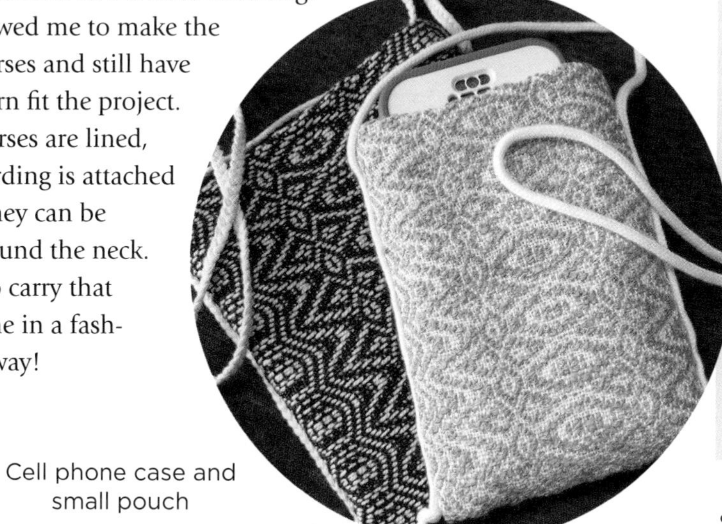

Cell phone case and small pouch

STARBURST SCARF

Dimensions: 7½ x 66 inches (19.1 x 167.6 cm), with 4-inch (10.2 cm) fringe

Pattern origin: variation of Maltese Cross

Warp

Sett: 24 epi; 12 dent reed, 2 threads per dent

Length: 3-yard (2.75-m) warp

Thread: 8/2 tencel, Tashkent, 195 ends plus 2 floating selvedges = 197 ends, 625 yards (572 m)

Floating selvedge: 8/2 tencel, Tashkent

Weft

Tabby thread: 8/2 tencel, Tashkent, 275 yards (252 m)

Pattern thread: RicRac Mill End, Persimmon, 275 yards (252 m)

Comparable:

- 5/2 Dragon Tale Rayon
- 5/2 perle cotton

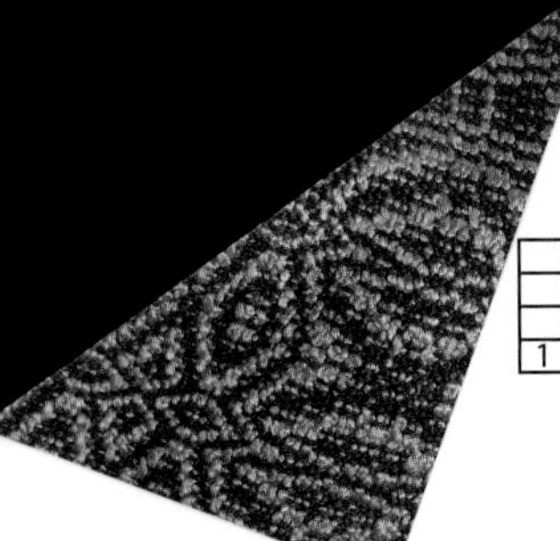

			4				4				4				4				4				4				4				4			
		3				3				3		3				3				3				3				3				3		
	2				2				2				2				2				2				2				2				2	
1				1				1						1				1				1				1				1				1

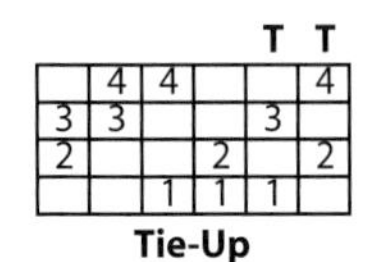

Tie-Up

Border 1—50 ends
1X

4				4										
	3				3				3				3	
		2				2		2		2		2		2
			1				1				1			

						4		4		4				4						4				4		4		4								4		4		4			
			3		3		3								3				3								3		3		3								3		3		
2		2		2								2				2		2				2								2		2		2								2	
	1								1		1		1				1				1		1		1								1		1		1						1

4								4		4		4				4						4				4		4		4								4				4	
					3		3		3								3				3								3		3		3										
		2		2		2								2				2		2				2								2		2		2				2			
	1		1								1		1		1				1				1		1		1								1		1		1		1		1

Motif—95 ends
1X

			4		4	
		3		3		
	2					
1						1

Threading and Tie-Up

Border 1: 1 time
Motif: 1 time
Border 2: 1 time

			4				4				4				4				4														4				4
		3				3				3		3				3				3				3				3				3				3	
	2				2				2				2				2				2		2		2		2		2		2				2		
1				1				1						1				1				1				1				1				1			

Border 2—50 ends
1X

			4				4				4
		3				3				3	
	2				2				2		
1				1				1			

STARBURST SCARF (RED AND WHITE)

Dimensions: 7½ x 66 inches (19.1 x 167.6 cm), with 4-inch (10.2 cm) fringe
Pattern origin: variation of Maltese Cross

Warp

Sett: 24 epi; 12 dent reed, 2 threads per dent
Length: 3-yard (2.75-m) warp
Thread: 10/2 perle cotton, White, 195 ends plus 2 floating selvedges = 197 ends, 625 yards (572 m)
Floating selvedge: 10/2 perle cotton, White

Weft

Tabby thread: 10/2 perle cotton, White, 275 yards (252 m)
Pattern thread: 5/2 perle cotton, Lipstick, 275 yards (252 m)
Additional materials: Small red beads that you can easily thread onto 10/2 perle cotton

1			
	2		
		3	
			4
1			
	2		
		3	
		3	
		3	
	2		
1			
			4
		3	
	2		
1			
	2		
		3	
			4
1			
	2		
		3	
		3	
		3	
	2		
1			
			4
		3	
	2		
1			
			4
			4
			4
		3	
		3	
		3	
	2		
	2		
	2		
1			
	2		
	2		
	2		
1			
	2		
	2		
	2		
		3	
		3	
		3	
			4
			4
			4
1			
1			
1			
	2		
	2		
	2		
		3	
		3	
		3	

			4
			4
			4
1			
1			
1			
			4
		3	
	2		
1			
	2		
		3	
			4
1			
1			
1			
			4
			4
			4
		3	
		3	
		3	
	2		
	2		
	2		
1			
1			
1			
			4
1			
1			
1			
			4
1			
1			
1			
	2		
	2		
	2		
		3	
		3	
		3	
			4
			4
			4
1			
1			
1			
			4
		3	
	2		
1			
	2		
		3	
			4

1			
1			
1			
			4
			4
			4
		3	
		3	
		3	
	2		
	2		
	2		
1			
1			
1			
			4
			4
			4
		3	
		3	
		3	
	2		
	2		
	2		
1			
	2		
	2		
	2		
1			
	2		
	2		
	2		
		3	
		3	
		3	
			4
			4
			4
1			
	2		
		3	
			4
1			
	2		
		3	
		3	
		3	
	2		
1			
			4
		3	
	2		
1			
	2		
		3	
			4
1			
	2		
		3	
		3	
		3	
	2		
1			
			4
		3	
	2		
1			

Motif
Repeat to desired length
Begin

			4
		3	
	2		
1			
			4
		3	
	2		
1			

Border 1
1X

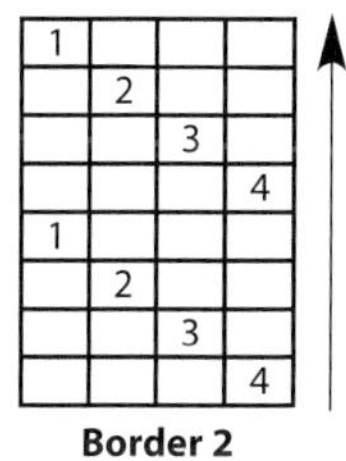

1			
	2		
		3	
			4
1			
	2		
		3	
			4

Border 2
1X

Treadling for Scarves

Add tabby.

Treadling sequence:

Border 1: 1 time

Motif: repeat to desired length

Border 2: 1 time

Read and weave treadling from the bottom up.

End last repeat with '1' to balance

1			

	2		
		3	
			4
1			
	2		
		3	
		3	
		3	
	2		
1			
			4
		3	
	2		
1			
	2		
		3	
			4
1			
	2		
		3	
		3	
		3	
	2		
1			
			4
		3	
	2		
1			

Treadling for Pouch

Add tabby.

Repeat motif to desired length.

End last repeat with 1 to balance.

Read and weave from the bottom up.

Stars and Stripes Table Runner

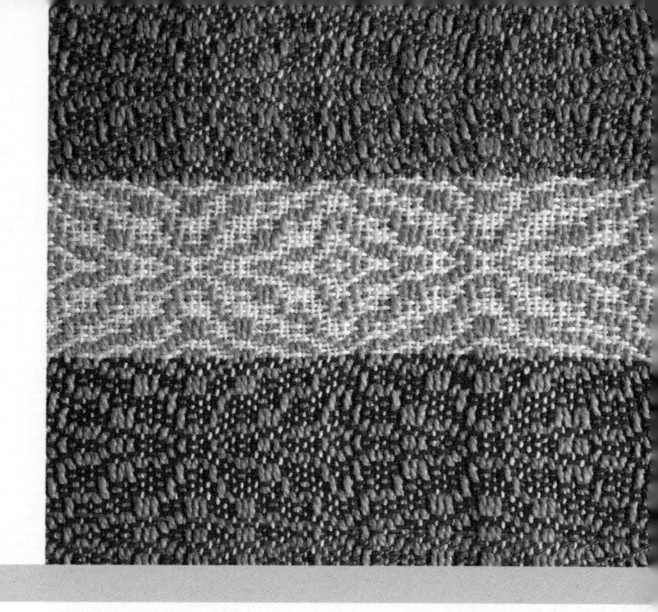

Every holiday needs its own table runner to brighten up your table! This is perfect for the Fourth of July, Memorial Day, and Veterans Day.

Set up the warp colors according to the color chart. When weaving, begin with the blue, and weave in 1½-inch (3.8-cm) blocks. Count your weft threads so they are consistent for each color but also measure and make sure your beat does not change. After the first blue, weave a red block, a white block, and another blue block, all with plain tabby weave. Then you will begin the overshot portion, weaving one repeat of the overshot pattern. Back to plain weave beginning with blue, white, red—for four times. Finish with a blue block and then back to one repeat of the overshot pattern. Finish the last section beginning with a blue, white, and red block, and finally the last blue block. Hem-stitch both ends of the piece. If you don't like the fringe, increase the first blue block 1 inch (2.5 cm) and do a rolled hem, but still keep the first block 1½ inches (3.8 cm) square.

COLOR SEQUENCE	
Color	**Ends**
Blue—Border 2	27 ends—1X
White	36 ends—1X
Red	36 ends—1X
Blue-White-Red	Each color section has 36 ends—3X
Blue—Border 1	28 ends—1X

Dimensions: 19 x 45 inches (48.3 x 114.3 cm) with 3-inch (7.6 cm) fringe

Pattern origin: Star of Bethlehem

Warp

Sett: 24 epi; 12 dent reed, 2 threads per dent

Length: 2½-yard (2.3-m) warp

Thread: 10/2 perle cotton

- White, 144 ends, 375 yards (343 m)
- Red, 144 ends, 375 yards (343 m)
- Royal, 163 ends plus 2 floating selvedges = 165 ends, 425 yards (389 m)

Floating selvedge: 10/2 perle cotton, Royal

Weft

Tabby thread: 10/2 perle cotton

- White, 250 yards (229 m)
- Red, 150 yards (138 m)
- Royal, 180 yards (165 m)

Pattern thread: 5/2 perle cotton, California Gold, 150 yards (138 m)

			4				4				4				4				4				4				4
		3				3				3				3				3				3				3	
	2				2				2				2				2				2				2		
1				1				1				1				1				1				1			

Border 1—28 ends
1X

				T	T
	4	4			4
3	3			3	
2			2		2
		1	1	1	

Tie-Up

			4						4		4		4				4		4				4		4		4						4		
		3						3		3						3				3						3		3						3	
	2				2		2								2						2								2		2				2
1				1		1						1		1				1				1		1						1		1			

Motif—36 ends
Repeat 11X

4				4				4				4				4				4				4		
	3				3				3				3				3				3				3	
		2				2				2				2				2				2				2
			1				1				1				1				1				1			

Border 2—27 ends
1X

Threading and Tie-Up

Border 1: 1 time
Motif: 11 times
Border 2: 1 time

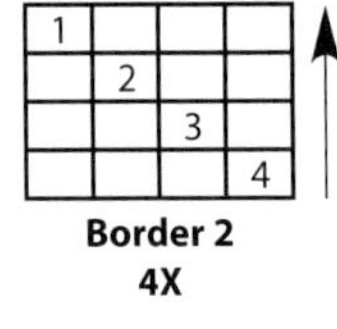

1			
	2		
		3	
			4

Border 2
4X

1			
1			
1			
	2		
		3	
		3	
		3	
			4
			4
			4
1			
	2		
		3	
			4
			4
			4
		3	
	2		
1			
			4
			4
			4
		3	
		3	
		3	
	2		
1			
1			
1			

Partial motif
1X

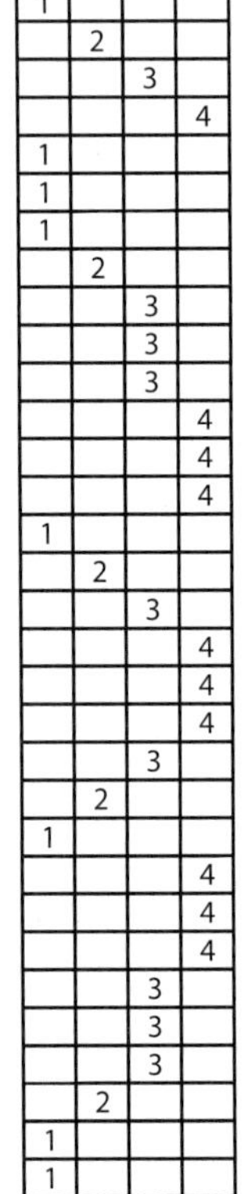

			4
		3	
	2		
1			
	2		
		3	
			4
1			
1			
1			
	2		
		3	
		3	
		3	
			4
			4
			4
1			
	2		
		3	
			4
			4
			4
		3	
	2		
1			
			4
			4
			4
		3	
		3	
		3	
	2		
1			
1			
1			

Full motif
1X

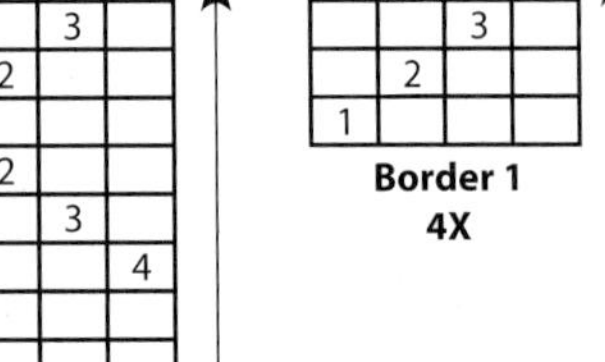

			4
		3	
	2		
1			

Border 1
4X

Treadling

Add tabby.
Treadling sequence:
Border 1: 4 times
Full motif: 1 time
Partial motif: 1 time
Border 2: 4 times
Read and weave from the bottom up.

Summertime Table Runner

This gamp is a beautiful piece to display but also serves as a great learning tool. Each time you treadle correctly for one tie-up, you are creating a new and different pattern with the other tie-ups. This is a wonderful example of how you can easily create your own patterns. Take the time to look carefully at each pattern that is created. You may find that you like a particular one enough to create a larger piece that just focuses on that pattern.

Additionally, note how your eye blends the colors used in the warp and tabby to create new colors. This happens because we are working with small threads. The mixture of the yellow warp with the pink tabby gives an orange hue to that block. The blue and yellow mixture makes a green block. Even though we are only working with five colors, this table runner exhibits many more colors, which makes it a very cheery addition to your table.

Begin and end this runner with ½ inch (1.3 cm) of green tabby and a hem stitch. If you don't want the fringe, weave 1½ inches (3.8 cm) of tabby and do a rolled hem.

When you weave the body of the runner, you will begin with the treadling for pattern A—cat tracks and snail trail. Because the warp for this pattern is green, use green for the tabby thread. Follow this pattern as you continue weaving.

Border and Block A, Green tabby Cat Tracks and Snail Trail
Block B, Wheel of Fortune, Violet tabby
Block C, Small honeysuckle, Light Yellow tabby
Block D, Leaves, Petal Pink tabby
Block B, Wheel of Fortune, King Blue Tabby
Border and Block A, Green tabby Cat Tracks and Snail Trail

You can easily increase the size of this runner by adding additional blocks. Change the colors and you can have a runner for another season, Christmas, fall, or just your favorite combination. Make this piece your own!

Dimensions: 18 x 32 inches (45.7 x 81.3 cm), with 4-inch (10.2 cm) fringe

Pattern origin: Leaves, Small Honeysuckle, Wheel of Fortune, Cat Tracks, and Snail Trail

Warp

Sett: 24 epi; 12 dent reed, 2 threads per dent

Length: 2½-yard (2.3-m) warp

Thread: 10/2 perle cotton

- Willow, 104 ends plus 2 floating selvedges = 106 ends, 275 yards (252 m)
- Petal Pink, 82 ends, 225 yards (206 m)
- Light Yellow, 65 ends, 175 yards (160 m)
- Violet, 110 ends, 290 yards (266 m)
- King Blue, 109 ends, 290 yards (266 m)

Floating selvedge: 10/2 perle cotton, Willow

Weft

Tabby thread: 10/2 perle cotton

- Willow, 90 yards (83 m)
- Petal Pink, 75 yards (69 m)
- Yellow, 45 yards (45.2 m)
- Violet, 70 yards (64 m)
- King Blue, 70 yards (64 m)

Pattern thread: 5/2 perle cotton, White, 350 yards (320 m)

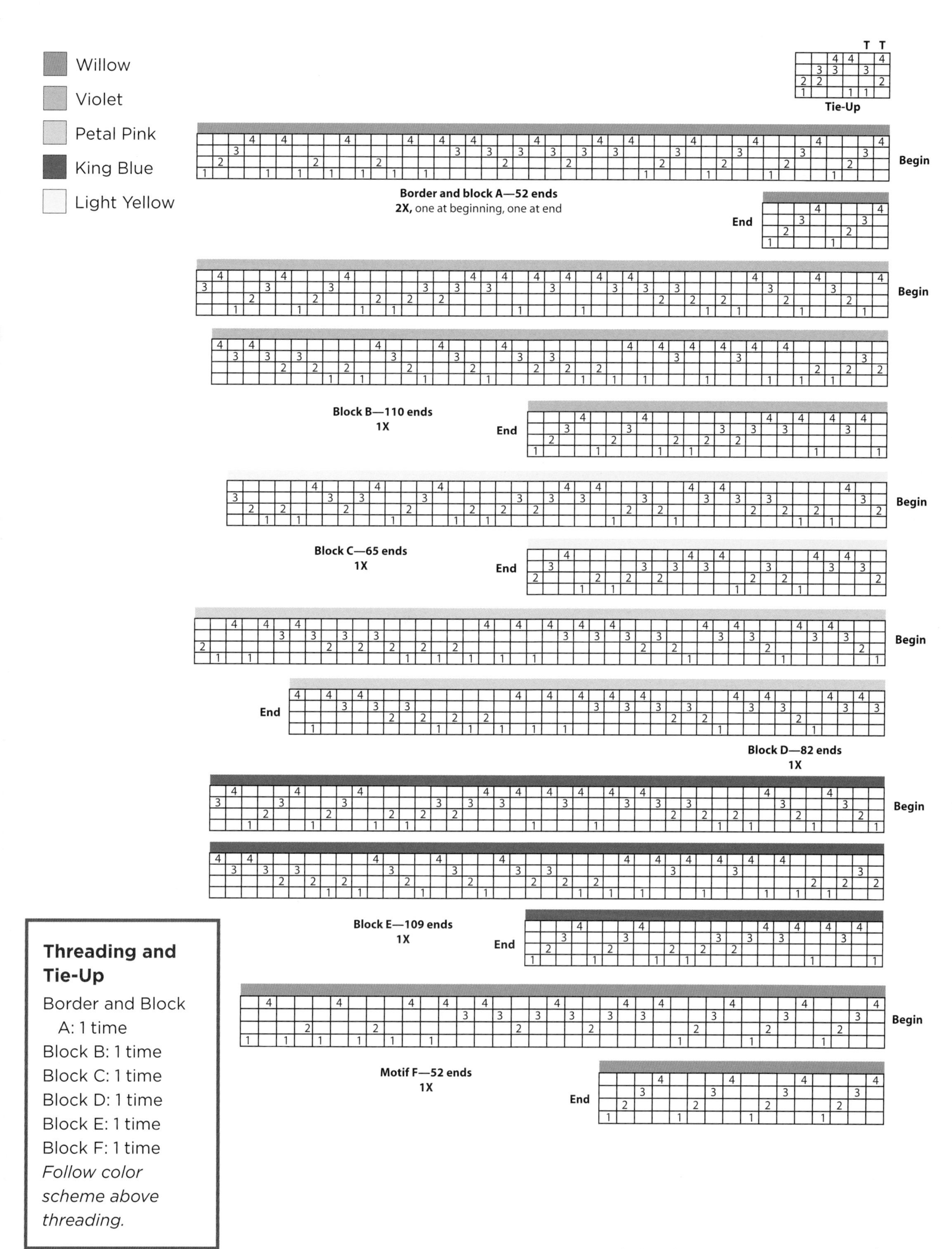

Willow
Violet
Petal Pink
King Blue
Light Yellow
T T
Tie-Up
Begin
Border and block A—52 ends
2X, one at beginning, one at end
End
Begin
Block B—110 ends
1X
End
Begin
Block C—65 ends
1X
End
Begin
End
Block D—82 ends
1X
Begin
Block E—109 ends
1X
End
Begin
Motif F—52 ends
1X
End
Threading and Tie-Up
Border and Block A: 1 time
Block B: 1 time
Block C: 1 time
Block D: 1 time
Block E: 1 time
Block F: 1 time
Follow color scheme above threading.

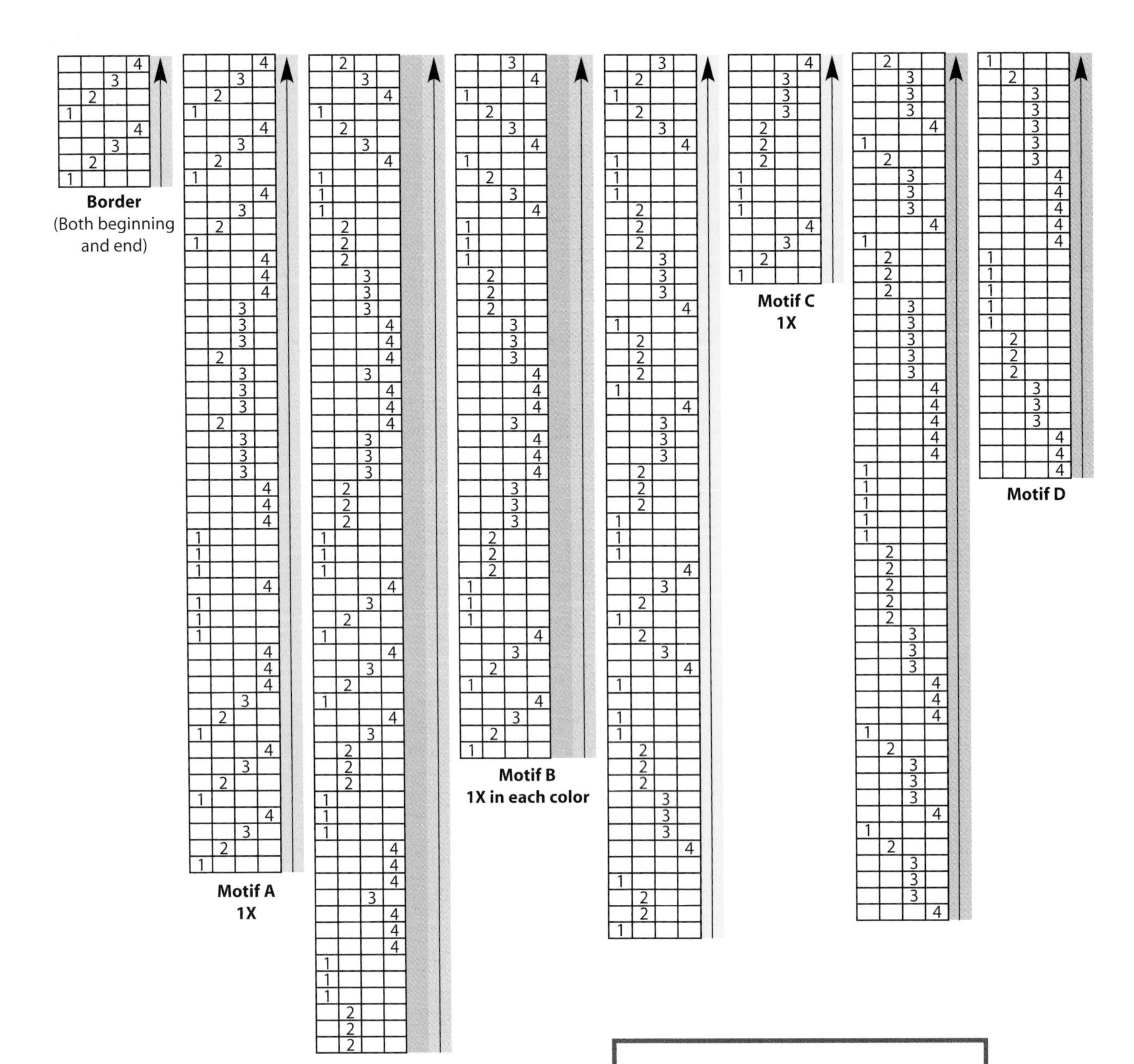

Treadling

Add tabby.

Treadling sequence:

Border: 1 time: Green Tabby

Motif A: 1 time: Green Tabby

Motif B: 1 time: Purple Tabby

Motif C: 1 time: Yellow Tabby

Motif D: 1 time: Pink Tabby

Motif B: 1 time: Blue Tabby

Motif A: 1 time: Green Tabby

Border: 1 time: Green Tabby

Pattern thread is White.

Read and weave treadling from the bottom up.

Wonderful Windows

A perfect and easy way to freshen up a room is with new valances. This duo certainly fits the bill for that project. The cheerful green will bring spring into your room, although any color combination would be just as amazing.

An easy adjustment to the draft would allow you to weave a matching table runner. Just simply center the stripes and make the piece the desired width. Place mats would be another project you could create with this pattern!

Weave a tabby border to begin and end each piece. Be sure to put a space or a different color thread to separate the two valances and then begin weaving the second one. After you have finished weaving, make a narrow rolled hem at each end. Finish the top of the valance with a 2-inch (5.1-cm) hem and edge-stitch the very top fold. Turn up the bottom edge until it meets the beginning of the first dark pattern. This will be approximately 1¾ inches (4.5 cm). You can hem by hand or on a sewing machine, although for the bottom hem I prefer handwork. This will allow for your valance to be finished at 18 inches (46 cm). The hems can easily be increased if the valance is too deep for you.

Hang them up and enjoy!

Dimensions: 18 x 32 inches (45.7 x 81.3 cm), with 4-inch (10.2 cm) fringe

Pattern origin: Original

Warp

Sett: 24 epi; 12 dent reed, 2 threads per dent

Length: 4½-yard (4.2-m) warp

Thread: 10/2 perle cotton

- Bali, 398 ends plus 2 floating selvedges = 400 ends, 1,850 yards (1,692 m)
- Dark Green, 131 ends, 600 yards (549 m)

Floating selvedge: 10/2 perle cotton, Bali

Weft

Tabby thread: 10/2 perle cotton, Bali, 1,500 yards (1,372 m)

Pattern thread: 5/2 perle cotton, White, 1,500 yards (1,372 m)

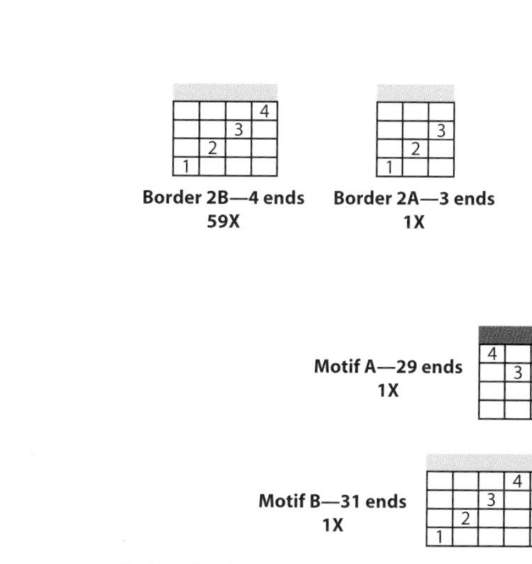

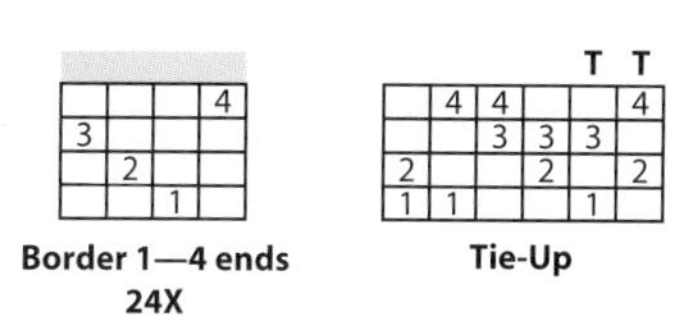

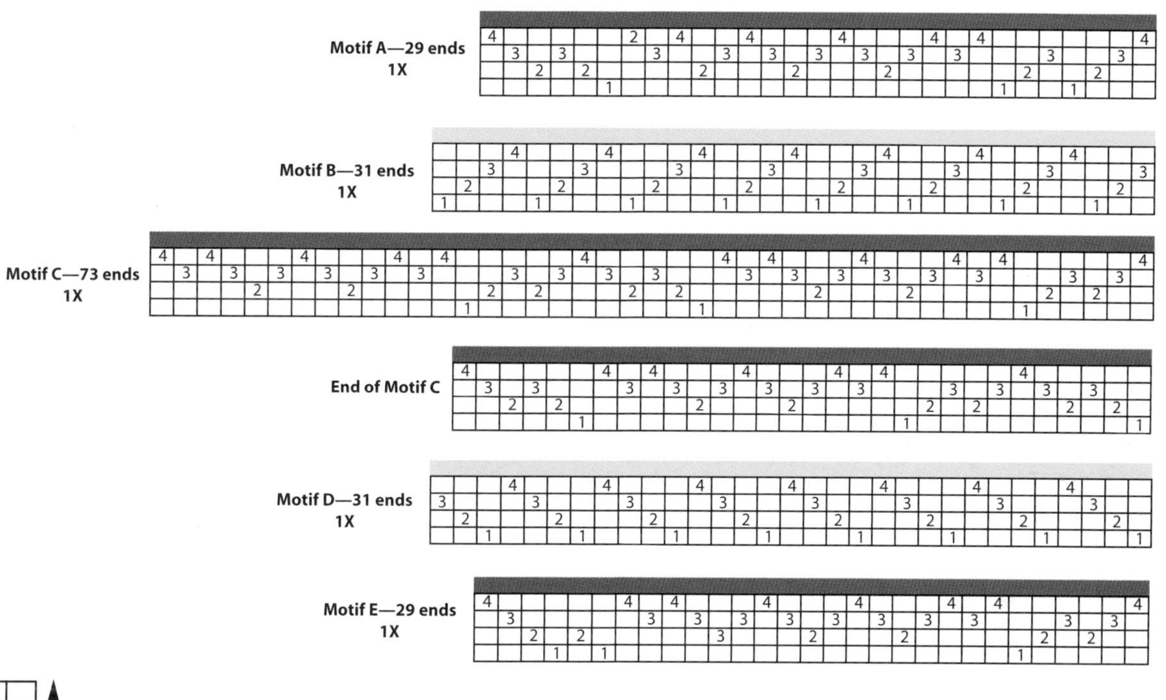

1			
	2		
	2		
	2		
		3	
			4
1			
	2		
		3	
			4
			4
			4
		3	
		3	
		3	
			4
			4
			4
		3	
	2		
1			
			4
		3	
	2		
	2		
	2		
	2		
1			
			4
		3	
		3	
		3	
	2		
		3	
		3	
		3	
	2		
		3	
		3	
		3	
			4

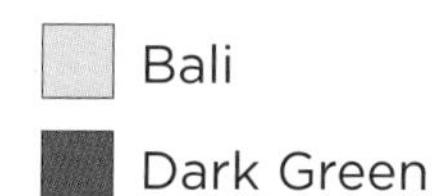

Threading and Tie-Up

Border 1: 24 times
Motif A: 1 time
Motif B: 1 time
Motif C: 1 time
Motif D: 1 time
Motif E: 1 time
Border 2A: 1 time
Border 2B: 59 times

Treadling

Add tabby.
Repeat treadling pattern to desired length of project.
Read and weave treadling from the bottom up.

Xs and Os Scarves

(Not the traditional Xs and Os)

Like all weavers, sometimes I do things a bit backward. I found this absolutely lovely yarn that has such a silky hand that I just had to create something wonderful. Naturally a scarf was my first choice. I created this draft with plenty of halftones that would allow the multiple colors in the warp to be emphasized, and named it Xs and Os because of its appearance. In addition, the choice of the black weft thread also emphasizes these colors. For the tabby I used a 16/2 cotton thread, because I wanted to use a finer thread so it would not compete with the multicolored warp thread. The tencel gives this scarf such a beautiful drape and the multiple colors allow it to be worn with many different outfits.

I made the second scarf using the same draft in Natural and Gold tones. This gives the piece a totally different look. I used mill end rayon for the weft thread. A comparable choice would be Dragon Tale 8/2 Rayon or 5/2 perle cotton. Have fun with this pattern, using your favorite colors and fiber choices. It is an easy pattern to weave, but it looks oh, so intricate!

Xs AND Os SCARF, GOLD

Dimensions: 6½ x 60 inches (16.5 x 152.4 cm), with 4-inch (10.2 cm) fringe

Pattern origin: Original

Warp

Sett: 24 epi; 12 dent reed, 2 threads per dent

Length: 3-yard (2.75-m) warp

Thread: 10/2 perle cotton, Natural, 625 yards (572 m), 201 ends plus 2 floating selvedges = 203 ends

Floating selvedge: 10/2 perle cotton, Natural

Weft

Tabby thread: 10/2 perle cotton, Natural, 375 yards (343 m)

Pattern thread: 6-ply rayon, Gold, Mill End, 375 yards (343 m)

Comparable: 5/2 Dragon Tale Rayon or 5/2 perle cotton

Weave ½ inch (1.3 cm) of tabby at beginning and end of project.

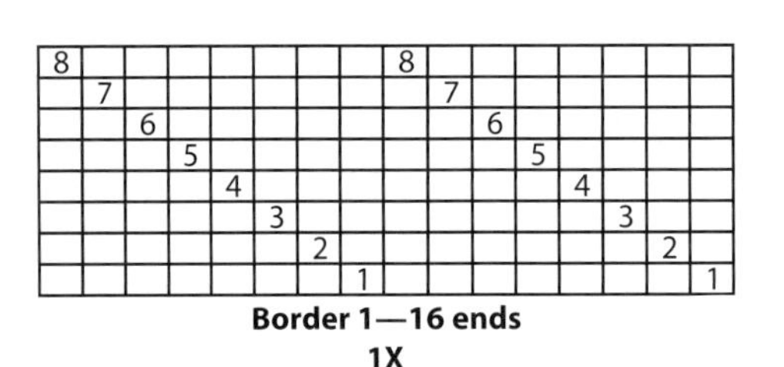
Border 1—16 ends
1X

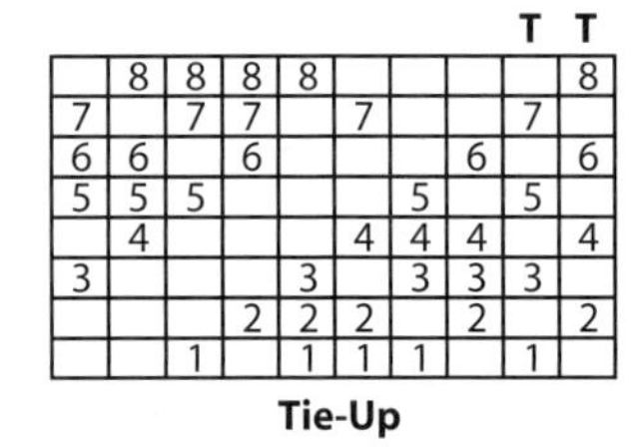
Tie-Up

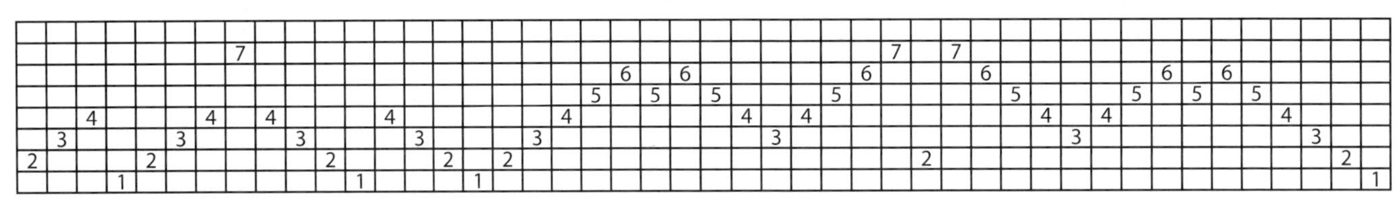
Motif—46 ends
3X

Threading and Tie-Up

Border 1: 1 time
Motif: 3 times
Partial motif: 1 time
Border 2: 1 time

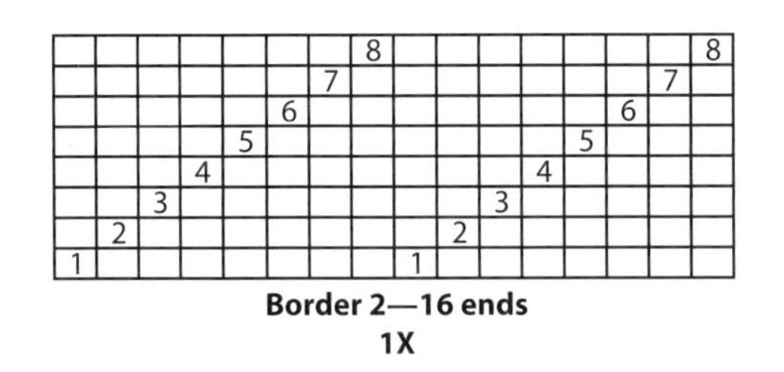
Border 2—16 ends
1X

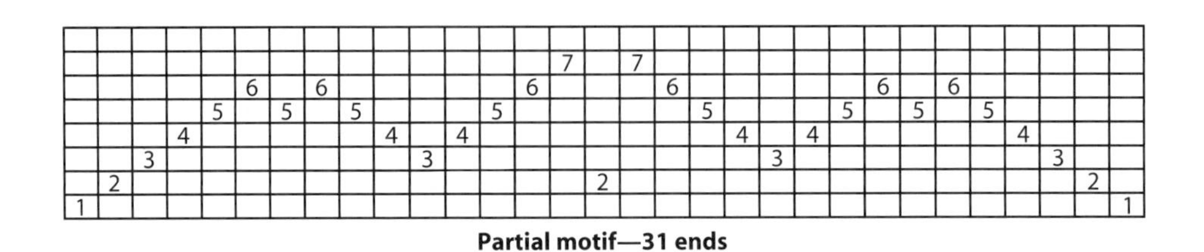
Partial motif—31 ends

Xs AND Os SCARF, MULTICOLORED

Dimensions: 6½ x 60 inches (16.5 x 152.4 cm), with 4-inch (10.2 cm) fringe
Pattern origin: Original

Warp

Sett: 12 dent reed, 2 threads per dent
Length: 3-yard (2.75-m) warp
Thread: Just Our Yarn, 100 percent tencel, Aziza, 500 yards (458 m), 155 ends plus 2 floating selvedges = 157 ends
Floating selvedge: Just Our Yarn, 100 percent tencel, Aziza

Weft

Tabby thread: 16/2 cotton, Green, 200 yards (183 m)
Pattern thread: 8/2 Dragon Tale Rayon, Black, 200 yards (183 m)
Weave ½-inch (1.3-cm) tabby at beginning and end of project.

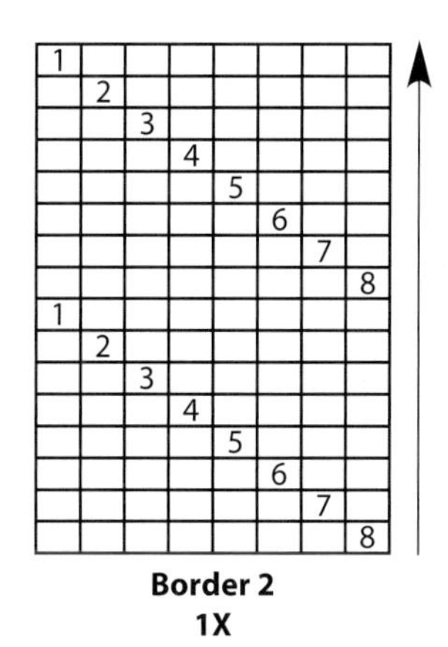

Border 2
1X

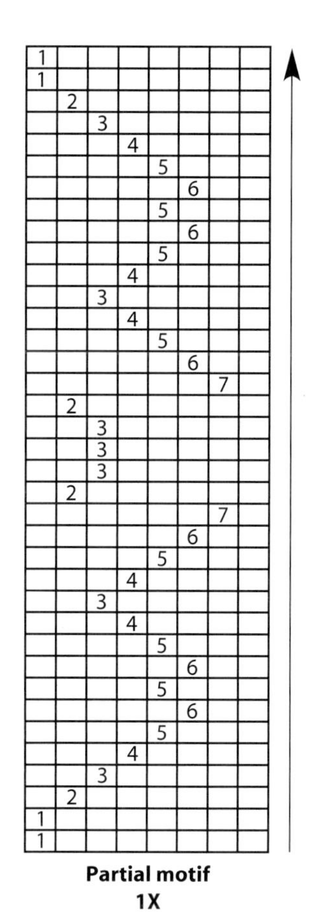

Partial motif
1X

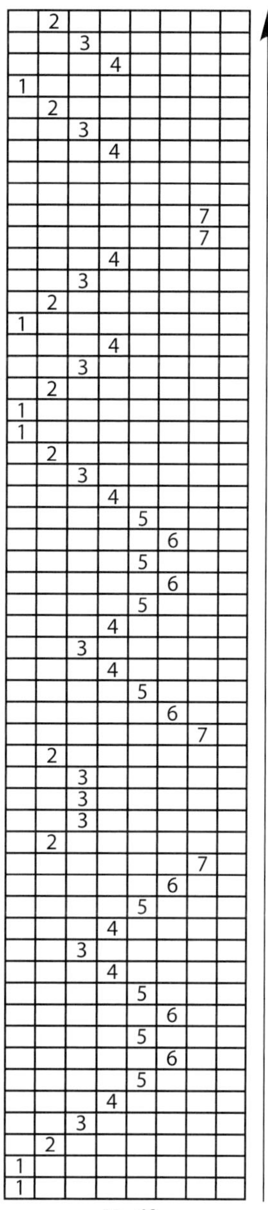

Motif
Repeat to desired length

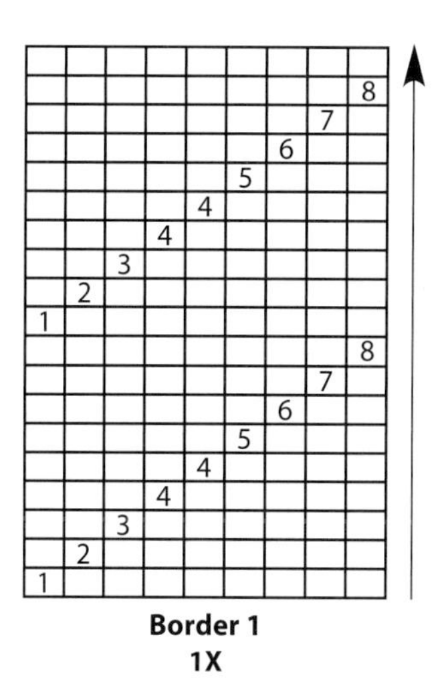

Border 1
1X

Treadling

Add tabby.
Treadling sequence:
Border 1: 1 time
Motif: repeat to desired length
Partial motif: 1 time
Border 2: 1 time
Read and weave from the bottom up.

RESOURCES

Learning to Weave. Deborah Chandler. Interweave Press, Loveland, CO.
The Handweaver's Pattern Directory. Anne Dixon. Interweave Press, Loveland, CO.
A Handweaver's Pattern Book. Marguerite P. Davison. Marguerite P. Davison, Swarthmore, PA.
Overshot for Rugs. Tom Knisely, *Handwoven* magazine. March/April 2007.

RESOURCES FOR FIBER

AC Moore: Arts and Crafts Store
www.acmoore.com

JoAnn Fabrics
www.joann.com

PRO Chemical & Dye
126 Shove Street
Fall River, MA 02724
(800) 228-9393

Red Stone Fiber Arts Center
435 Popps Ford Road
York Haven PA 17370
(717) 212-9022
http://redstoneglen.com

WEBS
75 Service Center Road
Northampton, MA 01060
(800) 367-9327
www.yarn.com

Yarn Barn of Kansas
930 Massachusetts St.
Lawrence, Kansas 66044
(785) 842-4333
www.yarnbarn-ks.com